Do It Gorgeously

ALSO BY SOPHIE ULIANO

Gorgeously Green

The Gorgeously Green Diet

Do It Gorgeously

How to Make Less Toxic, Less Expensive, and More Beautiful Products

SOPHIE ULIANO

Illustrations by Alexis Seabrook

voice

HYPERION • NEW YORK

Library of Congress Cataloging-in-Publication Data
Uliano, Sophie.
    Do it gorgeously : how to make less toxic, less expensive, and more beautiful products / Sophie Uliano.
        p.   cm.
    ISBN: 978-1-4013-4139-8
    1. Home economics.   2. Sustainable living.   I. Title.
    TX147.U45   2010
    640—dc22   2010009052

Hyperion books are available for special promotions and premiums. For details contact the HarperCollins Special Markets Department in the New York office at 212-207-7528, fax 212-207-7222, or email spsales@harpercollins.com.

Designed by Jessica Shatan Heslin/Studio Shatan, Inc.

FIRST EDITION

10 9 8 7 6 5 4 3 2 1

SUSTAINABLE FORESTRY INITIATIVE — Certified Fiber Sourcing — www.sfiprogram.org

THIS LABEL APPLIES TO TEXT STOCK

We try to produce the most beautiful books possible, and we are also extremely concerned about the impact of our manufacturing process on the forests of the world and the environment as a whole. Accordingly, we've made sure that all of the paper we use has been certified as coming from forests that are managed to ensure the protection of the people and wildlife dependent upon them.

To Lola and every girl out there who believes
that anything is possible

Contents

2 ❧ Miraculous Mama 71

3 ❧ Frugalista 133

Acknowledgments

As usual, my incredible husband and daughter get the first shout-out for putting up with me while I was writing this book. They have graciously allowed themselves to become guinea pigs for many of the projects, experiments, and recipes in these pages. Over the last year, my husband never knew what to expect upon walking in the door: oftentimes every available surface would be stacked with bottles, jars, bowls, bubbling saucepans, and the like. Every member of my family, including our Maltese, Phoebe, and many of my friends have tried and tested lotions, potions, and remedies galore. I want to thank them all for their valuable and encouraging feedback.

Brendan Duffy, my fantastic editor, and all the team at Voice have made the writing of this book pleasurable and fun. It's a joy to have found my home with such a collaborative and forward-thinking group of people.

I want to hug Kristie McNamara for her help and inspiration in formulating many of the skincare recipes. It's wonderful to work with an expert who is not only hugely talented at what she does but is also a force for Good. Ros, and the whole team at Hands-on Third, you girls rock and have shown me how I can transform just about anything old into something wonderfully hip and cool.

Thank you, Robert Rodriguez, for your perfect jacket illustration—you are the best.

Last but not least, I want to thank my mother and father, who passed on their "roll up your sleeves and get on with it" ethic. Their curiosity and passion for life and learning continue to inspire me and remind me of one of my favorite quotes:

"Whatever you can do, or dream you can, begin it. Boldness has genius, power, and magic in it."

—JOHANN WOLFGANG VON GOETHE

Do It Gorgeously

Introduction

Clueless Is Out and Crafty Is In

I am absolutely-not your average Do-It-Yourself type of girl. I have to make this disclaimer before we begin, because I suspect that you may be the same way. I've always secretly wished that I could be one of those really frighteningly capable moms who can turn a group of obnoxious kids into affable angels just by pulling out some old egg cartons and nontoxic paints. I wish I had the time to spend hours in my kitchen making jellies, breads, and cute menu charts for my daughter, Lola. I've had visions of building, plank by plank, the garden shed that I dream of having in my backyard. In short, I fancy myself as a bit of a homestead type—but substituting the loaf-of-bread shoes with a pair of Manolos.

Having trodden the green path for a few years now, I've realized that a green way of living has less to do with eco-chic iPhone covers and more to do with plain old common sense. The most important changes I have made in my life are things that my grandmother also did, and she obviously didn't call them "green." My grandmother, Belle, was a regular type of girl who, through necessity, had to recycle and reuse just about everything she could. Socks were darned or transformed into baby toys, stale bread was ground into breadcrumbs, and slivers of soap were balled together to make another bar. Of course, back then the "reduce" part of the dreaded 3R combo (reduce, recycle, reuse) didn't come into the picture, because conspicuous consumption wasn't what it is today.

Many of us are getting a bit fed up with our disposable society. It just doesn't feel that good anymore to be an obsessive shopper. As we become aware of barges of hazardous trash making their way to Brazil, maxed-out landfills, and dwindling natural resources, we're starting to think twice before clicking the "add to cart" button. Do we really want to deal with the packaging and transportation, much less the cost? Can we go without? Ugh—I hear my mother right now: "Do you really *need* it?" Much as I fight against it—because honestly, I want what I want and I want it now—I find myself yearning for something different. I'll always love shopping, but I find an even deeper satisfaction in actually making many of the things that I used to whip out the credit card for.

Over the past couple of years, it's astonished me how much I can actually make from scratch, how easy it is, and how much money I can save. Being thrifty is becoming a rather thrilling exercise. Making a beautiful sugar scrub for pennies, instead of buying the exact same item in a department store for the same price as a meal for five, gives me a bit of a high. As with many, my bank balance has seen better days, and environmental concerns aside, it just makes sense to cut corners wherever possible. Each time I nudge myself to get resourceful—dare I say, crafty—I realize that I'm putting the green back into my wallet as well as my life.

Making things from scratch is pretty much second nature to me. I think it has a lot to do with my mom, who has an amazing work ethic. If I ever needed anything, she'd roll up her sleeves and have a go at making it first. She's taught me how to cook from scratch and how to garden, and those two passions led me to learn how to make skincare products. I spent years in my 20s studying homeopathy, aromatherapy, and botany—always yearning for a completely natural solution for most any health or beauty problem. Making from scratch what I eat and put on my skin is tremendously empowering. I don't have to interpret complicated ingredients lists and marketing claims, and I get to keep a bunch of packaging out of the landfill.

When it comes to full-on DIY, I must confess, I rather enjoyed playing the ditzy blonde when it came to matters that hitherto seemed beyond my skill level. I depended on the hope that someone would eventually come to the rescue and fix that leaking pipe, jammed window, or crumbling grout. I relied on the kindness of strangers to make sure my car tires were pumped to the correct pressure. Hardware stores were fun if they had cute garden furniture or beautiful plants, but the nuts and bolts aisles left me cold. Don't get me wrong, I've made all kinds of half-hearted attempts at making and fixing things—clothes for my daughter's American Girl doll to avoid the sweatshop thing, and a ballet skirt because I erroneously thought it would take two minutes to whip up. Both had disastrous results, especially the former—my attempt at a sequined ball gown for the grinning doll had to be swiftly transformed into a fraying bandana (when in doubt, bandanas are the way to go). However, my efforts to live a more earth-friendly life have forced me to be more self-reliant. I've realized that it's no longer cool to be clueless. It's time to step up to the plate and learn the skills that my grandparents had to learn. If I get it wrong the first time, it doesn't mean I need to ditch the entire project and call myself useless. Self-deprecation is fun, but it can also be a cop-out. It's far more satisfying to pick myself up, brush myself off, and make a second and a third attempt. I've always believed that success is in the trying.

Deep down we all are infinitely resourceful—our latent skills are waiting to be honed. You can do anything you put your mind to. Perhaps it's time to experiment and to discover what you may be really good at. If you've found yourself commenting over the past few years that you are either "terrible at baking" or "can't sew to save your life," the time has come to remove that scratched record from the turntable and replace it with a snazzy mental application that will have you believing anything is possible.

What about the cool factor? In your community, is it considered cool or creepy to make a lot of your own stuff? Where I live, the tide is slowly turning. Up until a few years ago, whenever I thought of sewing, I couldn't shake this image of a family that sat in the front pew of the church I went to when I was growing up. The mom was obviously glued to her sewing machine 24/7 and spent every moment of her existence whipping up the most dreadful matching creations for herself and her two daughters. The three of them would arrive looking like pink, fluffy cupcakes—the henpecked husband trailing behind. Recently, however, hip and trendy sewing classes are cropping up all over town. A secondhand Singer sewing machine from eBay is a badge of honor—especially when you can rewind the bobbin while carrying on a juicy conversation with a girlfriend.

Women are hardwired to multitask, but sadly, much of this god-given talent goes into juggling e-mails, IMs, texts, tweets, and phone calls. Do you ever feel burned out at the end of the day just from sitting at your computer? Do you find yourself comparing prices at the grocery store while listening to your girlfriend whine about her husband on your earpiece? Do you sometimes crave silence, and yet you're too afraid to turn the whole blinking, beeping, ringing mess off? If your answers are affirmative, it might be time to wean yourself off the tech addiction.

The problem is that one addiction needs to be replaced with another. I can't turn everything off and then expect to slide into a dreamy, serene state. My mind is still working overtime and I need to be "doing." To my joy, I have found that sitting down to sew a few buttons on my daughter's shirt or putting aside an afternoon to bake has undreamed-of rewards. I not only get to focus on a single thing—which is basically meditation—but my breathing becomes deeper, my shoulders ease away from my ears, and I get the intense satisfaction of having gotten something done, when the afternoon might well have been spent dithering around on Facebook or deleting acres of spam e-mails.

My mission is to take DIY out of the pages of glossy magazines and the hardware store and make it a reality in my own life. I want to do it myself and do it gorgeously. I am ready to roll up my sleeves, get my hands dirty (feet still planted firmly in the Manolos), and be that force of nature that I saw in my grandmother. Being responsible and autonomous helps me tap into that wellspring of strength within. Through the pages of this book, I hope that I can help you become a "doer." I invite you to throw yourself in and try your hand at everything. If you're already a master baker, yippee—pass that skill on to your girlfriends; same thing if you're a wiz with a needle and thread. If, however, you are like the rest of us mere mortals, sharpen your tools—it's going to be a fun ride!

It's also exciting to realize that many of the products that you purchase and love, everything from soaps and bath oils to scrumptious cookies and artisan cheeses, started out being made in someone's kitchen. A little someone like you or me woke up with an idea, gave it a go, couldn't believe how beautifully it turned out, and started a business. Many of the companies I recommended in my two previous books started out exactly this way. Some of the projects in this book could plant a seed of an idea or inspire you to want to take your backyard efforts to the next level. As so many of us are now looking to work from home, in a job we love, a good starting point might well be some of the *Do It Gorgeously* projects—just a thought!

Getting Started

Since this book is all about putting the green back into your life and your wallet, I'm all about reusing, recycling, and reducing whenever I can. I invite you to start trawling thrift stores, garage sales, and flea markets for bits of old fabric, cushions, pillowcases, tablecloths, moth-eaten cashmere sweaters, and anything else that catches your eye. Keep a lookout for pretty prints and fabrics with interesting textures. One visit to my local thrift store had my car trunk loaded with a bounty of wonderful base materials for me to transform into purses, aprons, dog beds, even lingerie, and the whole lot only cost me 15 bucks.

You don't need to be able to sew for most of the projects. However, a few rudimentary sewing skills will come in handy. If you're a complete novice and you know anyone who can show you a few basic stitches (perhaps a teacher at your child's school, a grandparent, aunt, or neighbor), tell them you'll trade a jar of homemade jelly for a quickie lesson. What few sewing skills I have, I learned from my mother, which was like the blind leading the blind. But sewing is actually much easier than you think. I've put together all the projects in this book in a matter of minutes, not hours. I'm impatient and impulsive. Once I have a vision of what I want to make—a sassy summer skirt, for example—I haven't got the patience or skill to mess around with patterns and specialized stitches. What I'm trying to say is that if I can do it, so can you.

If you are up for a little investment, I cannot recommend a sewing machine strongly enough. If you are new to sewing, make sure the machine is simple so you don't set yourself up to fail. Perhaps someone has one that they'll lend you for a while. If not, I highly recommend the Brother CS-6000i machine. It's simple enough for a regular girl like me, yet has enough fancy stitches and attachments to satisfy an accomplished seamstress. You can whip it out of the box and start making the projects in this book right away. It might even whet your appetite to move on to more elaborate designs. *Project Runway,* here I come! The good news is that a machine like this costs less than a couple of pairs of designer jeans. I'm short, so every pair of pants I buy has to be hemmed. Even if I only use it for hemming, the machine will have paid for itself in less than two years.

You will also need basic sewing supplies such as needles, thread, and scissors—things you probably have on hand anyway.

You will need supplies for making your beauty products, and I provide all the resources so that you can easily order them. Keep in mind that ordering online is actually more eco-friendly than running around to dozens of health and craft stores. Better still to share an order/shipment with a friend.

Most of the other projects in this book, food recipes aside, will require you to reuse or recycle things you already have. A huge part of living a gorgeously green life is to take the clutter and put it to good use, so start looking around to see what you should keep rather than throw away—you never know when it might come in handy.

One

Do It Beautifully

Why Make Your Own Beauty Products?

Every time you rub something on your skin, imagine you are also rubbing it on your internal organs. We need to get over the notion that our facial skin is something separate from the rest of our body and that it requires ridiculously expensive and scientific-sounding potions to keep it youthful and glowing. We need to wise up to the marketing ploys of the giant corporations, whose advertising campaigns would have us believe that all our "fine lines" will be erased in a matter of weeks. The ubiquitous cliché "Beauty is from within" is mercifully true, so what we eat has to be the starting place for gorgeous skin. I say "mercifully" because what we ingest is totally within our control and doesn't cost as much as expensive skincare products. Filling your cart with fresh fruits, veggies, and grains—as opposed to pre-prepared convenience food—will pay huge dividends in the gorgeous department in just a few weeks. Having taken care of our insides, we can then learn how to nourish our skin instead of plastering it with synthetic chemicals that can actually *increase* the visible signs of aging.

A major concern about commercial skincare products is that they can be full of all kinds of chemicals that actually have an adverse affect on our health. Isn't it bizarre that there are no regulations to keep this in check? The reality is that many companies can pack their potions with preservatives, plasticizers, synthetic fragrances, and worse. Many of these chemicals, cumulatively and over a period of time, cause all kinds of health problems. Many preservatives are hormone disruptors. This doesn't just mean that you might get a few bad rounds of PMS; it means that, over time, your entire endocrine system will be nudged off course, which could ultimately lead to a plethora of diseases, including cancer. The synthetic fragrances are neurotoxins, which can cause allergies and affect your entire nervous system—and we haven't even gotten to the antifreeze, asbestos, and lead in your cosmetics bag.

Our skin has two major functions. The first is as a protective barrier against all kinds of horrors, including environmental pollutants. The second is as an organ of elimination. Through our skin, we detox many harmful pollutants and heavy metals. Our skin also absorbs as much as 60% of what we put on it. What it absorbs goes directly into our bloodstream. This is quite terrifying when you realize that scientists are discovering some commonly used skincare chemicals lead to the very diseases we take pains to avoid.

The number of green and eco-friendly skincare products is on the rise— there's even a section for them at many drugstores. There are two reasons for this. The first is that many large cosmetics corporations have had to face mounting pressure from online activists demanding safer cosmetics. The second is that by slapping an "organic" or "handcrafted botanicals" label on a bottle, they can jack up the price considerably. However, we need to be really savvy when it comes to forking out hard-earned cash for products that claim to be safer. The labeling loopholes are such that much of this natural-sounding terminology is intended to trick us into believing that the "organic" lotion in question was made by a team of herbalists on an organic farm—hmmmmmmm, not so sure about that!

Most of us can't possibly afford to replace our entire skincare/cosmetics line anyway. So what's a gorgeously green girl to do? The solution is DIY skincare— yes, making your own. I've been creating my own skincare products for years and not only am I guaranteed a top-quality product, but I'm saving myself oodles of cash. Many of you may be hesitant because you can't entirely trust that these products will be as effective as the store-bought ones you're used to.

Those of you who have specific skin conditions might worry that you won't get exactly what you need. The truth is that you can easily create a product that is much more effective, less toxic, and less expensive in a matter of minutes. Your products won't need any preservatives, which are the top toxic culprits, and they won't need synthetic fragrances, stabilizers, dyes, or anything else that doesn't belong on your body's largest organ.

You can make virtually everything, from hair conditioner to luxury anti-aging cosmetics, and you don't need to don a white lab coat or plan to spend hours in your kitchen sterilizing bottles. My recipes are quick, easy, and fun, and can be hilarious if you get a girlfriend to join you. Making cosmetics is especially entertaining—it beats finger-painting with a 5-year-old any day of the week—and can have you looking gorgeous for just pennies.

The Basics

Almost all skincare products contain oil and water. To prevent the oil and water from separating, wax or an emulsifier must be added. The difference between body/face oil and lotion is simply that the latter contains water. But the moment water is added to oil, the lotion becomes unstable—meaning it can go bad really quickly. That's why lotions and creams usually contain preservatives, while oils don't.

Look at the ingredients list on every product you currently have. Generally speaking, the longer the list, the more wary you should be. The joy of making your own products is that you'll begin to understand the basic components that make up a particular product and you'll see that most of the toxic chemicals are actually unnecessary. They're added to either stabilize or lengthen the life of a product or make it appear or smell nicer. These added chemicals do more harm than good to your skin.

The quality of the individual ingredients that make up most regular skincare products are unlikely to be top notch. Even if the company boasts that they use completely "natural" ingredients, they're likely to be the cheapest ones they can find. The joy of making your own is that you'll be able to source the best ingredients possible, for a fraction of the price. You won't, of course, be paying for packaging, marketing, travel, storage, or a storefront—ha-ha! Now *you're* the crafty one. So get ready to dive into an Aladdin's cave of fragrant and unctuous oils, pearly powders, and creamy balms. You're about to have a party.

History of the Lowly Moisturizer

The base of almost every skincare product you're going to make is cold-pressed plant oil. Ancient civilizations, including those in Egypt, China, and Rome, used cold-pressed vegetables oils for beautifying the skin, but nowadays using these oils is the exception. Why did we stop?

At the end of the 19th century, moisturizers began to be mass-produced. Demand became greater as more women started using commercial soaps and hot, chlorinated water to wash. Commercial soap strips your skin of all its natural oils, and hot, chlorinated water is horribly drying. So way back then, scientists got in their labs and started synthesizing petroleum, pig fat, lard, and whale oil into inexpensive/low-quality ingredients suitable for a moisturizer. They also had to synthesize emulsifiers and preservatives. Cold-pressed plant oils, however, contain natural preservatives. Nearly all the emulsifiers and preservatives you find in commercial skincare products are artificial. You may have heard of a class of preservatives called parabens. These are especially worrisome because they act like hormones and have been linked to reproductive and development problems in infants.

Most mass-produced commercial moisturizers today contain water, alcohol, coloring, mineral oil, and preservatives. All of the above interfere with the skin's natural production of sebum and are therefore aging. Even if the moisturizer contains minute amounts of antioxidants, botanical extracts, or whatever today's beauty buzzword is, these "nutrients" cannot be absorbed by the skin because they are not mixed with natural plant oils, which would aid in their absorption. Most of the more expensive department store moisturizers aren't any more effective than the cheaper drugstore brands. They still contain the usual synthetic chemical cocktail, which you want to avoid if you need a gentle and effective moisturizer. The greatest trade secret is known only by Mother Nature, and most mass-produced skincare product companies cannot afford her bounty.

Having now understood the basic components and history of what you have hitherto whipped out your credit card for, I hope you've realized that you can get a greatly superior product by making your own. The biggest advantage your own creation has over its store-bought equivalent is that you know exactly what's in it.

What Does "Natural" Really Mean?

The word "natural" is bandied about everywhere nowadays, but what does it actually mean? According to www.dictionary.com, the first definition of "natural" is "existing in or formed by nature." This gets us a little closer to the truth, but it's still a bit generic for our purposes. The Food and Drug Administration (FDA) states that a "natural" ingredient is "extracted directly from plants or animal products, as opposed to being produced synthetically." Because some of the ingredients you will be using for your recipes, especially essential oils, are extracted by distillation, which can create chemicals that didn't exist in the first place, I prefer the following definition from the *Encyclopedia of Common Natural Ingredients Used in Food, Drugs, and Cosmetics*: A natural product is one that is "derived from plant, animal, or microbial sources, primarily through physical processing, sometimes facilitated by simple chemical reactions such as acidification, basification, ion exchange, hydrolysis, and salt formation, as well as microbial fermentation." I know—that's a lot of information. So to keep things simple, here is what "natural" ingredients mean in my book:

- Grown, raised, harvested, and processed in an ecological manner

- Not produced synthetically*

- Do not contain petrochemicals

- Not extracted or processed using petrochemicals

- Not extracted or processed using anything other than natural ingredients as solvents

- Do not contain synthetic ingredients

- Do not contain artificial ingredients, coloring, or flavoring

- Do not contain synthetic or chemical preservatives

* The exceptions are emulsifying wax and L-ascorbic acid (vitamin C), which, although derived from natural vegetable sources, are produced in a lab and therefore synthetic.

WHY DOES MY SKIN NEED POLYUNSATURATED FATTY ACIDS?

Polyunsaturated fatty acids cannot be synthesized by the body and therefore have to be obtained through our diet, or through topical application to our skin. Skin that is deficient in these fatty acids has been shown to exhibit extreme water loss and can take on a scaly appearance. These fatty acids have excellent moisture-retaining properties and are easily assimilated by the skin. If skincare products contain these long carbon chain essential fatty acids, it makes their absorptive base highly emollient and facilitates penetration.

IS NATURAL ALWAYS BETTER?

The problem with synthetic is that it's a compound made artificially by using chemical ingredients—that is, it's made in a lab as opposed to being found in the great outdoors. I believe it's healthier for the most part to nourish yourself, food and skinwise, with what is actually found in nature. Obviously, not all things that are found in nature are good for us. Actually, some plants could literally kill us. However, through the ages many plants have been found to have incredible healing and beautifying properties. Most of the great benefits come without risk to your health or unpleasant side effects. The problem with many synthetics is that our bodies just weren't designed to deal with them. They may succeed in instantly making your skin appear softer, but you could also be throwing your endocrine system totally off balance or interfering with the neurological processes of your brain.

BEWARE

Green washing has become a bit of a problem. Many large companies want to appear greener than they actually are because it makes for good marketing. Now that you know the definition of the word "natural," you'll see that many products out there that use the word on their labels are misleading us. They may have *one* natural ingredient floating around in a sea of synthetic chemicals and still call the whole thing "natural." When you make your products from the recipes here, you can rest assured that it's the real thing, and you can and should proudly write the word "natural" on your labels.

Basic Ingredients You Will Need

Where do I find them?

Go to gorgeouslygreen.com and click on "Do It Gorgeously" to find an updated resource guide for absolutely everything you'll need for making your own skin-care products. You may also be able to find many of the ingredients in your local drugstore or health food store.

How safe are they and can anyone use them?

Although I try to use ingredients that are nontoxic—so much so that you could eat them—I don't recommend that you chug down a bottle of jojoba oil! Be particularly careful with the essential oils. Although nontoxic, they are extremely concentrated and so should be used exactly according to the recipe. And they should never be ingested.

PLANT OILS

Plant oils come from nuts, seeds, fruits, and veggies. These natural oils will be the mainstay or base oil of many of your preparations. They're also referred to as "carrier" oils.

You can use these oils on their own or mix them with all kinds of wonderful waxes, butters, and essential oils to make your potions. Don't skimp on quality when it comes to buying these beautiful oils. They need to be minimally processed because high temperatures, deodorizing, and bleaching can destroy the very nutrients in them that our skin needs. So look for one of the following terms on the label:

- Unrefined
- Expeller-pressed
- Cold-pressed

Because these oils are minimally processed, most of them have a relatively short shelf life. If you store them at room temperature for more than six months, they could go rancid, which means they oxidize and form free radicals—the very thing we want to avoid. Free radicals are one of the main culprits in aging skin, but they can be kept in check by using potent antioxidants. Your minimally processed oils, when they are fresh, are packed full of antioxidants—so buy only the amount you know you will use within six months.

Always store the products you make from plant oils in dark glass containers (either amber or cobalt blue glass are readily available; see the resource section, p. 379). Light and heat will cause your oils to oxidize faster. When you purchase your oils, they will arrive in clear or opaque plastic bottles, so keep these containers in a cool, dark spot until you use them. The shelf life of most of the following plant oils is about one year. Also start looking around for amber glass bottles that you can reuse. I keep a stash of old bottles, from ones that contained cough medicine to vanilla extract—they'll all be useful.

Sweet almond: This light but nourishing oil forms the base of many skincare products because it is easily absorbed (leaving no residue), and has a high concentration of fatty acids, which help regenerate facial tissue.

Sesame: Sesame oil is used extensively in Ayurvedic (traditional Indian) medicine due to its unique molecular structure, which enables it to penetrate all the way into the deeper layers of the skin. It is a very stable oil, so it has a longer shelf life than many other carrier oils.

Rosehip seed: Also known as *rosa mosqueta*, this extraordinary oil has been found to contain powerful anti-aging properties. It contains an extremely high concentration of essential fatty acids. It's the only vegetable oil that contains natural retinoic acid (vitamin A acid).

Apricot oil: Rich in vitamin A, this wonderful carrier oil is great for inflammation and/or sensitive skin conditions. It's also rich in polyunsaturated fatty acids.

Avocado oil: This rich and beautifully nourishing oil is green and brownish in color due to its chlorophyll content. It's useful in treating eczema, psoriasis, and sensitive skin conditions.

Jojoba oil: "Jojoba oil" is actually a liquid wax made from the jojoba bean. It contains essential fatty acids, proteins, minerals, and myristic acid (an anti-inflammatory agent). It attracts and holds in moisture to the skin and helps you increase collagen production. It's also great for your hair and scalp.

Virgin coconut oil: Made from fresh coconut meat, virgin coconut oil has a slightly sweet coconut scent. It is produced without chemicals. It forms a wonderful protective barrier around your skin. It's also useful in treating irritated or inflamed skin and is extremely soothing.

Evening primrose oil: Moisturizing, softening, and soothing, this oil is packed with gamma linolenic acid (GLA), an essential fatty acid that's great for your skin.

Wheat germ oil: Packed with nutrients such as vitamins A, D, and E, and lecithin and squalene, this light carrier oil is a perfect addition to facial skin-care products.

ESSENTIAL OILS

Essential oils are miraculous. I'm passionate about them because they have so many benefits—mental, physical, and spiritual. In times of anxiety or desperation, I've depended on specific oils to calm my nerves and soothe my soul. Essential oils are also medicinal in that they can alleviate everything from dandruff to staph infections.

Essential oils come from the leaves, stems, flowers, rinds, roots, berries, seeds, needles, or bark of a huge variety of plants. The oil contains the essence or life force of the plant. Strictly speaking, they aren't "oils," because they don't contain fatty acids. They are extracted by steam, hydrodistillation, or cold pressing. Because they don't contain fatty acids, they won't go rancid the way regular base oils do. Due to their molecular structure, they can penetrate the upper layers of the skin to nourish and renew skin cells.

What About "Anti-aging" Ingredients?

The skincare industry rakes in billions of dollars annually and uses all kinds of pseudoscientists, advertising agencies, and marketing/branding geniuses

ESSENTIAL OIL GUIDE

• Buying good quality essential oils is an investment. Unadulterated oils are expensive. However, you will only use a few drops in each recipe, so one bottle could last you for years. Stored properly, in a dark, cool cabinet, they can last up to 10 years. The exception is citrus oils, which will last up to 2 years if you keep them in the refrigerator.

• You need to be super savvy when it comes to choosing the company from which to buy your oils. Many companies dilute or adulterate their oils with cheap plant oils. I can usually tell by taking a sniff. An authentic essential oil should smell extremely strong. Make sure you research the company, asking them where they get their oils and how they are extracted. If the company can't answer, move on to a different company. You'll find the companies I like best in the resource guide (see p. 379).

• If you can buy organic oils, I highly recommend you do so. Paying a few dollars extra for oil that is pesticide-free and unadulterated is worth it. If you want to save a bit of money, buy nonorganic oils for cleaning products and room sprays, but I recommend going organic for skincare products.

• All essential oils are potent, so they should be treated with caution. Always do a skin test by mixing 2 drops of the oil with 1 teaspoon of base oil and apply to the delicate skin on the underside of your wrist. Wait 24 hours to see if you have a reaction. If you have high blood pressure, avoid rosemary and thyme oils. If you are pregnant, avoid basil, jasmine, peppermint, cedar wood, juniper, rosemary, chamomile, marjoram, fennel, thyme, and myrrh oils.

• Citrus oils can make your skin oversensitive to the sun. I prefer to use products containing these oils at night. If I use them in the daytime, I wait a couple of hours after applying before I go outside.

to get you to buy into the latest buzzword in anti-aging. What should we believe?

I'm fully into organic and natural, but I'm also fully into reversing the ticking of the clock where possible. The only ingredients in commercial over-the-counter products that have been clinically proven to improve the skin and in some cases make it look younger are vitamin C, alpha hydroxy acids, and retinol. It's vital to understand that these ingredients have to be present in a high enough concentration to be effective, and they often aren't. Moreover, they're often shoved into useless creams along with a bunch of toxic chemicals, so you really need to know what to look for.

VITAMIN C

Many creams boast a high concentration of vitamin C. It's an antioxidant, which is essential for the synthesis of collagen, which keeps the skin elastic and supple. The problem is that vitamin C is completely unstable except in its dry, powdered form. So when it's put into a liquid, it's incapable of performing the tasks it is supposed to (creating collagen or scavenging free radicals). Worse, when it oxidizes (which it does in most creams and lotions), it may even promote free-radical formation. The other problem with commercial formulations is that they

VITAMIN C CRYSTALS AND CAMU CAMU

It's important to realize that as natural as vitamin C sounds, all L-ascorbic acid (vitamin C) sold is a synthetic chemical. Most L-ascorbic acid is manufactured in just one facility in the United States, and different companies market it as they see fit. This doesn't take away from the fact that vitamin C or L-ascorbic acid is a fantastic topical antioxidant; however, if you want ingredients that really are natural and not synthesized in a lab, you may want to look out for a powder that comes from an Amazonian bush called Camu Camu. It contains more vitamin C than any other known plant. You can order it in powder form from Live Superfoods (www.livesuperfoods.com).

You can buy vitamin C crystals that have been specially formulated for your skin. The best I have found to date is Pure C by CosMedix (www .cosmedix.com). They come in a small shaker jar.

Put a dime-size dollop of your face cream or oil in the palm of your hand and add a generous shake of the C crystals or ¼ tsp of the Camu Camu powder. Rub your palms carefully together, blending the crystals/powder in, and apply to your face, neck, and décolleté.

need to have a really high concentration of vitamin C to be in any way effective. But our skin does benefit from vitamin C—so what's a girl to do? You can either add dry mixing crystals to your homemade products (see the box, p. 17) or you can make your own vitamin C serum and use it up quickly (see p. 40).

ALPHA HYDROXY ACIDS

Alpha hydroxies are a family of acids derived from fruit, which is why they are also known as fruit acids. They can effectively peel off the uppermost layer of your skin, allowing newer, softer skin to come through. In almost all commercial skincare products, they're added in concentrations below 10%. It's questionable whether, at this concentration, they can do anything at all. Cosmeticians usually use them on your skin at a 20% to 30% concentration. If you've ever had a glycolic peel (glycolic acid is a form of alpha hydroxy acid), you'll remember it because of the intense tingling sensation. Doctors often use an even higher concentration, which would result in your skin peeling, flaking, and looking horrendous for a week—until it drops off (much like a snake shedding its skin). These salon and doctor's office treatments can be extremely expensive, so I'll show you how to make your own AHA Mask (see p. 39).

THRIFTY GIRL TIPS

Since DIY is all about saving money, it's time to figure out where we need to spend and where we can cut corners. Your biggest initial expenditure will be your essential oils. Either:

1. Get two or three girlfriends to share your order. Each of you can choose your oils from the recipes here and write out a shopping list. Chances are you'll all need the same oils. If you do this, you can either get together one evening to make your products or pass the oils on to your friends when you are done.

2. Just swallow the initial expense and know that you will get literally dozens of bottles of cream out of this one order. Remember that the essential oils will last for years, so once you get a good collection going, you'll be in great shape to try out many wonderful future concoctions.

RETINOL (VITAMIN A)

This is the only commercial product that I add to my all-natural, homemade regime. Retinol is a derivative of vitamin A and is extremely effective at resurfacing the skin in a gentle, gradual way. If you are going to spend the money, make sure you buy a therapeutic-grade product with a high enough concentration to make a difference (at least 1.0%). Also make sure the product is nontoxic.

You can also add a little retinyl acetate (a natural fatty acid form of retinol) to your creams. Keep in mind that any kind of retinol product can cause skin sensitivity. If you use it and find that your skin gets a little red and dry in patches, you may need to decrease your dose. You should start off using a pea-size amount of the product every other night and increase to every night after two weeks. For a list of my favorite companies that sell nontoxic retinol (and other great ingredients), see the resource section (p. 379).

What Else Do I Need?

Waxes, butters, and emulsifiers: If you are going to make creams, lotions, and masks, you will need some or all of these ingredients, which include beeswax,* shea and coconut butters, and vegetable-based emulsifying wax from naturally occurring fats. These can be purchased from a number of web sites (see resources, p. 379, or go to www.gorgeouslygreen.com and click on "Do It Gorgeously") and are pretty inexpensive.

Infusions: Making an infusion is just as easy as making a mug of herbal tea. In the following recipes, you may need to prepare a lavender, chamomile, or rose infusion. You can use fresh or dried lavender. I like to use organic chamomile tea, and it's preferable to use dried rose petals. You can either dry your own or purchase all of these dried flowers from Mountain Rose Herbs (www.mountain roseherbs.com). Simply place about 1 tablespoon of fresh or dried herbs in a measuring cup and pour in ½ cup of water that has just been boiled. Steep for

If you are vegan, you may wish to substitute Jojoba Flakes for the beeswax (see resources, p. 379).

half an hour. Pour the infusion through a sieve into a small bowl or clean jar. Your infusion will keep for two days (covered), in the fridge.

Bottles and jars: You need to store all your preparations in dark glass jars or bottles to avoid light, which will turn your precious potions rancid or inactive. Amber or cobalt blue containers are inexpensive and readily available from the web sites in the resource section. You'll also find some amber bottles around your house that you can reuse—old cough syrup and medicine bottles are perfect. Whatever size or color container you choose, remember that when making gifts, they can be customized and made gorgeous with creative labels, ribbons, and other decorations.

Bowls, measuring cups, and spoons: No need to buy anything to prepare your products. Just use the bowls, saucepans, measuring cups, measuring spoons, and other items you already have in your kitchen. The only thing that may be useful is a set of little plastic funnels, which you should be able to find at your local hardware store.

Notebook and labels: Make sure you use a notebook to keep a record of your recipes. Write down dates and any problems or triumphs you encounter. You will also need sticky labels for each preparation. You can get really creative with your labels (see p. 67). You may want to cover a paper label with sticky plastic or tape to keep the oil from dripping down and spoiling it. You can also

IMPORTANT PREPARATION TIPS

• In many of the skincare recipes, you will be mixing water or floral-infused water into a blend of wax and oil. To keep the oil and water from separating, you must make sure the wax/oil mixture and the water infusion are the same temperature before you blend them. You don't need to fiddle around with a thermometer—just stick the tip of your finger in and make sure they feel about the same temperature.

• Many of the creams and lotions require refrigeration to prevent them from going rancid, so find a large, reusable container in which to keep all your bottles and jars. It should be big enough to fit three or four midsize jars and three or four bottles. Make sure you can see through it, so you can read the labels on your potions. I use a 9x13-inch Pyrex baking dish and I label it "Sophie's Potions" with a marker. That way, little fingers stay out of it. Before I get in the shower, I simply bring the container with my potions into the bathroom, and put it back in the refrigerator when I'm done.

• Make sure you create a label (see p. 67) for each potion you make and be sure to write the date on it.

• If you are traveling, one or two nights out of the fridge won't harm your preparations. However, if you are away for longer, you're better off taking just the oils, because they don't need refrigeration.

• Wrap a thick rubber band around any bottles that contain facial or body oil. This will prevent the bottom of your container from getting oily.

wrap a rubber band just below the rim of the jar or bottle and it will catch the drips.

Storage: If you are making a cream or lotion, you need to store it in the fridge because of the lack of preservatives. You can store your body and facial oils in a cool, dark cupboard or cabinet. I specify in each recipe exactly how long it can be stored; however, you may find it useful to purchase a Chek-It: Home Test Lab in a Box from www.snowdriftfarm.com. This way you can check if, after a few weeks, any bacteria or fungi have crept in!

Getting Started

Choose a cleanser, moisturizer, and toner for your skin type. Then, go shopping for what you need. Having picked your recipes and purchased your supplies, you're ready for some fun. I suggest putting aside no more than an hour. This will give you plenty of time to make a cleanser, toner, moisturizer, and body oil.

Set aside a large, clear space on your kitchen table or counter and set out all your supplies. Make sure you have a few clean rags or dish towels, and all your labeling supplies (see p. 67).

You may want to share this fun with a girlfriend or even an age-appropriate child. From my own experience, a 7- or 8-year-old will be able to participate without causing total mayhem. Keep in mind that you will be heating, stirring, and adding minute drops of essential oils, so a hyperactive child could have you tearing your hair out. My 8-year-old daughter got a strong prior word of caution (about heat and spilling), and now absolutely loves these sessions and even makes her own little potions.

STERILIZATION

You need to sterilize all your glass storage bottles and jars before filling them. The easiest way is to put them through a hot dishwasher cycle and allow them to air dry. If you don't have a dishwasher, you can boil your bottles and jars in a large pot of water for 5 minutes and remove carefully with tongs. Allow to air dry on a clean dishcloth.

Skincare Regime for Oily/Problem Skin

CLEANSER

....

Citrus Cleansing Cream

....

For those of you who are prone to oily skin, this is perfect for removing dirt, grime, and even makeup.

Yields: approximately 2 oz. of cream

Application: use every evening to remove makeup and the day's dirt

Storage: 2-oz. dark glass jar in the fridge

Shelf life: 3 months

¼ cup apricot oil	¼ tsp. borax
1 tbsp. virgin coconut oil	½ tsp. vitamin E oil
1 tbsp. beeswax	20 drops grapefruit essential oil
1 tsp. anhydrous lanolin*	20 drops lavender essential oil
½ cup distilled water	

Anhydrous lanolin is the waxy coating from sheep's wool after it's been sheared. Getting it doesn't hurt the animal in any way. "Anhydrous" means it's made without adding water. It's wonderfully emollient, which is why it's an excellent ingredient in skincare products. Some people can be allergic to lanolin, and if you're one of them, simply substitute an extra 1 tsp. of virgin coconut oil. Look for 100% pure lanolin (available on Amazon, www.amazon.com).

1. Place the base oils, beeswax, and lanolin in a small bowl set over a saucepan of boiling water and heat until the wax melts. Remove the bowl and leave it to cool for 10 minutes.

2. In another pan or in the microwave, warm the water and stir in the borax. Remove the bowl from the heat and allow it to cool.

3. Spoon the base oil mixture into a blender and blend on a high speed as you slowly drizzle the water through the hole in the lid. Blend for 15 seconds or until it is a smooth consistency.

4. Add the vitamin E and essential oils and pour into the jar. Allow it to cool completely before screwing on the cap.

How to use: Scoop out a dime-size dollop of the cream and massage into your face. Add some warm water, massage again, then rinse with cool water.

TONER

Pure Aloe Vera Toner

This is a wonderful, inexpensive toner for oily skin. If you have combination skin, it might be a good idea to use this toner only on your T-zone. You can store it in an old jelly jar.

Yields: approximately 16 oz. of toner

Application: use in the morning to refresh before moisturizing and in the evening after cleansing

Storage: 16-oz. glass jar in the fridge

Shelf life: 3 months

12 oz. pure, organic aloe vera juice	2 oz. distilled water

1. Pour the aloe vera juice and the water into the jar and gently shake.

2. Store in the fridge.

How to use: When you are ready to tone, dip a cotton pad or ball into the juice and gently wipe across your face and neck.

Lavender and Rosemary Moisturizer

This is a beautifully therapeutic moisturizer for oily skin. The combination of the essential oils is antiseptic and antibacterial, so it can help with skin that is prone to pimples or acne.

Yields: approximately 2 oz. of cream

Application: use morning and evening, after toning

Storage: 2-oz. dark glass jar in the fridge

Shelf life: 3 months

1 tsp. beeswax	4 tbsp. lavender infusion*
2 tsp. cocoa butter	5 drops rosemary essential oil
4 tbsp. jojoba oil	5 drops lavender essential oil
4 tsp. emulsifying wax	5 drops chamomile essential oil

Lavender infusion is made by pouring ½ cup of boiling water over 1 tbsp. dried lavender flowers. Leave it to steep for half an hour. Drain off the lavender water and discard the flowers.

1. Heat the beeswax, cocoa butter, and jojoba oil in a bowl set over a saucepan of boiling water. Stir until the wax has melted. Remove the bowl from the heat.

2. Place the emulsifying wax and lavender infusion in another bowl and put it over the same saucepan of boiling water, stirring until the wax dissolves.

3. It's vital that you make sure the base oil mixture and the lavender infusion are about the same temperature before you combine them. Dip the tip of your finger in each bowl to see that it's warm (not too hot and not too cool). Very slowly add the infusion to the oil mixture, whisking vigorously. Be very sure you add the infusion mixture extremely slowly to keep the preparation from separating.

4. When the mixture cools, stir in the essential oils.

5. Spoon the mixture into a jar and only screw on the lid when it's completely cooled.

Balancing Oil for Clogged Pores

You can either use this oil on just your nose/T-zone area (where the blackheads and enlarged pores will be worse), or if your skin is particularly oily, use it all over your face. Jojoba oil will help unclog your pores. It mimics your body's natural sebum, so rubbing it into your clogged pores will tell them that they can stop overproducing sebum (which causes the blackheads). The molecules of jojoba oil are small enough to penetrate your skin pores, so the antibacterial tea tree oil that I've used in this recipe will be drawn into your pores.

Yields: approximately 2 oz. of oil

Application: use every evening after toning

Storage: 2-oz. dark glass bottle in a cool, dark cupboard

Shelf life: 3 months

2 oz. jojoba oil	10 drops rosemary essential oil
15 drops tea tree essential oil	

1. Sterilize your bottle by filling it with boiling water or putting it through a hot dishwasher cycle.

2. Pour in the jojoba oil, then add the essential oils and shake gently.

How to use: Gently rub in and around your nose and T-zone area. Then soak a little cotton pad in witch hazel and gently wipe over the area of application.

Skincare Regime for Normal/Combination Skin

Chamomile and Aloe Cleansing Cream

This is a wonderfully creamy, soothing concoction that will completely remove all traces of grime and makeup (even stubborn mascara).

Yields: approximately 2 oz. of cream

Application: use every evening to remove makeup and the day's dirt

Storage: 2-oz. dark glass jar in the fridge

Shelf life: 3 months

¼ cup sweet almond oil	1 tbsp. vegetable glycerin
2 tbsp. virgin coconut oil	¼ tsp. borax
1 tbsp. beeswax	1 tsp. vitamin E oil
1 tsp. anhydrous lanolin*	15 drops lavender essential oil
¼ cup aloe vera juice	10 drops rosemary essential oil
3 tbsp. chamomile infusion**	8 drops chamomile essential oil

Anhydrous lanolin is the waxy coating from sheep's wool after it's been sheared. Getting it doesn't hurt the animal in any way. "Anhydrous" means it's made without adding water. It's wonderfully emollient, which is why it's an excellent ingredient in skincare products. Some people can be allergic to lanolin, and if you're one of them, simply substitute an extra 1 tsp. of virgin coconut oil. Look for 100% pure lanolin (www.amazon.com).

**Chamomile infusion is made by pouring ½ cup of boiling water over 1 tbsp. of dried chamomile flowers. Leave it to steep for half an hour.*

1. In a small bowl set over a large saucepan of boiling water, melt the base oils, beeswax, and lanolin until the wax has just melted. Remove from the heat.

2. In another pan, heat the aloe vera juice, chamomile infusion, glycerin, and then stir in the borax until it dissolves in the liquid. Remove from the heat.

3. Pour or spoon the beeswax mixture into a blender and leave it to cool a further 5 minutes or until it begins to thicken. Stir the mixture, loosening it from the sides of the blender with a spatula.

4. Turn the blender on high and, through the removable plastic center of the lid, very slowly pour the aloe vera and chamomile liquid. Blend for 15 seconds. Check that the consistency is smooth (you may need to scrape some more away from the sides of the blender) and blend 10 seconds more or until the cream is smooth.

5. Add the vitamin E oil and the essential oils and blend 5 more seconds.

6. Pour or spoon the cream into your glass storage jar. Screw on the cap only when you are sure the cream has completely cooled.

TONER

Rose and Aloe Softening Toner

This is the most wonderfully soothing toner for those of you with dry skin.

Yields: approximately 4 oz. of toner

Application: use every morning to freshen up before moisturizing and every evening after cleansing

Storage: 4-oz. dark glass bottle in the fridge

Shelf life: 3 months

½ cup aloe vera juice	2 tsp. vegetable glycerin
½ cup rosewater	

1. Blend all the ingredients together in a measuring cup and pour into the glass bottle.

MOISTURIZER

....

Geranium and Apricot Moisturizer

....

This is my favorite moisturizer for normal to dry skin. It's perfectly smoothing for under makeup, and the essential oils are joyously uplifting.

Yields: approximately 2 oz. of cream

Application: use every morning and evening after toning; allow 5 minutes for absorption before applying makeup.

Storage: 2-oz. dark glass jar in the fridge

Shelf life: 3 months

2 tsp. beeswax	4 tsp. emulsifying wax
2 tsp. cocoa butter	20 drops geranium essential oil
2 tbsp. apricot oil	½ tsp. rosehip seed oil
2 tbsp. jojoba oil	½ tsp. vitamin E oil
4 tbsp. rose petal infusion*	

Rose petal infusion is made by pouring ½ cup of boiling water over 1 tbsp. of dried rose petals. Leave it to steep for half an hour.

1. Heat the beeswax, cocoa butter, and base oils in a bowl set over a saucepan of boiling water, until the wax has dissolved. Remove the bowl from the saucepan. Let it cool for 5 minutes.

2. Heat the rose infusion and the emulsifying wax in a small bowl set over the same pan of boiling water, until the wax has dissolved. Remove from the heat and allow it to cool.

3. It's vital that you make sure the oil mixture and the rosewater/emulsifying wax mixture are the same temperature. Dip the tip of your finger in both bowls to make sure. They should both be warm (you'll know they're getting too cool if they begin to thicken and become opaque). Very slowly add the infusion to the oil mixture, whisking vigorously.

4. When the mixture cools down, add the essential oil, rosehip seed oil, and vitamin E oil.

5. Spoon the mixture into your jar. Leave the cream to cool completely before screwing on the top.

Skincare Regime for Dry/Mature Skin

INSIDE OUT

As we age, it's vitally important that we focus on good skin from the inside out. Make sure that you are eating plenty of omega-3 fatty acids, which can be found in high amounts in salmon, sardines, trout, walnuts, and flaxseed. You could also take a fish oil supplement. I love every blend from Nordic Naturals (www.nordicnaturals.com).

Make sure you get as many antioxidants as you can through your diet. The foods containing the highest amounts of antioxidants include prunes, raisins, blueberries, blackberries, strawberries, raspberries, plums, kale, spinach, alfalfa, broccoli, and beets.

I highly recommend adding the anti-aging ingredients listed on pp. 17–19 to your skincare regime. You can add a small scoop of vitamin C crystals or Camu Camu powder (a scoop the size of your pinky fingernail) to any of my cream and lotion recipes. I also sometimes add a retinol powder to the next recipe.

It's vital that you exfoliate at least twice a week. Dry skin brushing (see p. 44) will help exfoliate your body, and I recommend the following gentle recipe for your face. Remember, if you don't exfoliate, you are just sticking dead skin cells back onto your face with lotion!

Gentle Facial Exfoliating Scrub

This is a very inexpensive scrub made from basic kitchen ingredients.

Yields: approximately 16 oz. of scrub

Application: use three times a week

Storage: 16-oz. plastic or glass container

Shelf life: 6 months

1 cup ground oatmeal	2 tsp. cornmeal
½ cup dry lavender flowers, stripped off stalks (optional)	Filtered water
½ cup powdered milk (whole or nonfat is fine)	

1. Mix all the dry ingredients in a bowl.

2. Transfer to a container with a lid.

How to use: Combine 1 tbsp. of your scrub with enough filtered water to form a thick paste. Gently massage in circular motions over your face and neck. Rinse with warm water and pat your skin dry.

India Rose Luxurious Oil for Dry/Mature Skin

This is the finest treatment oil for mature skin that you can find. It's made with rose absolute and frankincense essential oils—both historically renowned for deeply nourishing dry skin. It also contains rosehip seed oil, which contains natural retinoic acid—perfect for gently resurfacing the skin.

Yields: approximately 1 oz. of oil

Application: use every evening after toning

Storage: 1-oz. dark glass bottle with dropper in cool, dark cupboard

Shelf life: 1 year

1 tbsp. rosehip seed oil	10 drops rose absolute essential oil
1 tbsp. sweet almond oil	10 drops galbanum essential oil
1 tbsp. avocado oil	½ tsp. Antioxidant Booster*
10 drops benzoin resin essential oil	(optional)
10 drops frankincense essential oil	

*You can purchase a small bottle of Antioxidant Booster from Skin Actives (www.skin actives.com).

1. Combine all the oils in a small glass measuring cup.

2. Carefully use a funnel to pour the oils into your bottle. Shake gently and allow the oil to sit for a few hours before using.

Sunscreen

Many of you already have sunscreens that you know and love. Here are my favorite nontoxic brands for your face:

- Solar Rx from Keys (www.keys-soap.com)

- Reflect and Serious Protection, both by CosMedix (www.cosmedix .com)

- All Lavera sunscreens (www.lavera.com)

Although many of you may want to stick to commercial sunscreens, where you know the exact SPF, you can make your own by simply adding 2 tsp. of zinc oxide powder to 2 oz. of any of the face cream recipes in this chapter (so if you have made a 4-oz. jar of cream, you'll need 4 tsp. of zinc oxide). You could also try the following recipe.

Sesame Sunscreen

Coconut and sesame oils have been used as natural sunscreens for ages. This is a buttery sunscreen for your entire body. Coconut oil liquefies when it's warm, so if you want a firmer butter, keep it in the fridge.

Yields: approximately 2 oz. of butter

Application: use half an hour before going in the sun

Storage: 2-oz. dark glass jar in the fridge

Shelf life: 6 months

2 tbsp. coconut oil	½ tsp. aloe vera gel
1 tbsp. shea butter	2 tsp. zinc oxide (see the resource
½ tsp. sesame oil	section, p. 379)

1. Place the oils and shea butter in a small bowl set over a saucepan of boiling water and heat until the shea butter has melted.

2. Pour into a glass measuring cup and stir in the aloe vera gel and the zinc oxide.

3. Pour into your jar.

Eyes

Gentle Eye Makeup Remover

I need something unscented and super-gentle to remove my makeup, especially if I've really gone to town with the mascara and eyeliner. This is perfect.

Yields: approximately 4 oz. of lotion

Application: use every evening to remove eye makeup

Storage: 4-oz. dark glass bottle with pump dispenser, in the fridge

Shelf life: 3 months

2 tsp. beeswax	4 tsp. emulsifying wax
1 tsp. shea nut butter	1½ tsp. aloe vera juice
½ tsp. cocoa butter	½ cup chamomile infusion*
4 tsp. almond oil	

Chamomile infusion is made by placing either 1 tsp. of dried chamomile flowers or a chamomile tea bag in a cup. Pour in ½ cup of boiling water and allow it to steep for half an hour.

1. Melt the beeswax, shea nut butter, cocoa butter, and almond oil in a bowl set over a pan of boiling water until the wax and butters have melted. Remove the bowl from the saucepan and let it cool for 5 minutes.

2. Meanwhile, in a small pan, heat the emulsifying wax, aloe vera juice, and chamomile infusion. Remove from the heat and let it cool.

3. Make sure the oil mixture and the emulsifying wax mixture are the same temperature by dipping the tip of your finger in the bowl and pan. Both should be warm, not hot.

4. Mix the aloe and chamomile mixture into the oil mixture and whisk vigorously for about 30 seconds, or until well blended.

5. Allow it to cool for 5 minutes and then, using a funnel, pour the lotion into the bottle.

Pomegranate Eye Serum

This deeply nourishing eye serum would cost you more than a pair of designer jeans at a department store. It's packed with antioxidants. I always pop a bottle in my purse when traveling, as it helps combat unavoidably dehydrated skin.

Yields: approximately 1 oz. of serum

Application: use a few drops under your eyes, in the morning and evening after moisturizing

Storage: 1-oz. dark glass bottle with dropper

Shelf life: 1 year in a cool, dark cupboard

1 tbsp. grapeseed oil	1 tsp. carrot seed oil
1 tsp. pomegranate seed oil	1 tsp. wheat germ oil

Simply pour the oils into your bottle, shake gently, and you're ready to go.

Soothing Eye Gel

This is so easy and inexpensive to make, and works wonderfully for "morning-after" eyes.

Yields: approximately 2 oz. of gel

Application: shake gently before using

Storage: 2-oz. bottle with pump dispenser, in the fridge

Shelf life: 3 months

2 oz. aloe vera gel	¼ large cucumber, washed, unpeeled, and cut into cubes

1. Place the cucumber in your food processor or blender and blend until it's liquid.

2. Strain through a fine mesh sieve into a glass measuring cup.

3. Place the aloe gel in a small bowl and add 1 tbsp. of the cucumber juice. Blend well and use a funnel to pour into the bottle. Shake gently and place in the fridge to chill before using.

How to use: Apply under and around eyes when needed.

Salon Alternatives

Having now made your basics, you may want to choose a treatment or two from the recipes that follow. These are all extremely inexpensive and easy to make. It always thrills me to think I can create treatments that are just as effective as salon treatments, in the comfort of my own kitchen.

DIY Salon-Style Facial

Salon facials not only are prohibitively expensive, but also often use products that aren't in the least bit effective. It's a win/win to learn to do it yourself in the comfort of your own home. The following is really fun to do with your partner or a good friend.

HOW TO

1. Thoroughly cleanse your face of all makeup, dirt, and grime with one of the homemade cleansers in this chapter.

2. Tone by dipping a cotton ball in fresh, chilled aloe vera juice and wiping across your face.

3. Perform a facial steam with the Facial Steam Blend (below).

4. Sit in front of a strong magnifying mirror. If you don't have one, it's worth borrowing a really strong one, ideally one with a light. Examine your skin, especially around your nose and the top of your upper lip. Check to see if there are blackheads that need removing. There are several ways in which you can attempt to remove blackheads/pimples; however, you need to be really careful not to damage the delicate tissue around the spot. Choose from a variety of blackhead-extracting implements from your local beauty supply store. (I have the Blackhead Remover kit from www.venusworldwide.com.) When your extracting session is done, pour 1 tbsp. of aloe vera juice into a small glass and add 4 drops of tea tree oil. Dip a cotton ball into the mixture and wipe over the infected area.

5. Having de-clogged your pores, it's now time for either a Clay (p. 38) or AHA Skin-lightening Mask (p. 39).

6. Rinse off your mask, then apply the vitamin C serum and leave it to soak in for 5 minutes.

7. Massage in the Restorative Facial Oil (p. 40).

8. Perform the Acupressure Face Lift (p. 42).

Facial Steam Blend

Prepare a small 1-oz. bottle of this extraordinary blend and use it as a facial steam once a week. If you have blackheads, acne, or problem skin, use it twice a week for 6 weeks.

Yields: approximately 1 oz. of oil blend

Application: see above

Storage: 1-oz. dark glass bottle in a cool, dark cupboard

Shelf life: 2 years

4 drops bergamot essential oil	4 drops grapefruit essential oil
4 drops chamomile essential oil	2 drops juniper essential oil
4 drops geranium essential oil	2 drops patchouli essential oil

Drop each of the oils straight into the bottle and shake gently.

How to use: For your facial steam, boil a teakettle of water and pour carefully into a large stainless steel or ceramic bowl. Add 4 or 5 drops of your blend and immediately cover with a small towel. When you are ready to steam, sit in front of the bowl, put the towel over your head, and breathe in the delicious aroma until the water stops steaming.

Gorgeously Green Purifying Clay Mask

This mask is made with green clay, which is high in chromium, copper, and nickel. It works well for oily skin, as it helps minimize sebum production, which can lead to clogged pores.

Yields: enough for 1 application

Application: use when your skin feels in need of a deep cleanse

1 tbsp. green clay (also known as French clay) Approximately 3 tsp. aloe vera juice	3 drops chamomile essential oil 2 drops lavender essential oil

1. Mix the clay with the aloe vera juice until it forms a smooth paste.

2. Mix in the essential oils.

How to use: After cleansing your face of grime and makeup, apply the mask with your fingertips. Allow it to dry for half an hour. Rinse off well with warm water. Moisturize with the oil or cream of your choice.

AHA Skin-lightening Mask

If your skin is sun-damaged or blotchy with high pigmentation, before you succumb to expensive laser treatments, give this natural alpha hydroxy acid mask a try.

Yields: enough for 1 application

Application: use once a week for 6 weeks

1 fresh papaya, peeled, seeds removed, cut into small cubes	½ fresh pineapple, peeled, cored, cut into small cubes

1. If you have a juicer that has a setting for soft fruit, this will be perfect for extracting the juice (you also don't need to peel or core the fruit).

2. If not, crush the fruit cubes with a mortar and pestle and then press through a sieve to extract the juice.

How to use: Saturate a cotton pad or ball in the juice and apply to your décolleté, neck, and face in upward strokes. Leave the juice to dry for 15 minutes, then rinse off with warm water and moisturize as usual. A tingling sensation is normal, as the acids are clearing away those dead skin cells. If the sensation becomes too much, rinse it off sooner.

Vitamin C Serum

This is more effective/active than any vitamin C product you can buy in a store. When you're next in a fancy department store, just take a look at some of the serums that boast a high vitamin C content and check out how expensive they are! L-ascorbic acid is vitamin C and is available as a powder at most drugstores and health food stores.

Yields: approximately 1 oz. of serum

Application: use every morning and evening under your moisturizer

Storage: 1-oz. dark glass bottle with pump dispenser

Shelf life: 1 month in the fridge*

* If your serum becomes discolored (yellowish), discard it; this means that it has oxidized.

¼ tsp. L-ascorbic acid	1 tsp. distilled water
1 tsp. vegetable glycerin	

1. Dissolve the L-ascorbic acid in the water in a small measuring cup. When it has fully dissolved, mix in the glycerin.

2. Pour into the glass bottle.

Restorative Facial Oil

This nourishing oil is fantastic for stressed-out skin.

Yields: approximately 1 oz. of oil

Application: at night, once or twice a week

Storage: 1-oz. dark glass bottle in a cool, dark cupboard

Shelf life: 1 year

1 tbsp. apricot oil	6 drops calendula essential oil
1 tsp. rosehip seed oil	6 drops rose absolute essential oil
1 tsp. macadamia nut oil	

1. Blend all the ingredients in a small glass bowl.

2. Carefully pour (a funnel is useful here) into the bottle.

Regenerative Floral Beauty Balm

This is an especially nourishing balm for tired and maturing skin. It works wonderfully as a treatment cream after a facial steam. The difference between a balm and a cream is that a balm is thicker and more concentrated. You may need to warm it up in the palms of your hands before applying.

Yields: approximately 2 oz. of balm

Application: use once a week, or whenever your skin feels in need of some extra TLC

Storage: 2-oz. dark glass jar in the fridge

Shelf life: 3 months

2 tbsp. apricot oil	½ tsp. vitamin E oil
2 tbsp. rosehip seed oil	10 drops geranium essential oil
1½ tsp. beeswax	10 drops neroli essential oil
1 tbsp. rose infusion*	8 drops ylang ylang essential oil

This rose infusion is made by pouring ½ cup of boiling water over 1 tbsp. of dried rose petals. Leave to steep for half an hour, then drain off the rosewater.

1. Heat the base oils and beeswax in a small bowl set over a pan of boiling water, until the wax melts.

2. In another pan, heat the rose infusion.

3. Remove both pans from the heat and cool until the wax mixture just begins to thicken.

4. Very slowly drizzle the infusion into the wax mixture, vigorously whisking for 3 or 4 minutes or until a creamy emulsion forms.

5. Add the vitamin E oil and the essential oils and stir rapidly for another 4 minutes.

6. Spoon into the glass jar and allow it to cool completely before screwing on the cap.

Acupressure Face Lift

Some of the best facials I've ever had have involved acupressure. This is similar to acupuncture and serves to stimulate the meridians (energy centers) of the face as well as tighten the muscles and smooth the skin. You can perform a wonderful acupressure session on your own face very easily. The whole session takes me no more than 10 minutes and I can see visible results.

HOW TO

The following shows you 26 pressure points on the face and neck, lettered A to Z. I recommend using a blunt/rounded object to stimulate the pressure points. The end of a medium-size cosmetic brush or a lip/eye pencil is perfect. You need to start at A and work through to Z. It's much like following a dot-to-dot picture! You will be moving from one side of your face to the other, back and forth. At each pressure point, press your blunt tool into the point with a medium pressure and gently rotate in a clockwise direction for 5 to 10 seconds.

1. Forehead area: To soften forehead lines, begin at point A and move consecutively through points B, C, and D.

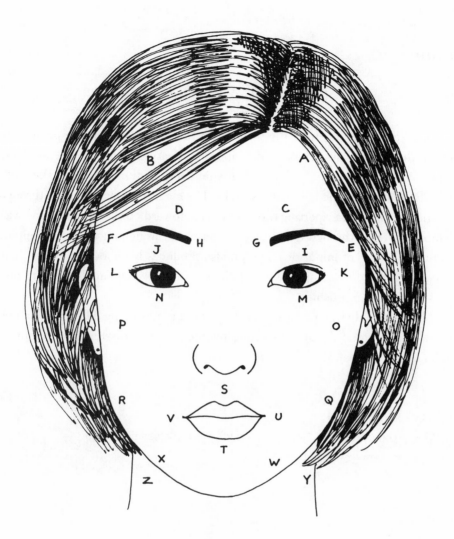

2. Eye area: To soften lines around the eyes, including crow's feet, start at point E and move through to point N. As the skin tissue is delicate around the eyes, apply a more gentle pressure than other areas of the face.

3. Cheeks and mouth: You can apply a little more pressure to these areas as you work through points O to X.

4. Neck: Finally, a gentle pressure is needed to stimulate points Y and Z in order to activate a gentle lifting of the neck muscles.

Body

Dry Skin Brushing

I highly recommend getting the hang of dry skin brushing—a European technique that is used in Britain and France for treating cellulite, illnesses, and lackluster skin. The idea is that the brushing not only removes dead skin cells but also stimulates the lymphatic system. The clear fluid, lymph, runs through a series of valves, transporting the lymph back toward our heart. Along the way, lymph is filtered through lymph nodes scattered throughout the body, helping to rid our bodies of impurities. Lymph also produces lymphocytes, which help keep our immune system strong and illness at bay. We can aid this entire process by daily skin brushing.

About the only thing I have ever discovered to make any difference on cellulite is a vigorous dry skin brushing regime, combined with toxin-removing cellulite oil (see p. 45).

YOU WILL NEED

☐ Soft, natural fiber brush with a long handle (available at most health food stores)

HOW TO

1. Begin at your feet and brush vigorously in circular motions.

2. Continue brushing up your legs.

3. Proceed to your hands and arms, with circular motions on the hands and long, sweeping brushes up your arms toward your heart.

4. Brush your entire back and abdomen area, shoulders, and neck.

5. Use circular, counterclockwise strokes on the abdomen.

6. Lightly brush the breasts.

7. Brush upward on the middle and lower back and down from the neck on the upper back. Better yet, have your partner do it for you.

8. After brushing, take a hot 3-minute shower with some gentle soap, followed by a 10- to 20-second cold rinse. Repeat this 3 times. If the hot/cold showers are too extreme, try a warm shower.

9. Follow the shower with a rubdown with either a sponge or a towel to remove dead skin.

Cellulite Oil

This oil is *amazing*—you'll be hard-pressed to find anything as effective in any store. I know this is a horribly long list of essential oils, but remember that once you've got them, they'll last for years, plus you're only using a few drops per bottle for this miracle oil. Make a few bottles and combine them with a dry skin brush and a bar of organic dark chocolate for a great girlfriend gift!

Yields: approximately 2.2 oz. of oil

Application: use daily after skin brushing

Storage: 2–3 oz. dark glass bottle

Shelf life: 1 year

3 tbsp. sweet almond oil	8 drops sandalwood essential oil
2 tbsp. evening primrose oil	10 drops frankincense essential oil
4 tsp. wheat germ oil	2 drops juniper essential oil
5 drops lemon essential oil	2 drops black pepper essential oil
5 drops orange essential oil	2 drops eucalyptus essential oil

1. Combine all the oils in a measuring cup.

2. Using a funnel, pour into your bottle.

After-Shower Spritzing Oil

I love this oil because I'm able to spritz difficult-to-get-to areas. Keep in mind that there's very little oil in commercial body lotions—most of the product is made up of water and chemicals. By using this spray, you'll know that you're nourishing your skin with the best, even if you're in a hurry.

Yields: approximately 8 oz. of oil

Application: use every morning and evening after showering

Storage: 8-oz. dark plastic bottle with sprayer

Shelf life: 6 months in a cool, dark cupboard

4 oz. sweet almond oil	5 drops geranium essential oil
4 oz. olive oil	(optional)
10 drops lavender essential oil	

1. Carefully pour the almond and olive oils directly into the bottle (a funnel will help).

2. Add the essential oils.

3. Screw on the top and enjoy!

Vanilla Body Cream

The combination of this four-ingredient cream is delicious—the subtle scent of coconut and vanilla makes you want to eat it. It'll take you 3 minutes to prepare in a food processer.

Yields: approximately 4 oz. of cream

Application: use after showering and whenever you're in the mood for a treat

Storage: 4-oz. dark glass jar in the fridge

Shelf life: 6 months

2 tbsp. shea butter	4 tbsp. sweet almond oil
2 tbsp. virgin coconut oil	½ tsp. pure vanilla absolute oil

1. Blend all the ingredients together in a food processer.

2. Spoon into your jar.

Orange and Apricot Body Cream for Dry Skin

This is an extremely emollient cream for very dry skin. A little goes a long way, so this 4-oz. jar will last you a long time.

Yields: approximately 4 oz. of cream

Application: use on heels, knees, and elbows when they feel very rough and dry

Storage: 4-oz. dark glass jar in the fridge

Shelf life: 3 months

6 tbsp. apricot oil	½ cup lavender infusion**
2 tbsp. beeswax	2 tsp. vegetable glycerin
1 tbsp. virgin coconut oil	½ tsp. borax
1 tbsp. cocoa butter	35 drops orange essential oil
1 tsp. anhydrous lanolin*	25 drops geranium essential oil

*Anhydrous lanolin is the waxy coating from sheep's wool after it's been sheared. Getting it doesn't hurt the animal in any way. "Anhydrous" means it's made without adding water. It's wonderfully emollient, which is why it's an excellent ingredient in skincare products. Some people can be allergic to lanolin, and if you're one of them, simply substitute an extra 1 tsp. of virgin coconut oil. Look for 100% pure lanolin on Amazon (www.amazon .com).

**Lavender infusion is made by pouring ½ cup of boiling water over 1 tbsp. dried lavender flowers. Leave it to steep for half an hour. Drain off the lavender water and discard flowers.

1. Heat the apricot oil, beeswax, coconut oil, cocoa butter, and lanolin in a bowl set on a large saucepan of boiling water, until the wax has melted.

2. In another pan, warm the lavender infusion, glycerin, and borax until warm.

3. Remove both the bowl and the pan from the heat and allow them to cool for 10 minutes or until the oil mixture begins to thicken. Dip your finger in to see that both the oil mixture and the infusion mixture are body temperature.

4. Time to move fast! Pour the oil mixture into a blender. Remove the plastic plug top from the top of the blender and blend. After 10 seconds, begin to slowly drizzle the infusion into the blender. After you have poured in half the infusion, stop the blender and scrape down the sides, making sure that all the ingredients stay in the mix. Add the remainder of the infusion. You may need to scrape down the sides a few times before everything is well blended.

5. Add the essential oils and blend for another 10 seconds.

6. Swiftly pour the cream into the glass jar.

7. You will need to make sure that you scrape all the cream out of the blender (I recommend wiping out the blender and bowls with paper towels, which you can then compost). Then put everything in the dishwasher on the hottest cycle. The creams and waxes can be pretty hard to hand-wash off, so you'll use a lot less water by flinging them all in the dishwasher.

Spicy Holiday Sugar Scrub

Because of its spicy aroma, this sugar scrub makes a wonderful holiday gift. It's an incredible exfoliating potion for skin that gets dry in the winter.

Yields: approximately 8 oz. of scrub

Application: massage onto damp skin (during a shower), twice a week. Use circular motions to exfoliate dry/dead skin, then rinse.

Storage: 8-oz. dark glass jar in a cool, dark cupboard

Shelf life: 6 months

¾ cup organic sugar	2 tsp. grated orange zest
2 tsp. ground cloves	1 cup sesame oil
1 tbsp. dried rose petals	

1. Combine all the ingredients in a bowl, making sure that everything is well mixed.

2. Spoon into your jar.

Minty Foot Scrub

This is a perfect salt scrub for exfoliating all that dead, dry skin, and works really well when used with a foot file. It also makes a lovely gift.

Yields: approximately 8 oz. of scrub

Application: use whenever your feet are in need of a bit of love!

Storage: 8-oz. dark glass jar in cool, dark cupboard

Shelf life: 6 months

6 oz. sea salt or kosher salt (if you want to get really fancy, you can use pink Himalayan sea salt) 1½ cups sweet almond oil	30 drops peppermint essential oil 15 drops tea tree essential oil 1 tbsp. dried mint leaves, crushed (optional)

1. Fill the jar with the salt.

2. Slowly pour the almond oil over the salt and gently mix it in with a teaspoon.

3. Let the oil and salt settle for 5 minutes.

4. The oil should just cover the salt, so add a little more if you need to (the salt will soak up a lot of the oil).

5. Mix in the essential oils and dried mint.

How to use: Soak one foot in a large bowl of warm water for 5 minutes. (I place one large towel under my bowl and one over my knee, as it can get messy.) Cross the soaked foot across your other knee. Scoop out a generous dollop of the foot scrub and, starting on the top of your foot, massage it in, using circular motions. Work the scrub up to your ankle and around your toes and heel. Rub a small dollop of the scrub on a foot file to use for extra-rough skin on your heel. Rinse off in the bowl, dry off, and repeat with the other foot.

Double Mint Foot Lotion

This tingly, refreshing lotion pairs beautifully with the Minty Foot Scrub. Mint is antiseptic, antifungal, and cooling. It helps tremendously with tired, achy, and swollen feet.

Yields: approximately 4 oz. of lotion

Application: use when your feet are hot and tired

Storage: 4-oz. dark glass jar in the fridge

Shelf life: 3 months

2 tsp. cocoa butter	2 tbsp. mint infusion*
2 tsp. beeswax	2 tsp. emulsifying wax
2 tbsp. sweet almond oil	20 drops peppermint essential oil
1 tbsp. wheat germ oil	5 drops tea tree essential oil

Mint infusion is made by pouring 1 cup of boiling water over 1 tbsp. of fresh mint leaves. Leave it to steep for half an hour.

1. Heat the cocoa butter, beeswax, and almond and wheat germ oils in a bowl set over a pan of boiling water, until the beeswax has melted. Remove from the heat.

2. Place the mint infusion in a small bowl over the pan of boiling water, add the emulsifying wax, and heat until the wax has dissolved.

3. Dip your fingertip in both the oil and the infusion mixture to check that they are a similar temperature (if the oils have cooled down, heat them up a little).

4. *Slowly* add the infusion mixture to the oils, whisking vigorously.

5. Add the essential oils.

6. Spoon into your jar and, when cool, screw on the lid.

Delightfully Cooling Deodorant

Natural deodorants can be so expensive, so I was relieved to find a recipe that really works. It also smells wonderful.

Yields: approximately 4 oz. of deodorant

Application: use in the morning and before you go out in the evening

Storage: 4-oz. dark glass bottle with a sprayer closure, in a cool, dark cupboard

Shelf life: 1 month

1 tsp. vegetable glycerin	3 tsp. zinc oxide*
½ cup witch hazel	20 drops bergamot essential oil
½ cup aloe vera juice	10 drops grapefruit essential oil

You can buy zinc oxide from Natural Health Supply.com (www.naturalhealthsupply .com). It's sold as Deodorant Zinc Oxide.

1. In a measuring cup, combine the vegetable glycerin and the witch hazel.

2. Add the aloe vera, the zinc oxide, and the essential oils.

How to use: You will need to shake before using. The spray will leave a non-staining white residue that will wear off during the day.

Nail Care

DIY NAILS

I have always been envious of girls who have the knack for painting their own nails perfectly. I'm okay with my left hand, but my right (because I'm right-handed) can be a disaster. Over the past few years I have gotten better, and now I can perform a very decent manicure and pedicure as long as I use a pale-colored polish. I've also realized that if I cut my salon visits down to a quarterly trip, I can save enough to buy a very nice pair of eco-friendly designer boots or shoes, or I can earn brownie points by stashing away an extra few hundred in my retirement account.

I recommend learning to do a weekly DIY manicure and pedicure and then visiting the salon every three months to give your cuticles and hangnails a good going over. I actually found that when I started going to the salon less, my cuticles didn't grow so fast and furiously—I think they're happier when left to do their own thing.

PEDICURE

1. Prepare a large plastic bowl or tub with warm water. Place it on a towel and add 10 drops of tea tree essential oil.

2. Trim your nails with a nail clipper. Toenails should always be slightly longer than your toe. They look terrible if clipped too short, so be careful.

3. File them in one direction only and buff around the edges with a nail-buffing block.

4. Soak your feet in the warm water for 10 minutes. Use the Minty Foot Scrub (see p. 50) to exfoliate dry skin.

5. Use a rough grit file to file away any rough skin on your heels.

6. Rinse and dry off your feet and massage the Double Mint Foot Lotion (see p. 51) into them. Use your thumbnails to push your cuticles down—this often works better than a cuticle stick.

7. Clean off your nails with a nontoxic polish remover—I love the polish removers from SpaRitual (www.sparitual.com)—or white vinegar.

8. Apply a clear base coat of nail polish, followed by two coats of a pale pink (unless you're really adept at painting), and finish with a top coat. I always use nontoxic polishes and love both SpaRitual and Zoya (www.zoya.com) polishes.

WINTER TOES

In the winter months, I allow my nails to breathe—and save money—by letting my toenails go bare. If you want to get rid of that horrid yellow stain that results from wearing polish (especially dark colors) all the time, you need to give your nails a rest. In the winter, I rarely have my toenails on display, and if I have a special romantic evening coming up, I'll give them a quick coat of a pearly pink polish and whip it off straight after.

I recommend these weekly practices for winter maintenance. If you keep them up, you'll eventually see baby pink nails appearing. This is exciting, as it means fewer visits to the salon. And you may even want to show off your pearly shells in summer sandals when the time comes. There's nothing prettier than well-kept au naturel nails—especially when they're paired with a healthy tan.

• Make a paste with 2 tablespoons of baking soda and 1 tablespoon of fresh lemon juice. Stand in the shower once a week and massage the paste into your nails before you turn the water on. Leave for five minutes before rinsing off. It's a good time to apply a facemask, as you'll get it all done at once.

• While sitting at the kitchen table, pour some 3% hydrogen peroxide into a small plastic container and dip your toes into it, one foot at a time. Leave your toes in for as long as you can. When you're done, push back your cuticles with a warm, wet washcloth.

• Invest in a good buffing/shining block. Each time you perform one of the above treatments, give your nails a good buff and shine.

Nail and Cuticle Conditioning Oil

It really helps to regularly condition and nourish your nails with therapeutic oils. It'll help your cuticles become more pliable and thus easier to push back, and it'll help eliminate skin peeling (which can happen after a manicure if the manicurist is a little too cuticle-clipper happy) and hangnails.

Yields: approximately 4 oz. of oil

Application: apply daily to your nails with a cotton swab (after a few weeks, you'll notice a huge difference)

Storage: 2-oz. dark glass bottle in a cool, dark cupboard

Shelf life: 6 months

2 tbsp. sweet almond oil	4 drops sandalwood essential oil
1 tsp. vitamin E oil	2 drops cypress essential oil

1. Blend all the oils together in a small bowl.

2. Use a funnel to pour them into your bottle.

Your Pearly Whites

Whitening Peppermint Toothpaste

This is so easy and inexpensive to make. It will make your teeth shiny and your mouth tingle.

Yields: approximately 1 oz. of toothpaste

Application: use morning and evening

Storage: 1-oz. dark glass jar in a cool, dark cupboard

Shelf life: 1 month

2 tsp. baking soda	1 tiny pinch powdered stevia* (it's
2 tsp. vegetable glycerin	so concentrated that you will
2 tsp. hydrogen peroxide	only need as much as goes on the
6 drops peppermint essential oil	tip of a teaspoon)

* *Stevia is a natural sugar, which is extracted from the stevia plant. It contains zero calories and is much sweeter than regular sugar.*

1. In a small bowl, mix all the ingredients together to form a paste.

2. Spoon into your jar.

Mint Zinger Mouthwash

I rarely buy mouthwash. Most of them contain a high percentage of alcohol, which alters the pH of the mouth and is associated with increased risk of mouth and throat cancer. They also contain harsh detergents, and sorbitol and saccharin, which cause bladder cancer in animals. Finally, most lurid-colored mouthwashes contain synthetic colors, aromas, and flavorings, which alter our healthy mouth flora. The alternative/healthy ones can easily be made at home for a fraction of the price. This mouthwash is antibacterial and will help conquer bad breath!

Yields: approximately 14 oz. of mouthwash

Application: use morning and evening

Storage: 16-oz. plastic bottle (an old mouthwash bottle is ideal)

Shelf life: 2 weeks in a cool, dark cupboard

1 cup aloe vera juice	2 tsp. baking soda
½ cup distilled water	20 drops peppermint essential oil
1 tbsp. witch hazel	

Mix all the ingredients in a glass bowl or pitcher and pour into the bottle.

Remedies

There are so many remedies for common ailments that you can easily make yourself for pennies. Many of the commercial preparations we buy, such as cough syrups and lozenges, are expensive and pretty useless, and they can contain a number of horrendous dyes and additives. I always make my own.

I highly recommend starting a medicinal herb garden (see p. 289), as it'll save you a lot of money and ensure you have a supply of all the herbs you need. If you don't have the time or space, you can buy all the herbal ingredients for the following remedies from grocery stores or from Mountain Rose Herbs (www.mountainroseherbs.com).

The healing properties of the herbs I recommend in the following recipes are gentle, safe, and extremely effective. However, if you are seriously ill, you should consult your physician before using them.

Best Ever Cough Syrup

This is easy to make and magically helps even the most stubborn of coughs. It's a great general cold remedy, as it helps you expectorate the mucous.

Yields: approximately 12 oz. of syrup

Application: use when coughing (see Dose, below)

Storage: 14-oz. dark glass bottle (an old cough medicine bottle would be perfect) in a cool, dark cupboard

Shelf life: 3 months

1 tbsp. dried sage	15 cloves
1 tbsp. dried thyme	½ tsp. ground ginger
1 tbsp. dried chamomile flowers	4 cups filtered water
1 tsp. fennel seeds	2 tbsp. raw honey

1. Place all the ingredients except the honey in a large saucepan and bring to a boil.

2. Cover the pan and simmer for 20 minutes.

3. Strain off the solids and return the liquid to the pan.

4. Simmer until the liquid has reduced down to about 1½ cups.

5. Remove from the heat and allow to cool for 5 minutes.

6. Add the honey and stir.

7. When the syrup is cool, transfer to your bottle.

Dose: Children under 12 years: 2 tsp. three times a day

Adults: 3 tsp. three to four times a day

Cough Syrup for Dry Coughs

I know from raising a little girl who's prone to coughs that not all coughs are alike. Lola's dry cough needs an entirely different treatment than the one she gets with a cold. This recipe will help coat the throat and ease the annoying tickle of a dry cough.

Yields: approximately 8 oz. of syrup

Application: use as needed for a dry throat and cough (see Dose, below)

Storage: 8-oz. glass jar, in the fridge

Shelf life: 1 month

2 cups water	1 tbsp. slippery elm*
1 tbsp. marshmallow root*	1 tbsp. raw honey

These herbs come in powder form and can be ordered from Mountain Rose Herbs (www.mountainroseherbs.com).

1. Place the water, marshmallow root, and slippery elm in a saucepan over medium heat.

2. Bring to a boil and allow it to simmer for half an hour, or until the liquid has reduced down to about 1 cup.

3. Remove from the heat and allow it to cool for 5 minutes before stirring in the honey.

4. Pour into your jar and seal tightly.

Dose: 2 tsp. up to four times a day

Cough Drops

Lola loves these cough drops because she thinks they're just candy. It's a great way of getting these healing herbs into a little one, and I love them, too. The process is similar to that of making cough syrup, only this time you're using sugar instead of honey. The herbs used are decongestants. They are also anti-bacterial and antiviral, as well as soothing. You will need a candy thermometer for this recipe.

Yields: approximately 2 cups of drops

Application/directions: suck on a drop every 3 hours

Storage: glass or plastic container with air-tight lid (a mason jar is perfect)

Shelf life: 1 month

2 tbsp. dried thyme	3 cups boiling water
2 tbsp. dried horehound	3½ cups soft brown sugar
2 tbsp. dried marshmallow root	2 tbsp. slippery elm powder

1. Place all the herbs (except the slippery elm) and the boiling water in a large saucepan, cover, and simmer gently for 20 minutes.

2. Strain the herbs and pour the liquid back into the pan.

3. Add the sugar and boil until the thermometer reaches 290 to 300°F.

4. Pour onto a greased baking sheet and allow to cool.

5. Cut or break this herby taffy into small pieces and roll each piece in the slippery elm powder.

Warming Chest Rub

Many of the commercial chest rubs are made with petroleum jelly or mineral oil, which I try to avoid. Instead, you can prepare this incredible healing balm with oils and butters that will feed your skin.

Yields: approximately 4 oz.

Application: Rub a quarter-size dollop of balm onto your chest before going to sleep.

Storage: 4-oz. dark glass bottle with a sprayer closure, in a cool, dark cupboard

Shelf life: 1 month

4 tbsp. jojoba oil	30 drops eucalyptus essential oil
1 tbsp. beeswax	10 drops ravensara essential oil
1 tbsp. cocoa butter	10 drops thyme essential oil
1 tbsp. shea butter	10 drops tea tree essential oil

1. Heat the jojoba oil, beeswax, and butters in a bowl set over a large pan of boiling water, until everything has melted.

2. Remove the bowl from the heat and set it aside to cool for 5 minutes.

3. Mix in the essential oils and, before it thickens too much, pour into a dark glass jar. Wait until it has completely cooled before you screw on the cap.

How to use: Scoop out a teaspoon-size dollop and work between your fingers before rubbing on your or your child's chest. You can also apply a dab under your nose.

Antiviral Steamy Inhalation

I live in a very dry region and I am very susceptible to sinus infections. I prepare this steam inhalation at the first sign of any trouble and it nearly always works well enough to keep me from having to take any medication.

Yields: enough for 1 application

Application: use inhalation up to 3 times a day when congested

4 cups boiling water	5 drops tea tree essential oil
5 drops eucalyptus essential oil	

1. Boil 4 cups of water in a teakettle. The moment it comes to a boil, carefully pour the water into a large bowl and cover the bowl with a towel.

2. Add the essential oils to the bowl. It's best to have the bowl placed right at the spot where you're going to sit for your inhalation. You don't want to have to move an open bowl of boiling water!

3. Lift the edge of the towel and poke your face in, so that your mouth and nose are a few inches away from the water. Try to keep the towel over your head to prevent any steam escaping.

4. Take at least 10 long, deep breaths. Rest and then repeat.

Soothing Acne Gel

Bright orange marigold flowers are also known as calendula flowers, and they are enormously helpful in treating all kinds of skin conditions, especially acne. They contain salicylic acid, which is found in many commercial acne creams. However, commercial creams also contain other harsh ingredients that can dry out your skin. This preparation is a cooling gel for inflamed skin.

Yields: approximately 4 oz. of gel

Application: use morning and evening, after cleansing and toning

Storage: 4-oz. dark glass bottle with pump dispenser, in the fridge

Shelf life: 8 weeks

2 cups filtered water	4 tsp. vodka
15 marigold flowers	15 drops tea tree essential oil
1 packet vegetable gelatin (available from most grocery stores)	

1. Boil the water. Place the flowers in a large glass bowl and cover with the boiling water. Steep for half an hour.

2. Place the flower and water mixture in the blender and process for 30 seconds.

3. Strain the mixture through a piece of cheesecloth into a glass measuring cup.

4. In another glass bowl, dissolve the gelatin in 2 tbsp. of cool, filtered water. Slowly add the marigold infusion, stirring constantly.

5. Add the vodka and the tea tree oil. You may need to stir and mash the mixture to make sure you break up any lumps of gelatin.

6. Use a funnel to pour into your bottle.

Best Hand Sanitizer

Most hand sanitizers contain toluene, a solvent that is toxic for you and the environment. This recipe contains specific essential oils that will fight even the toughest germs out there. I suggest making it in 2-oz. bottles and giving one to everyone in your family to carry around with them. I made one for each child in Lola's classroom. Because the bottle is less than 3 oz., you should be able to travel with it on an airplane, which is the kind of place where you'll really need it. You can make an alcohol-free version by substituting water for the alcohol, but it won't be quite as potent.

Yields: approximately 2 oz.

Application: spray on hands and wrists repeatedly throughout the day

Storage: 2-oz. dark plastic bottle with a sprayer closure, in a cool, dark cupboard

Shelf life: 6 months

1 oz. water	2 drops each cinnamon, clove,
1 oz. vodka (80 proof)	rosemary, eucalyptus essential
1 tsp. aloe vera gel	oils
½ tsp. vegetable glycerin	10 drops each lemon, tea tree
	essential oils

1. Pour the water and vodka into the bottle, leaving half an inch empty at the top of the bottle.

2. Add aloe vera, glycerin, and the essential oils. Shake gently.

Insect Repellent Spray

Now that DEET, a pesticide that is typically found in insect repellents, has been found to be extremely toxic, I like to make my own spray. There are plenty of great natural alternatives that you can buy, but they are pricey and this works just as well for the whole family.

Yields: approximately 2 oz.

Application: use morning and before you go out in the evening

Storage: 2-oz. dark glass bottle with a sprayer closure, in a cool, dark cupboard

Shelf life: 3 months

| 3 tbsp. lavender water* | 6 drops citronella essential oil |
| 2 drops sandalwood essential oil | 6 drops eucalyptus essential oil |

Lavender water is made by pouring half a cup of boiling water over 1 tbsp. of dried lavender flowers. Leave it to steep for half an hour.

1. Add the essential oils to the lavender flower water and pour into your bottle.

PMS Reliever

Rose (*Rosa centiflora, R. damascena*) is the ultimate essential oil for helping to relieve those PMS blues. It's cooling, relaxing, and is commonly used as an antidepressant. It's expensive, but since you use just a few drops at a time, a ⅛-oz. bottle should last you a long time.

Yields: enough for 1 application

2 tbsp. sweet almond oil	8 drops rose essential oil

1. Place the sweet almond oil in a small jar or mug and stand it in a bowl of hot water until the oil has warmed through.

2. Add the essential oil and gently massage over your neck, chest, arms, and belly.

Period Pain Soothing Pack

A castor oil pack is a magical remedy for relieving period pains and any menstrual disorders. It's the ultimate TLC remedy for when you just want to curl up and get cozy.

YOU WILL NEED
- ☐ 2 cotton facecloths
- ☐ 1 cup castor oil
- ☐ Plastic wrap or an old plastic bag
- ☐ Hot water bottle

HOW TO

1. Soak the facecloths in the oil until they are saturated but not dripping with oil.

2. Cover your bed or couch with old towels or sheets (castor oil does stain).

3. Have your hot water bottle and plastic ready. Lie down and place the castor oil pack on your belly. Cover it with plastic and place the hot water bottle on top.

4. Relax! See if you can lie for 15 to 30 minutes as you practice slow, deep breathing.

5. Wash off the oil with baking soda and warm water—this is to prevent any residue from staining your clothes. You can reuse the pack up to 20 times, so place it in a resealable bag in your fridge.

Achy Muscle Soak

Epsom salts are magical for soothing tired and achy muscles. They are also wonderfully inexpensive and can be found at any grocery or drugstore.

YOU WILL NEED
- ☐ 1 cup epsom salts
- ☐ 5 drops lavender essential oil

HOW TO

Run a hot tub of water, add the epsom salts and lavender, and soak away.

Hot Flash Reliever

One of my best friends, who will remain nameless, says she can't live without this tea when she's having a bad bout of hot flashes. Thank goodness it's so easy to prepare.

Yields: 1 cup of tea

1 tsp. dried sage leaves (if you have fresh sage leaves, use ½ tbsp.)	1 tsp. dried raspberry leaves 8 oz. boiling water

1. Place the leaves in a mug and cover with the water, which should be just off the boil.

2. Leave the tea to steep for 10 minutes. Strain.

3. Pour half the tea into a glass or teacup and sip every few hours. Refrigerate the remainder of the tea for another day. Store in a covered container for up to 3 days.

Labels

If you've gone to the trouble of making all your own skincare products, you want the packaging to be as beautiful as possible. An attractively packaged jar of cream can work like a placebo: Even if it's filled with rubbish, we tend to imagine that our skin looks 10 years younger after the first application. Given that your new potions are likely better than what you'll typically find in a store, you want the packaging to reflect the quality of the actual product. All these homemade products make fantastic gifts, and lovely labels will showcase your creative flair, as well as delight your girlfriends.

REUSE

Get into the habit of keeping all kinds of interesting scraps of paper or cards that find their way into your home or office. If you see a brightly colored envelope, don't throw it away; same with magazines that are made out of that lovely thick matte paper. Remember that you only need tiny squares of paper for each label.

DESIGN

Take a look at all your bottles and jars and decide on the look you want. Do you want a brightly colored eclectic look or something more uniform? I've had a go at all kinds of different styles. My favorite is the "apothecary" look, where I find a cream or beige card and write with brown ink in curly writing.

GLUE

You'll need some good strong glue. It's very important to buy nontoxic glue, as many of the white glues contain chemicals that are extremely bad for the environment.

I recommend the Natural Glue from Green Crafts (www.green-crafts.com). You can also make your own glue—give it a go, as it's really easy.

Homemade Glue

Yields: 1 quart

Storage: in sealed container in fridge

Shelf life: 1 week

1 quart skim milk	¾ tsp. baking soda
1 tbsp. white vinegar	10 oz. water

6. Turn the bear right side out.

7. Stuff the bear with the kapok or cushion stuffing and gently spoon in the dried lavender, making sure it's evenly dispersed around the bear's torso.

8. When the bear is at the desired level of firmness, turn the edges of the opening under and hand sew to close.

9. Sew on the buttons for eyes.

10. Use a running stitch and the black yarn to create a nose and mouth.

11. Customize your bear by putting a little ribbon around his neck. You can always make a ribbon from a strip of the remaining cashmere.

Pillowcase Laundry Bag

When my daughter was a baby, I was given a very expensive laundry bag that tied onto her crib. I didn't love it because I was always afraid of the ties (cords and ribbons make me nervous when they're within the reach of tiny hands). I came up with an easy and perfect solution. I had a number of really pretty odd pillowcases, so I created a laundry bag out of one of them.

YOU WILL NEED
- ☐ 1 old pillowcase
- ☐ 1½ yards ribbon, ¾ inch wide
- ☐ Large safety pin
- ☐ Basic sewing supplies

HOW TO

1. Cut a 6- to 8-inch opening down one of the long sides of the pillowcase.

2. Tack the bottom of the opening with several stitches to make sure it's really secure.

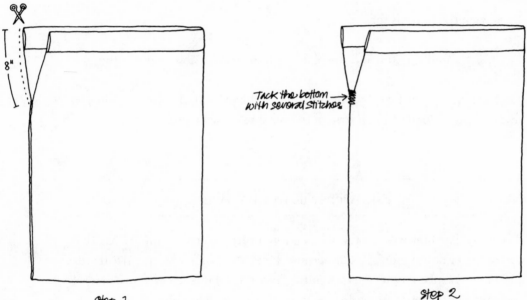

8"

Tack the bottom with several stitches →

step 1   step 2

3. Turn under a ¼-inch seam along the raw edges and pin. Sew them up.

4. Fasten a large safety pin to one end of the ribbon and thread it through the casing (the top hem of pillowcase). Tie the ends together in a double knot. If the pillowcase doesn't have a casing/hem, create one by turning the top over 1 inch and sewing it down.

5. Find a vintage hook to put on your nursery wall in a convenient spot for you to hang your laundry bag.

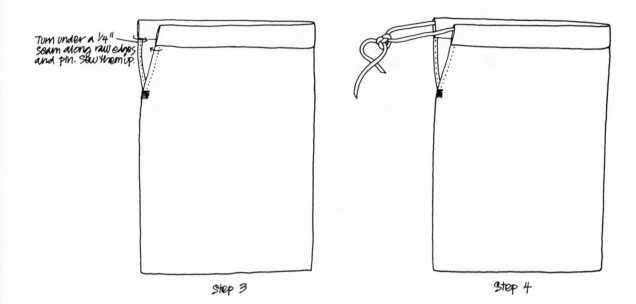

Turn under a ¼"
seam along raw edges
and pin. Sew them up.

step 3

step 4

Jeans Diaper Bag

Another rather costly item that everyone expects a mother to have is a diaper bag. Many of them come with a huge flap, which makes the bag really annoying to reach into when you have a screaming, dripping baby in the other arm. It's a great idea to save your baby shower gift requests for things you cannot make (like a breast pump), and get sewing on the things you can make yourself. This diaper bag can be customized to look extremely chic.

YOU WILL NEED

☐ 1 pair old jeans (use women's XL or men's jeans)
☐ Pinking shears
☐ Basic sewing supplies

HOW TO

1. Cut off the legs 2 inches below the crotch of the jeans.

2. Turn the jeans inside out and sew a hem about ½ inch away from the raw edge. Cut off the raw edges with pinking shears to avoid fraying.

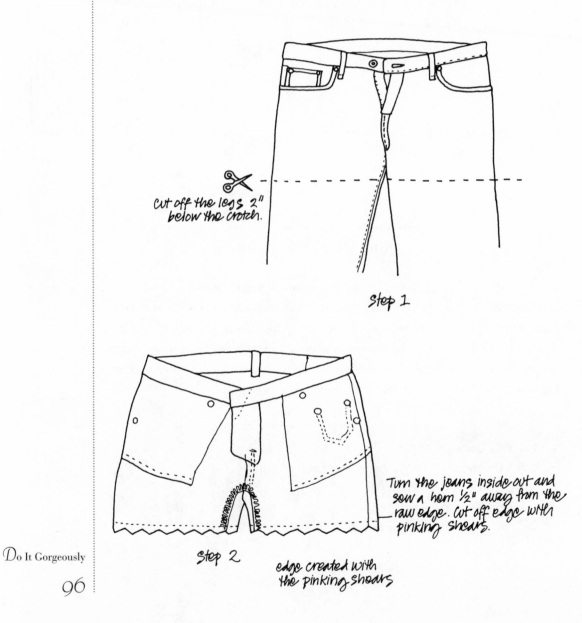

Cut off the legs 2"
below the crotch.

step 1

Turn the jeans inside out and
sew a hem ½" away from the
raw edge. Cut off edge with
pinking shears.

step 2

edge created with
the pinking shears

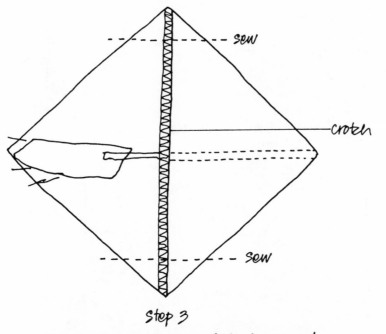

sew

crotch

sew

Step 3

Grab the front and back of the jeans and
pull apart so that the crotch is facing you.
You should see a diamond shape. Sew off a
triangle at the north and south tips of the
diamond to create the base of the bag.

3. Grab the front and back of the jeans and pull apart and turn so that the crotch is facing you. You should see a diamond shape. Sew off a triangle at the north and south tips of the diamond to create the base of the bag.

4. Turn the jeans the right way and you'll see you have miraculously created a bottom for your bag.

5. Take one of the discarded legs and cut off both side seams. Measure over your shoulder to see how long you need the shoulder strap to be.

6. Cut a 3-inch-wide strip of fabric from the leg. The length will be what you have measured.

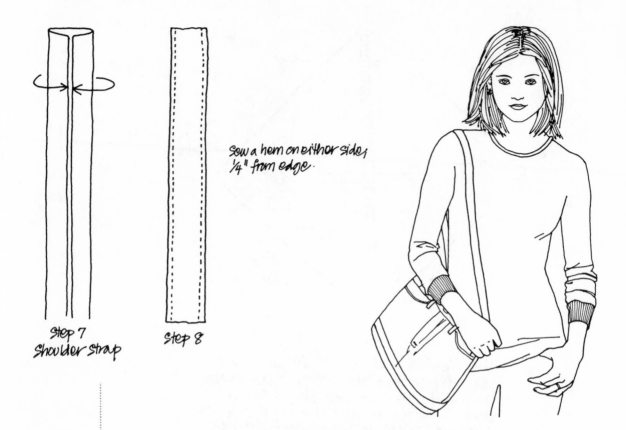

step 7
shoulder strap

step 8

Sew a hem on either side, ¼" from edge.

7. Fold in the sides of the strip to meet in the middle and then fold in half like a sandwich.

8. Sew a hem on either side of the strap, ¼ inch from the edge.

9. Attach the strap to the inside of either side of your bag, backstitching several times so it's super-secure.

No-sew Perfect Baby Sling

A baby sling is ideal, especially for a newborn who wants to stay as close to your heartbeat as possible. My daughter lived in her stretchy sling until she was at least 6 months old. There's no need to buy an expensive sling—many of which are annoying and don't work as well as you really need them to. Making your own will take you 10 minutes!

YOU WILL NEED
- [ ] 2½ yards (XS–M) or 3 yards (L–XL) jersey knit fabric

HOW TO

1. Using a pair of sharp fabric scissors, cut your fabric so that your piece measures 25 inches wide. Don't throw out the remainder of the fabric, as you can use it for all kinds of other wonderful craft projects.

2. Hang about 20 inches of the fabric over your left shoulder, then pull it down across your back until it reaches the front of your right hip.

3. Tie the two ends of the fabric together with a strong double knot. Keep in mind that the weight of the baby will pull the sling down lower than it is at this point.

4. Always sit down to place your baby in the sling. You should have enough fabric to create a really cozy cocoon around your baby once he/she is installed in the sling.

Baby Mobile

This is so much better than anything you will find in a store. The store-bought mobiles may look cute to adults, but babies want to see bright colors and flashing shapes—which is where your old CDs come in.

YOU WILL NEED
- ☐ Large piece of cardboard or a large paper plate
- ☐ Ball of string
- ☐ 1 old cereal box
- ☐ 1 old CD or DVD

HOW TO

1. Cut out some animal and flower shapes from your old cereal box.

2. Either cut a circle out of your cardboard by turning a bowl upside down and drawing around it with a marker, or have your paper plate ready. With a skewer or a sharp scissors point, make a hole in the center of the circle.

3. Cut a length of string and tie a few knots (to form one large knot) in one end. Thread through the center hole from underneath the cardboard.

4. Draw two diagonal lines across the plate, crossing over the center hole. Make four more holes on the diagonal lines, about ½ inch away from the edge of the circle.

5. Take 4 lengths of string and knot their ends. Thread each one through a hole from the top of the cardboard circle.

6. Attach a shape or a CD to each length of string.

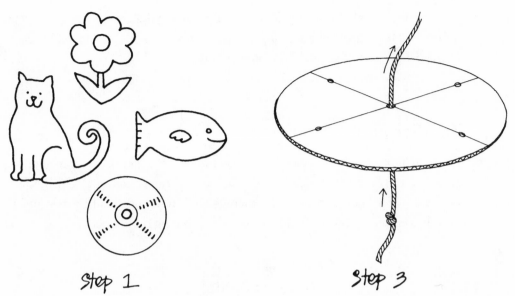

Step 1   Step 3

Step 6

7. Hang the mobile from a hook in the ceiling above the crib, making sure that it's extremely secure and hung high enough so that it's completely out of reach of the baby—even if the baby should stand up.

Toddler and Beyond

It's even more fun when you can make things for a child who can join in. Lola loved to help me design her Pillowcase Nightgown and pick out the fabric squares for her comforter. The nightgown is now too small for her, but is proudly sported by the stuffed bear who sits grinning on her bed.

Pillowcase Nightgown

This was the most thrillingly easy thing I've ever made for Lola, and it's sooooo pretty.

YOU WILL NEED
- ☐ 1 old pillowcase (search around to see what you have and look for an odd one with embroidery or polka dots—if you don't have any, you'll find one in a thrift store or flea market)
- ☐ 1 yard ¼-inch silk ribbon
- ☐ Basic sewing supplies

HOW TO

1. If the pillowcase has embroidery/lace at one end, decide if you want it to be the top or the bottom of the nightgown. You are better off having the opening of the pillowcase as the bottom of the nightgown—that way, there's less hemming. Hold up the pillowcase against your child to see how long you want it to be. If the pillowcase is too long, mark with a pin how much you need to cut off. A standard pillowcase should work as a long nightgown for ages 5 through 7 and a shorter one for ages 8 through 10.

2. Measure your child from the top of her shoulder to under her arm. My daughter measured 7 inches.

3. With a pencil or tailor's chalk, mark 2 rectangles in both top corners. The length will be the measurement you just took in step 2 and the width should be 2 inches. Cut out the rectangles.

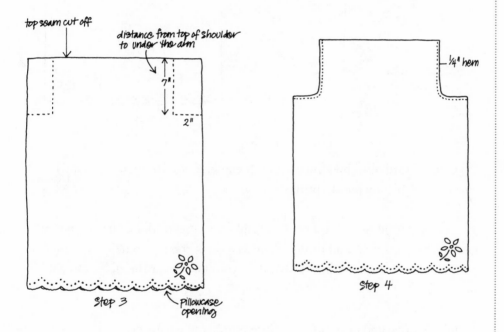

4. Tuck under the raw edges of the armholes ¼ inch and then another ¼ inch to create a seam, and sew.

5. Fold over the top edge (front first) ¼ inch and then 1 inch to create the casing.* Press. If your pillowcase is 100% cotton, the pressing will keep your seam in place and you won't need to pin it. Repeat for the back and then sew both hems.

*A casing is a large seam that you can run ribbon, elastic, or binding through.

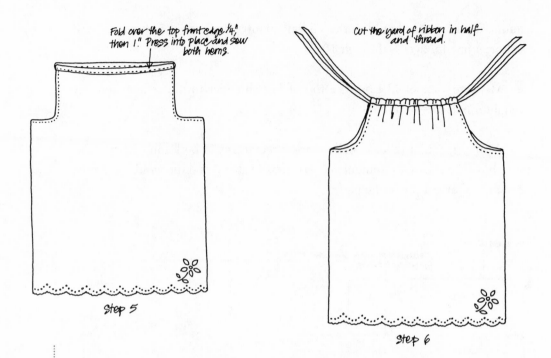

Fold over the top front edge 1/4", then 1." Press into place and sew both hems.

Step 5

Cut the yard of ribbon in half and thread.

Step 6

6. Cut the yard of ribbon in half and thread half of it through the front 1-inch casing with a safety pin. Repeat for the back.

7. Bunch the fabric together on the ribbon to create the desired amount of gathering. You can sew a button on either side of the top to hold the ribbon in place. You don't have to, but it's handy if you don't want the ribbon to get lost in the wash!

8. Get creative and decorate your little number in whatever way you can think of. I added a little pink and green button to mine and then cut a large letter L out of a scrap of green fabric. I sewed it on the front with a zigzag stitch to prevent the edges from fraying. You can cut flowers, hearts, letters, or even animals out of old scraps, and with a sewing machine, you'll have it done in under 5 minutes.

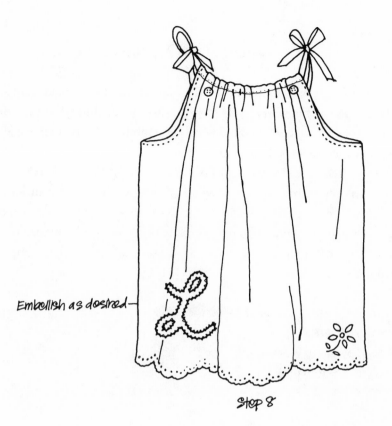

Embellish as desired —

Step 8

Easy Gathered Skirt

Lola and I used to drool over the fancy skirts in a pricey kid's boutique around the corner, until I realized how incredibly easy they were to make. The joy of making your little girl's skirts is that she can go to the fabric store and have the fun of picking out exactly what she wants. You can always whip one up for yourself at the same time (not in the same fabric *please!*). There are directions on p. 146 for how to make the skirt for an adult. You'll obviously need to adjust the measurements accordingly. No pattern required!

Boiled Wool Mittens

Boiled wool is just what sounds like: To create it, you take an old wool sweater and "boil" it in the hot water cycle of your washing machine. You then dry it to a crisp and voilà—a piece of boiled wool! It's a fabulous fabric to make all kinds of things out of—purses, hats, and little mittens.

You may have ruined a sweater or two by putting it through a machine wash, so here's an opportunity to redeem yourself. If not, check out your local thrift store for some sweaters in fun colors. Kids' sweaters are great and you'll be able to pick them up for pennies from a garage sale. Boiled wool mittens are perfect for very cold, snowy weather because the close weave of the knit simply won't allow the cold in.

YOU WILL NEED

☐ 1 old sweater, washed and dried as hot as possible
☐ Basic sewing supplies

HOW TO

1. Place your child's hand on the spread-out sleeve of the sweater.

2. Measure your child's hands from the tip of the fingers to a couple of inches past the wrist.

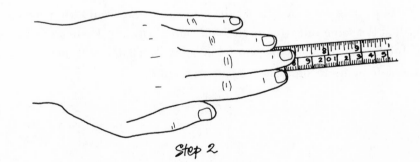

Step 2

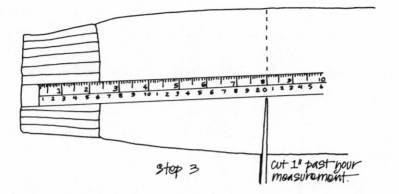

Step 3

Cut 1" past your measurement.

3. Cut off the sleeve of the sweater 1 inch past the measurement you made.

4. With a marker, draw around your child's hand, leaving 1 inch around the fingers and ½ inch around the thumb.

5. Cut out the mittens with sharp scissors.

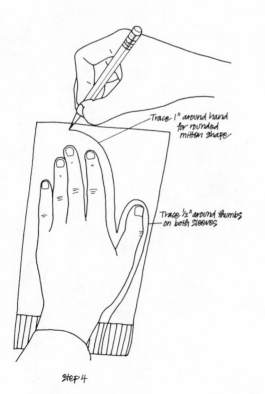

Trace 1" around hand for rounded mitten shape

Trace ½" around thumbs on both sleeves

Step 4

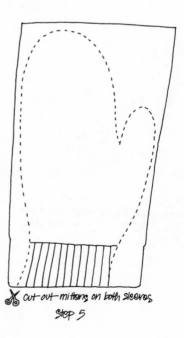

Cut out mittens on both sleeves

Step 5

6. Place the right sides of the mittens together and, using a backstitch (see p. 137), sew a seam all around the edges, ¼ inch away from the raw edges.

7. Make a small snip in the wool between the thumb and first finger to avoid wrinkling (be very careful that you don't snip your stitches).

8. Turn the mittens the right way out and customize with little buttons or a bow made from an odd bit of ribbon.

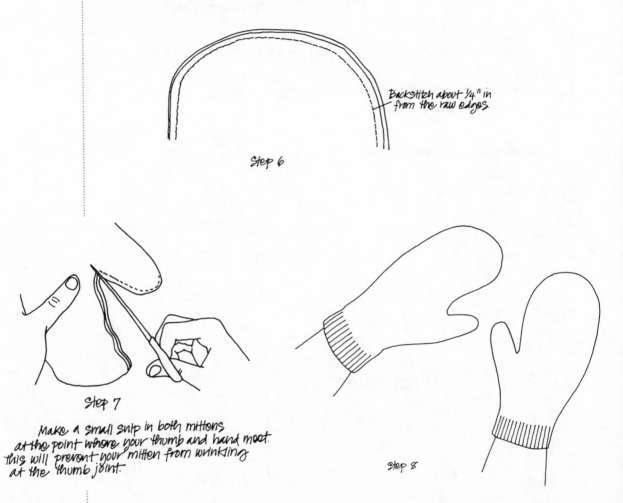

Backstitch about ¼" in
from the raw edges.

Step 6

Step 7

Make a small snip in both mittens
at the point where your thumb and hand meet.
this will prevent your mitten from wrinkling
at the thumb joint.

Step 8

Patchwork Comforter Cover

This is my daughter's favorite comforter cover. It is enormously pleasurable to put together, as you can use up all kinds of little scraps of fabric. You can also use some of your own or your child's worn-out clothes. I once had a skirt that was made of adorable fabric, but it looked a bit Pollyannaish on me, so it got cut up into dozens of squares and became part of my daughter's cover.

YOU WILL NEED
- ☐ Old fabric scraps
- ☐ 1 empty cereal box
- ☐ Basic sewing supplies

HOW TO

1. Cut a square out of an empty cereal box or a spare piece of cardboard. This will become your template. Your square should be about 6 to 8 inches wide.

2. Work out approximately how many squares you'll need. The first time I made this, I laid out an existing comforter cover on the bed and figured I'd need 5 6-inch squares for the width and 10 for the length—so in all, I would need 50 squares for the back and 50 for the front. Keep in mind that each square will end up ½ inch smaller, as there'll be a ¼-inch seam around each side. Also be sure to make your cover larger than the comforter that you're making it for.

3. Place your template on your scraps of fabric and draw around them with a wax crayon. Cut out the squares with sharp fabric scissors. Arrange the squares on the floor in the pattern you want.

4. Mark the back of each square with a number. Grab a piece of paper and draw a plan of your cover, so you'll know where each numbered square goes.

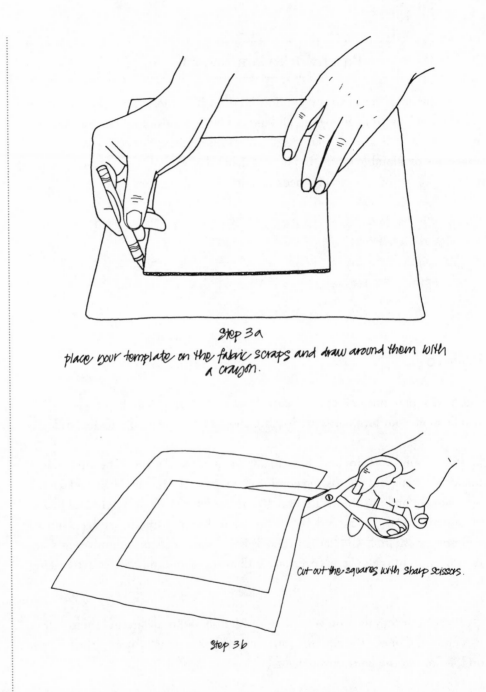

step 3a

place your template on the fabric scraps and draw around them with a crayon.

cut out the squares with sharp scissors.

step 3b

5. Take 2 squares and put their wrong sides together. Pin one edge and sew ¼ inch away from the raw edge. Join all the squares together until you've created the front of your cover. Repeat for the back.

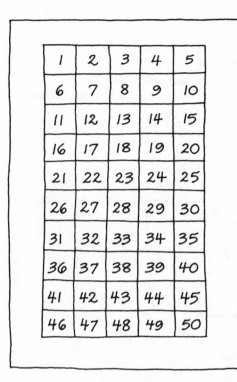

1	2	3	4	5
6	7	8	9	10
11	12	13	14	15
16	17	18	19	20
21	22	23	24	25
26	27	28	29	30
31	32	33	34	35
36	37	38	39	40
41	42	43	44	45
46	47	48	49	50

Draw a plan of your cover, so you'll know where each numbered square goes.

Step 4

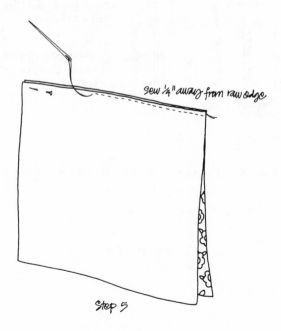

Sew 1/4" away from raw edge

Step 5

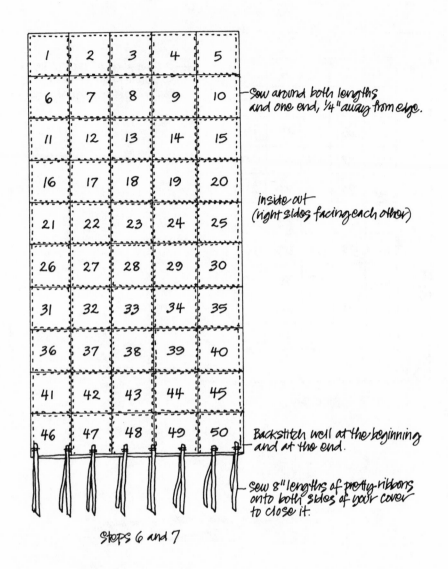

1	2	3	4	5
6	7	8	9	10
11	12	13	14	15
16	17	18	19	20
21	22	23	24	25
26	27	28	29	30
31	32	33	34	35
36	37	38	39	40
41	42	43	44	45
46	47	48	49	50

Sew around both lengths and one end, ¼" away from edge.

inside out (right sides facing each other)

Backstitch well at the beginning and at the end.

Sew 8" lengths of pretty ribbons onto both sides of your cover to close it.

Steps 6 and 7

6. Join the right sides of the front and back of the quilt together and pin. Sew all around both lengths and one end, ¼ inch away from the edge. Make sure you backstitch (see p. 137) at the beginning and end, as this will be your opening.

7. To close the comforter cover, you can either sew on large snaps or cut 8-inch lengths of pretty ribbon to sew onto either side of the opening as ties, to make sure the comforter stays inside the cover.

How to Cut Your Child's Hair

I have always cut Lola's hair. I once (and only once) took her to a madly expensive kids' hair salon in Los Angeles, where she got lollipops and stickers and I got a whacking bill. After forking out the tip and dragging a bad-tempered toddler home, I vowed to learn to do it myself, and have had great success. You just need a good pair of haircutting scissors and some knowledge of the basics.

For a Baby or Toddler

YOU WILL NEED

- ☐ 1 sheet
- ☐ 1 towel
- ☐ Comb
- ☐ Pair of sharp hair-cutting scissors (a worthwhile investment)
- ☐ 1 lollipop or video (or both!!)

HOW TO

1. Since attention is a major issue at this age, you may only get 10 minutes max, so get ready with a video that will keep your precious one amused. If your baby/toddler still fits, put her in her highchair, as this will bring her to the right level for you. You might want to place the highchair on a sheet. Put a little towel around the baby's neck and tuck it into her collar.

2. Comb all the baby's hair forward from the crown of the head over the baby's eyes. Lay the closed scissors flat on the baby's head for her to know that she's safe, then cut about ½ inch above the eyebrow line. Cut *only* from edge of one eyebrow to edge of the other. You don't want your child to look silly.

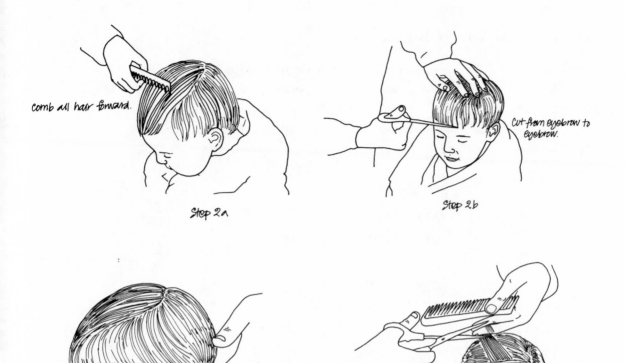

comb all hair forward.

Step 2a

Cut from eyebrow to eyebrow.

Step 2b

Trim around the ears.

Step 3

Step 4

3. Cut a little longer in a line around the temples, ears, and down the back of the head. Repeat on the other side.

4. If you can buy another 2 or 3 minutes, give your baby a few layers by anchoring a 2-inch section of hair between your index and middle fingers. Pull the section of hair until it's straight. Holding your fingers at an angle, snip at an angle. You can pull up as many sections as you have time to before your little one has had enough.

For a Little Girl

YOU WILL NEED
- ☐ Mirror
- ☐ 1 sheet
- ☐ 1 towel
- ☐ Sprayer with water
- ☐ Sharp haircutting scissors
- ☐ 4 or 5 large hairdressing clips

HOW TO

1. Give your little girl a mirror or set yourself in front of a mirror, as it's fun for her to see what you're doing. Place a sheet beneath her chair and a towel around her neck.

2. If her hair isn't wet, spritz with water to make sure it's pretty damp all the way through.

3. If she has bangs, begin trimming them. Take half a section of half the bang between your index and middle fingers, pull it straight, and snip off the ends (no more than ¼ inch or your child will never forgive you!).

4. Gather your child's hair into two large knots on top of her head and secure with clips.

5. Pull down the first section of hair about ½ inch above the hairline and cut straight across. I start with one side, then continue around the back and the other side. This is where you determine the correct length, so make sure it's right before continuing.

6. Get your child to sit up straight, legs uncrossed, and pull down the two front pieces of her hair on either side of her face to see if they're the same length.

7. Draw the next section of hair (1½ inches above hairline) out of the topknots, and cut to the same length as the layer below. Continue until you have pulled all the hair out of the knots.

8. Add a few layers for bounce by pulling 2-inch sections of hair away from the crown of the head, straight up toward the ceiling, between your index and middle fingers. Snip off the ends at an angle.

Step 4

hairdressing clip

Step 5

Step 8

Making Shoes Last Longer

When I was little, getting a pair of new shoes was a huge treat and an adventure. I remember the excitement of having my feet measured and walking out of the store in a brand-new pair of shiny party or school shoes that I could show off to my friends. I'd love to say it's the same with my daughter, but sadly, things have changed and her shoe shelf is crammed with flip-flops, tennis shoes, and sequined ballet slippers. Footwear clearly isn't the extravagance it used to be. However, when I buy her a more expensive pair of fancy shoes, I teach her to take care of them by using the following techniques. She knows that if we take care of them, we can then hand them down to a smaller friend who may need them.

SOCK-STUFFING

As it's hard to find good shoe trees for kids, I just ball up odd socks and stuff them into the toes of the shoes when Lola's not wearing them.

Leather Protector

How annoying is it when you splurge and buy your child a pair of smart, expensive leather shoes, and after just one outing, they come back scuffed and scratched? It's a great idea to apply this nontoxic leather protector as soon as you get the shoes out of the box. Keep in mind that regular leather and suede protectors contain chemicals that are toxic.

YOU WILL NEED
- ☐ 1 oz. beeswax
- ☐ ½ cup safflower oil

HOW TO

1. Place the beeswax and the oil in a bowl set over a saucepan of boiling water and warm until the beeswax has melted.

2. Apply to shoes with a clean rag while the wax is still warm.

3. Buff with another clean rag.

SHOE POLISH

As almost all shoe polishes contain horribly toxic ingredients, the best thing you can use to keep your kids' shoes gleaming is olive oil. Just pour about ½ teaspoon of oil onto a clean, dry rag and buff up until the shoes shine.

CLEANING TENNIS SHOES

The best thing for cleaning up an old pair of tennis shoes is to make a paste of baking soda and water. Scrub the canvas, toes, and soles by dipping a toothbrush or old nailbrush into the paste. Rinse with water and leave to air dry outside in the summer, and on top of your dryer in the winter.

Baby Skincare Products

Most of the mainstream baby skincare products that we were raised with have that ubiquitous "baby" smell—a scent that conjures up images of pink, fluffy bunnies and daisy-filled meadows. The truth is that the "meadow sweet" scent you are filling your baby's nostrils with is likely to contain a cocktail of toxic chemicals. It's vital that you start recognizing that smell as totally fake. In the same way that apple-flavored candy tastes nothing like an actual apple, there is nothing in nature that is anything like that baby scent.

As a society, we are obsessed with cleanliness and we've taken it a bit too far. We obviously want everything to be clean and sanitary, especially around our babies. However, our fixation with antibacterial products is not healthy. Most antibacterial products—wipes, sprays, body lotions, and hand sanitizers—contain yet another cocktail of toxic ingredients that you would be wise to avoid. It's far safer, more effective, and satisfying to make all your own products. I promise that your baby will still smell like a little angel, and you'll still be able to keep harmful germs at bay.

I went shopping the other day, planning to buy a basket of organic baby products for a friend's baby shower. The first shocker was how expensive every single one of these products was. The second shock was how *many* products there are for you to choose from. I know that these well-intentioned companies are trying to sell us everything they can, but when you really think about it, what do you actually need? The following recipes will cover everything you'll need for a baby or child, and you will save a fistful of cash by making your own.

Diaper Cream

This is an extremely effective, gentle diaper cream.

Yields: approximately 2 oz. of cream

Application: use as often as your baby needs, to avoid chafing and diaper rash

Storage: 2-oz. dark glass jar in a cool, dark cupboard or the fridge

Shelf life: 1 month in the cupboard, 3 months in the fridge

2 tbsp. organic olive oil (use cold-pressed)	1 tsp. beeswax
	½ tsp. vitamin E oil
2 tbsp. caster oil	1 tsp. zinc oxide*

You can find zinc oxide at Natural Health Supply (www.naturalhealthsupply.com). It is sold as Deodorant Zinc Oxide and comes in a large jar that will last you awhile.

1. Gently heat the oils and beeswax in a small bowl set over a pan of boiling water. When the wax has melted, remove from heat.

2. Allow to cool for 5 minutes and then stir in the vitamin E oil and the zinc oxide.

3. Pour into your glass jar.

Baby Wipes

I recommend avoiding scented baby wipes, as the "fragrance" could be toxic. Making your own is terribly easy and cost-effective.

YOU WILL NEED
- ☐ 1 roll unbleached paper towels (preferably made from recycled paper)
- ☐ 2 cups boiled, then cooled, water
- ☐ 2 tsp. liquid castile soap
- ☐ 1 tbsp. organic sweet almond oil
- ☐ 3 drops Roman chamomile essential oil
- ☐ 1 large, round plastic container (you could use an old wipes container) with a tight-fitting lid

HOW TO

1. With a sharp serrated knife, cut the paper roll in half so that you end up with two toilet paper–size rolls. You may need to use a sawing action with your knife to cut through the layers.

2. Remove the inner cardboard rolls from one of the rolls. (Store the other for a second use.)

3. Pour the water, soap, oil, and essential oil into the plastic container.

4. Place the half paper roll, cut side down, into the container.

5. Pull the towels out from the center of the roll.

6. Keep the container tightly sealed to ensure freshness.

Baby Bubble Bath/Shampoo

Since a baby's skin is so delicate, I recommend avoiding most drugstore bubble baths, as many of them contain harsh and toxic ingredients. There are some great natural alternatives, but like many of the nontoxic baby products, they can be really expensive.

You don't need a separate product for your baby's body and hair—let's face it, we're not talking about much hair anyway! This simple recipe meets your needs and is cleansing yet very gentle—perfect for a baby under 1 year old.

YOU WILL NEED
- ☐ 1 cup distilled water
- ☐ 2 tbsp. liquid castile soap (unscented)
- ☐ 1 tbsp. vegetable glycerin
- ☐ 6 drops Roman chamomile essential oil

HOW TO

1. Mix all the ingredients together in a measuring cup and pour into a plastic bottle (a used and rinsed-out shampoo bottle is a good idea).

2. Keep for up to 1 month.

Fizzy Orange Bath Bomb

It's fun for toddlers and kids to have a bath bomb that'll fizz around their tub, leaving a beautiful scent and even a few rose petals. I suggest doubling up the amounts, so you can give some as gifts. These bath bombs contain oils that are safe for a child over 1 year of age.

HOW TO

1. Mix all the ingredients together in a small bowl, making sure that you mash the oils well into the powder.

2. Press into an ice cube tray. Leave the tray at room temperature for a few hours so that the bath bombs can harden. You should get 2 or 3 small bath bombs (cubes) from this recipe.

3. You can wrap your bath bombs in pretty remnant squares and tie with a ribbon for a cute gift. Store them in an airtight container for up to 3 months.

Baby Balm

This simple yet softening balm is perfect for your little baby's delicate skin after a bath.

Yields: approximately 4 oz. of balm

Application: use after a bath and massage into your baby's body

Storage: 4-oz. dark glass jar in a cool, dark cupboard

Shelf life: 3 months

5 tbsp. sweet almond oil

2 tbsp. beeswax

1 tbsp. cocoa butter

10 drops Roman chamomile
   essential oil

5 drops lavender essential oil (this
   should only be added for a baby
   who is 12 months or older)

1. In a small bowl set over a large saucepan of boiling water, place all the ingredients except the essential oils and warm until the beeswax has melted.

2. Remove from the heat and allow to stand for 5 minutes before adding the essential oils.

3. Pour into your jar.

Baby Powder

Since talc, the main ingredient in most baby powders, is a proven carcinogen, here's a safe and effective alternative.

YOU WILL NEED

☐ ½ cup cornstarch*

☐ ½ cup arrowroot powder*

☐ 20 drops Roman chamomile essential oil

Find in the baking aisle of most grocery stores.

HOW TO

1. Simply place all the ingredients in a shaker (a flour/sugar shaker is ideal).

2. Store your powder out of direct sunlight for up to 6 months.

Shampoo

Shampoos are tough because they contain so many questionable ingredients. This recipe is simple to prepare and does the job. You can also mix and match the scents.

Yields: approximately 8 oz. of shampoo

Application: for a baby, use once a week; for a toddler 18 months and up, use 2 to 3 times a week

Storage: 8-oz. plastic bottle (an old shampoo bottle will do)

Shelf life: 6 months

1 cup liquid castile soap	5 drops lavender essential oil*
½ tsp. jojoba oil	5 drops grapefruit essential oil*

* For a baby under 12 months old, skip the essential oils.

1. Mix all the ingredients together in a measuring jug and pour into a plastic bottle.

Conditioner

I never used a conditioner on Lola until she was about 4. She has really thick hair, and because we live in a very dry climate, I give her hair a little "treatment" once a week as follows.

YOU WILL NEED
- ☐ ½ cup virgin coconut oil
- ☐ 12 drops ylang ylang essential oil

HOW TO

1. If it's really warm in your house, your coconut oil will be liquid, in which case just stir in the essential oil.

2. If it's chilly and the oil is solid, gently heat the jar in a bowl of hot water before you add your essential oil.

3. It's best to apply this conditioner to only the ends of *dry* hair. My daughter is too impatient to wait for anything, so I just have to get her to stand still for 10 seconds while I work about ½ tsp. into the ends of her hair. I do this about half an hour before her shower. When in the shower, I shampoo her hair as usual with a gentle, nontoxic shampoo (see p. 124).

Useful Remedies for Little Ones

Head Lice Treatment

Most of the commercial head lice treatments aren't effective or safe. I always make my own, and I have found this remedy to be 100% effective.

Yields: approximately 4 oz.

Application: Comb your child's hair to eliminate any tangles. Apply to dry hair, making sure you cover the entire scalp, and take the oil down to the ends of the hair. Cover your child's head with a shower cap and leave it on overnight. In the morning, shampoo twice and condition with a few drops of jojoba oil. Comb the hair thoroughly with a lice comb. Repeat this entire procedure a week later.

Storage: 4-oz. plastic bottle with pop-up cap (an old shampoo bottle is perfect)

Shelf life: 6 months

6 sprigs fresh rosemary	4 garlic cloves, minced
6 tbsp. neem oil	Cheesecloth for straining
2 tbsp. jojoba oil	1 tbsp. tea tree essential oil

1. Strip the rosemary leaves off their stalks and mash them down with a mortar and pestle.

2. Place the neem and jojoba oils in a metal bowl set over a pan of boiling water and add the rosemary and the garlic. Heat gently for 15 minutes.

3. Strain the oil mixture through a piece of cheesecloth into a glass measuring cup. Allow the mixture to cool. Add the tea tree oil.

4. Pour into the plastic bottle.

Earache Drops

These easy-to-make drops are great and are completely safe for babies, kids, and adults, too. As you need to let the flowers infuse into the preparation for a couple of weeks, make a batch now so you'll be prepared in case of an emergency.

YOU WILL NEED
- ☐ 2 tbsp. dried mullein flowers (mountainroseherbs.com)
- ☐ 1 clove garlic, crushed
- ☐ 1 cup cold-pressed olive oil

HOW TO

1. Simply place all the ingredients in a screw-top glass jar (an old jelly jar is perfect). Shake the jar and place it in a cool, dark spot for 2 weeks. It'll take that long for the flowers and garlic to infuse their healing properties into the oil.

2. Strain the oil through a fine mesh sieve and decant the mixture into a couple of dark glass bottles with droppers.

3. At the first sign of an earache, place 2 or 3 drops in each ear and plug with cotton to keep the oil from running out.

Baby Food

There's no need to buy baby food in jars, cans, or packages. It's so easy to make and store that if you care about your baby's health, your bank account, and the planet, you'll get yourself in the kitchen for a quick hour once a week and get things going.

Alternative to Buying Jars

Buy yourself a set of Baby Cubes (www.babycubes.com). These are BPA-free small plastic containers with snap-on lids. BPA (Bisphenol A) is a hormone-disrupting chemical that can leach from plastic into food and beverages. The cubes are stackable and are a perfect alternative to jars for storing baby food. Each container is a perfect size for one meal, and if your baby is really hungry, you can give him/her two of them. I also use them for storing homemade chicken and veggie stock.

Store-bought jars of organic baby food can be pricey and are obviously less fresh and nutritious than food made by your sweet self. It'll take you all of 15 minutes to make a batch—so you have no excuse!

The best vegetables for making baby food are sweet potatoes, corn, squash, green beans, zucchini, peas, and carrots. The best fruits are apples, pears, and plums. Try to buy organic if possible.

If you want to give your baby some interesting combos, try these:

Sweet potatoes and corn

Carrots and zucchini

Peas and green beans

Apples and pears

Apples and plums

Apples and squash or pumpkin

Add steamed brown rice to any of the above combos for babies 6 months and older. Add the rice *before* you blend.

YOU WILL NEED
- ☐ Steamer
- ☐ Blender, immersion blender, or food processor
- ☐ Baby Cubes or tiny glass jars with lids (Pyrex makes a small, round glass container with a BPA-free plastic lid that will store enough for 2 or 3 meals)

HOW TO

1. Wash and/or peel your fruits and veggies. Use homemade veggie wash (see p. 304).

2. Steam food until soft and tender, but be careful not to overcook until it's gray and soggy.

3. Drain. If you're using soft or watery fruits or veggies (zucchini, carrots, peas, and fruit) use an immersion blender, as it's so much quicker and easier. I love to skip having to wash up a blender or food processor whenever possible. You may need to use a food processor for the potatoes and green beans.

4. Spoon into your containers and allow them to cool completely before fitting on the lid.

5. Chill for a few hours in the fridge.

6. Place in the freezer. They will keep for up to 3 months.

Organic Teething Biscuits

Making your own organic teething biscuits will cost you way less than the ones you'll typically find in a health food store.

Yields: approximately 12 medium biscuits

Storage: airtight container

Shelf life: 10 days

1 cup organic whole-wheat flour	3 tbsp. virgin coconut oil
1 cup organic dry baby cereal	Ice water

1. Preheat oven to 425°F.

2. Mix the flour and rice cereal in a medium bowl.

3. Stir in the oil.

4. Add enough ice water to create a big, sticky ball of dough.

5. Transfer the ball to a pastry bag or a plastic bag with the bottom corner snipped off (see p. 317).

6. Pipe out onto a greased baking sheet any shape that takes your fancy. I like to pipe out ring shapes.

7. Bake for 10 to 12 minutes. Transfer to a wire rack to cool.

Baby Berry Cereal

This is delicious and nutritious for a baby 4 to 12 months old.

Yields: enough for 1 serving

4 tbsp. water ½ tbsp. organic rice cereal	½ banana, finely chopped 10 organic berries (blueberries, raspberries)*

Berries are on my "Top Five Must-Buy-Organic" list.

1. Bring the water to a boil in a small saucepan and add all the ingredients.

2. Simmer on a low heat for 5 minutes.

3. Puree in a blender and add more water if it's too thick.

Apricot and Banana Porridge

This is a warming meal for a baby 4 to 12 months old.

Yields: enough for 1 serving

½ tbsp. oats ⅔ cup water 1 small banana, mashed	5 dried apricots (unsulphured), finely chopped

1. Place all the ingredients in a small saucepan, cover, and bring to a boil.

2. Simmer gently for 5 minutes.

3. Puree in a blender, adding more water if it's too thick.

Apple and Walnut Porridge

This warming porridge can be given to a baby 1 year and older. It's perfect for adults, too!

Yields: enough for 1–2 servings

1 cup water	4 walnut halves, crushed into tiny
½ cup oats	pieces
1 apple, peeled, cored, and cut into	Cinnamon
cubes	Raw honey

1. Place all the ingredients, except the honey and cinnamon, in a small saucepan and bring to a boil. Turn the heat down and let it simmer for 5 minutes.

2. Spoon into bowls and sprinkle each bowl with a little cinnamon and ½ tbsp. raw honey.

Three ❧

Frugalista

I adore beautiful clothes. I've spent way too much of my hard-earned money over the years on can't-live-without dresses, shoes, sweaters, and purses. I'm not a slave to fashion and couldn't care less about the "it's sooooo last year" thing, but I have to admit that it can be heart-flutteringly delicious to pull a brand-new little something out of wisps of tissue paper, only to marvel at its wrinkleless perfection. A few washes later, when the excitement has worn off, the cute little something will be relegated to the back of my closet or sit for weeks in the ironing pile in my laundry room, leaving me to wonder what on *earth* I'm going to wear that day!

Growing up in the English countryside, quite a few miles away from the nearest town, if I wanted something—a new skirt, a doll, candy, almost *anything*—my mother suggested that I have a go at making it. When you *need* the new miniskirt that all your friends are wearing and your mom won't buy it for you, you find a way of making it. I remember Mom's black and gold hand-crank Singer sewing machine. With visions of a fire-engine red miniskirt that I'd seen in a magazine, I got that thing cranking like never before. I didn't bother with patterns, no way! I just draped the fabric around my hips, marked with a ballpoint where it needed to be cut, and got going. Admittedly, much fabric was wasted in my quest for a garment that actually fit, but I did figure out how to make darts, waistbands, hems, and even linings in a matter of days. Sewing clearly wasn't my strength—and it still isn't today—so if I can easily throw together the following useful items, so can you.

Since attempting to live a greener life, I've had to put away the plastic and seriously cut back on the shopping sprees. I've learned the pleasures of window shopping. I go out *sans* credit card and allow myself to just look. I've taught my Lola to do the same, and we've often come back from one of these little adventures thrilled with ourselves that we didn't buy that ridiculously expensive skirt that on first sight had made us swoon. There's a massive feel-good factor to knowing that we *can* live without something—that we won't spontaneously combust if we don't get this season's boots on our feet right away. I'm secretly rather pleased with myself when I see women in the mall decked out head to toe in this month's fashion must-haves. I just know that those pointy boots or Grecian sandals will end up in the thrift store by this time next year—and I didn't succumb!

Flicking through the pages of a fashion magazine can be a little depressing: 14-year-old models in sickeningly expensive shoes that were probably made for less than 10 bucks by impoverished workers in India. Moreover, the fashion industry, unless otherwise stated, can be a hideous polluter. If you care about nontoxic water and soil, and the human rights of the workers stitching your sassy purse, you will probably think twice about buying it.

So what's a fashionista to do? The most important thing is to find your own signature style. It's important to create a look that expresses who you really are. After all, just because you're not diving into the latest pricey trends doesn't mean you must make style sacrifices. A gorgeous women who is sexy, stylish, and comfortable in her own skin (and shoes!) is the furthest thing from a fashion victim. There's nothing less sexy than seeing someone hobbling along the sidewalk in a pair of excruciatingly uncomfortable shoes—shoes she has to wear because this month's *In Style* says they are in.

I can't count the number of times I've asked someone where she got that skirt or sweater, and she either says it's years old or from some obscure vintage store. I'm beginning to think that being a *frugalista* is a great thing. It encourages me to dust off my sewing machine or to trawl thrift stores for some fabulous finds. Becoming frugal in the fashion department also encourages me to use my imagination and find a style that really fits.

Do I still need a shopping fix of the tissue paper and bag-with-fancy-cloth-handles variety? Yes, I absolutely do, but once or twice a year will suffice. And nowadays if I buy something expensive, it needs to be a classic, a piece that'll last me a few seasons. Beautiful leather shoes and cashmere should be purchased with a very long life in mind. I've discovered many ways in which I can make my clothes and shoes last longer, and how to make do with what I've got—without feeling hard done by.

It's Sew Easy

If you can get your sew on, do it! By learning the basics of sewing, you can save yourself wads of cash. You'll be able to mend, alter, and even put together simple and sexy outfits. I'm not talking about homemade-*looking* clothes, I PROMISE. Trust me, the thought of wearing a dress that really *looks* homemade is abhorrent. You know the deal—bunchy seams, badly constructed darts, puffy hemlines, and stray threads, all rendered in a somewhat suspect fabric. We're not talking about homesteading or pioneer-style living here. Rather, we're talking about getting crafty enough to make something that will knock the socks off your friends when they find out where it came from.

I've become a regular at my local sewing store in Los Angeles. It's been in operation since the 1940s and has signed photographs on the walls of stars from back in the day when they all had dressmakers. The women who work there are all about 108 and move extremely slowly. I never go there in a hurry, as they painstakingly measure out each millimeter of fabric with massive scissors hanging on elasticized ribbons around their necks. I love this musty old store with a passion. It slows me down considerably as I wander the aisles of enormous fabric bolts, dreaming of what I could—skill permitting—create. The bargain bins overflow with rolls of embroidered ribbon, outdated buttons, and fabric remnants galore. Best of all, this kind of store makes me want to go home and pull out my sewing basket.

A basic sewing machine is one of the best investments you can make. It'll cost you less than a fancy outfit, and even if you only pull it out to hem a few pairs of pants, it'll pay for itself handsomely. I bet you know someone who'll lend you a machine to have a go, but you might want to ask for a good new one for your next birthday. I love the Brother CS-6000i. It's a very well-priced machine that's so easy to work that a total novice can get it up and running

BEGINNER'S SEWING GUIDE

If you decide to go the hand-sewing route, you will only be required to know a couple of different stitches. If you can do these and thread a needle, you're good to go.

NEEDLES

Buy a packet of different size needles, as you'll need a thinner needle for soft, flimsy fabric and a thicker one for a hefty job.

THREAD

Buy as many colors as you want of an all-purpose thread. For hand sewing, it doesn't matter if you use polyester, cotton, or a blend of both. If you are buying thread for your sewing machine, check with the manufacturer to see what type of thread they recommend. To create a basic sewing kit, start with black, white, and beige thread. If you're buying for a specific project, you'll know what colors to pick based on the fabric colors.

THREADING THE NEEDLE

My eyesight is annoyingly not what it was, so I use a needle threader for tiny needles. Poke the wire loop through the eye of the needle, put the thread through the wire loop, and pull through. If your needle has a big enough eye, snip the end of the thread with sharp scissors, wet it with saliva, and just poke it through. Don't forget to knot the other end of your thread. If you are trying to thread yarn or embroidery thread, you may need to use the double-fold technique, where you fold over the end of the thread/yarn and squeeze it through the eye.

STITCHES

For most of the projects in this book, you will need just two stitches.

Running stitch: You will use this stitch for seaming, mending, and gathering. Simply weave your needle in and out of the fabric, creating short stitches, and then pull the needle and thread through the fabric.

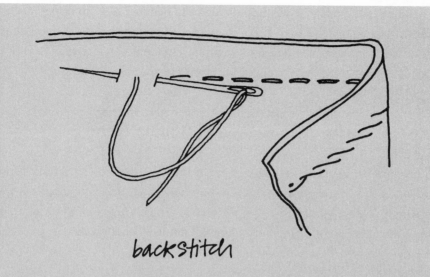

backstitch

within an hour. It also has a bunch of really fancy stitches to choose from. I had a blast just spending an entire evening trying out all the stitches on an old pillowcase. It amazed me that with one touch of a button and a press on the foot pedal, I could produce embroidery that would've given my grandmother a run for her money.

If you can't get a sewing machine right now, at least pull a little sewing basket/box together. You can use an old shoebox, and if you want to customize it, cover it with magazine photos of sewing/fashion-related things, then give it a coat of nontoxic varnish. You can also line it with felt to prevent everything from sliding around. You can find scissors, thread in basic colors, needles, a package each of straight and safety pins, and a tape measure in most grocery stores, to get your "basket" started. You might also want to include Stitch Witchery (a kind of iron-on tape that's the cheat's tool for hemming), a pin cushion, a small measuring tape, a package of multiuse darning needles, a seam ripper, a small jar or tin of assorted buttons, tailor's chalk, a thimble, pinking shears (jagged edges, which prevent fraying), and anything else that catches your eye. It all depends on how much you're going to commit to your new sewing self!

How to Sew on a Button by Hand

You have probably got quite a collection of buttons by now. Extra buttons are provided with most every garment you buy nowadays, and you should always keep them. Even if you don't lose a button from the corresponding garment, it's a lot of fun to start collecting buttons for all kinds of craft projects.

YOU WILL NEED
- ☐ Medium needle
- ☐ Thread
- ☐ Toothpick

HOW TO

1. Use a marker to mark the spot where you want your button to be sewed on.

2. Thread your needle. Your thread should be about 20 inches long, so that it won't tangle. Knot the end.

3. Poke the needle through the fabric on the point you have marked. Bring it all the way up and then create a tiny stitch to the side of the mark.

4. Thread the button on the needle, through the left hole, and push the button against the fabric.

5. Place a toothpick under the thread between the two sets of holes. This creates a "spacer," which will ensure that the button can rise up enough to go through the buttonhole.

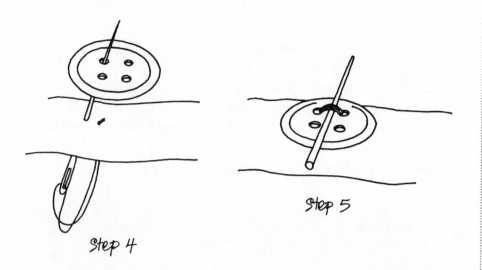

Step 4

Step 5

6. Push the needle down through the right hole and pull the thread tight. Repeat (up through the left, down through the right) four more times.

7. Repeat for the second set of holes.

8. Remove the toothpick.

9. Wind the thread 3 times around the threads that connect the button to the fabric, and tie a knot by threading the needle through a thread loop as it goes around the connecting threads. Clip the thread.

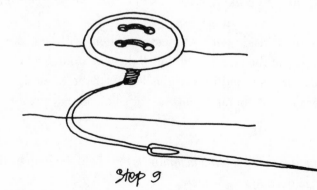

Step 9

How to Hem a Pair of Pants or a Dress

You can put away your money and stop going to the tailor to have things altered, as it's so very easy to do it gorgeously yourself! If you have a really nice pair of work or evening pants or a dress, you will want to sew a "blind" hem, where the stitches are barely visible. This is very easy to sew by hand, but obviously a little speedier with a machine. Machine hems are more visible, though.

YOU WILL NEED
- [ ] Ruler
- [ ] Thin needle
- [ ] Thread that matches your fabric

HOW TO

1. Measure the length you want your pants to be. It's really helpful to have someone help you at this point. Stand on a chair in front of a full-length mirror with a pair of heels on (if there's any chance you'll wear heels with the pants/skirt). Have your friend help you decide on the perfect length and mark it with a pin.

2. If you have a lot of excess fabric, you will need to cut it off. If you are using a machine, sew the raw edge with a zigzag stitch to prevent fraying. If not, cut the excess fabric off with pinking shears, as this, too, will help prevent fraying.

3. Turn the garment inside out and press your hem with a steam iron. You need to make sure that the hem is uniform all the way around, so I always have a little ruler close at hand and measure as I iron. If the fabric is cotton, you won't need to pin it. If it contains polyester or silk, you may want to pin it for stability.

4. *The most important part of blind hemming is this:* Fold the hem back on itself with the raw edge overlapping ¼ inch.

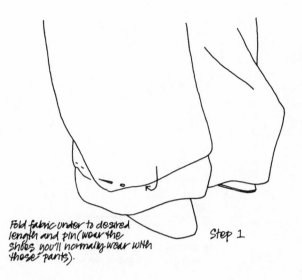

Fold fabric under to desired length and pin (wear the shoes you'll normally wear with those pants).

Step 1

5. If you are using a sewing machine, line up the divider in the foot with the folded edge and sew. If you are hand sewing, which I recommend as it's so easy, choose a matching thread and sew your first tiny stitch on the fabric just above the fold and the second stitch on the fold.* Repeat all the way along the folded edge.

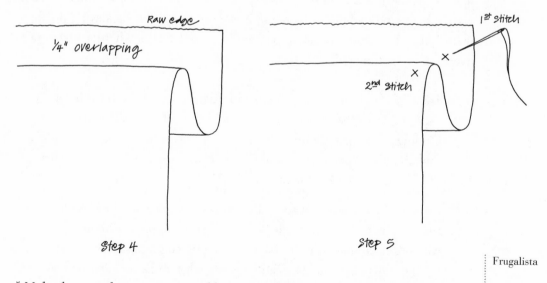

Raw edge

¼" overlapping

Step 4

1st stitch

2nd stitch

Step 5

Make these stitches as tiny as possible, just catching a few threads of the fabric.

Step 6
Turn the pants back out,
press the hem, and voilà!

6. Turn right side out and press. Voilà! You've saved yourself 10 to 20 bucks!

COOL AND CRAZY HEMMING

If your pants/skirt are more on the casual side, there are a number of time-saving hemming techniques you can easily do. If you have a sewing machine with a few different stitches, you're golden—and this is where a machine is worth its weight in gold.

- Turn the raw edge under ¼ inch and then another ½ inch (or however wide you want the hem to be). A thinner hem often looks better here. Use the zigzag or any other cool-looking stitch and a *contrasting color* thread. I just hemmed a pair of cream jeans with a bright yellow zigzig stitch and they look amazing.

- For skirts, you may want to find a contrasting color bias binding (double fold). Bias binding is like a long strip of cotton ribbon, which is used to bind or fold over raw fabric edges to prevent fraying. This way, you get to add a pretty edge and a hem in one fell swoop.

- If you want to do a quick hem on a patterned skirt, just fold under the raw edge ¼ inch, then fold under another ½ inch and use a simple running stitch all the way around. This will only look good if the hem is thin.

- If you can't be bothered to get out a needle and thread, much less a machine, buy yourself some Stitch Witchery tape from most large grocery or craft stores. This is an iron-on tape, which will give you a perfectly good stitchless hem. Keep in mind that it's not suitable for any fabric containing polyester because you need to use a fair amount of heat to get the tape to stick. You don't want your ball gown shriveling up.

As Good as New

I get enormous pleasure from transforming something old into something new. Transforming an antique sheet into a sexy chemise makes me feel rather clever, as do all of the following projects. Every time you keep something out of the landfill and choose *not* to use up more of this planet's dwindling resources, you'll get a kick out of it. Transforming old clothes and fabrics into something new will encourage you to get creative by fashioning bold and unique new styles for yourself. It's your opportunity to become a style maker instead of a fashion victim!

SEVEN NEW LOOKS

The first thing you want to do before you add anything to your wardrobe, home-made or otherwise, is to see what you already have and get rid of all the clutter. If you get a full-on eyeful of every garment you own, you might be surprised at the many new looks that you can put together. I know women who have hired stylists and the like to go through their closets, but you don't need a professional. If you really can't trust your own judgment, ask a good friend to join you.

I want you to commit to creating seven totally new looks out of what you already have.

1. Lay out all your clothes on the bed or on a large table. If you have a lot of clothes, you may need to do it in two batches. You could start

- Look for soft, long fibers. Cheaper cashmere won't feel so silky smooth.

- If you find vintage cashmere at a flea market, grab it because it has clearly stood the test of time.

The two things that can ruin your sweaters are:

1. Washing them incorrectly

2. Moth holes

PERFECT HAND WASHING

If you can hand wash instead of dry-cleaning your cashmere and wool, do. If the label says "dry-clean," it means you can hand wash it. If it says "dry-clean only," you may need to send it out. Poorly made sweaters often say they must be dry-cleaned.

1. Fill the kitchen sink with warm water and add a capful of natural shampoo. Gently agitate and swish around your sweater. If you know it has a stain, put a tiny dab of dishwashing liquid over the stain and rub in with your finger.

2. Gently squeeze out the excess water and carry the sweater in a towel to the tub.

3. Run a heavy stream of cold water over the sweater as you turn it over and gently squeeze out the soap. Rinse until the water runs clear.

4. Very gently twist the sweater into a loose twist and place lengthwise in the center of a large, dry towel. Have your partner or a friend hold one end of the towel while you hold the other. Both of you should begin to twist at the same time, squeezing out all the excess moisture.

5. An alternative method for squeezing out excess water is to use a salad spinner, but this will only work if your sweater is lightweight and not too large. If it fits easily into the bowl of your salad spinner, give it a go.

6. Lay the sweater out flat to dry. If it's warm outside, use a drying rack or even a hedge with a dry towel on it. If it's winter time, place it on a towel over your clothes dryer or a table in a warm room. It will even dry if placed on a towel on a bed in a warm and well-ventilated room.

MOTH AWAY

The best defense against chomping moths is a steam iron or the freezer. It's the larvae, not the actual moths, that eat the wool. The heat of the steam iron will kill the larvae, as will leaving them in the freezer overnight.

I take all my sweaters at the end of the season and turn them inside out. I then steam iron, fold, and put them away in plastic bags with zips. I never buy sweater bags because I hang on to the bags that I purchase pillows, cushions, and comforters in. This is the most inexpensive and least toxic way of keeping the moth holes away.

NEW SWEATER LIFE

If your sweaters are looking a bit tired, I suggest depilling them. You can buy a battery-operated gadget, but they can take a few too many fibers off your sweater. I prefer an inexpensive De-Fuzz It from Woolen Mill (www.woolen mill.com). It's a comb that removes fuzz balls.

If the cuffs or waistbands of your sweaters have become stretched out, dip them in a pot of very hot water (just off the boil) and dry with a hair dryer.

I encourage you to have a go at some of the projects in this chapter. Whether it's giving a second use to an old, frayed T-shirt, figuring out how to sew something simple, learning how to preserve a precious piece of cashmere, or even simply darning a sock, you will feel more connected to the earth and to a naturally slower rhythm of life. Days at my computer go by horribly quickly. Dozens of e-mails and tweets later, the sun's already setting, my eyes are tired, and my back is aching. When we have a wonderfully fruitful family day, my husband calls it "living in *real* time." I don't mean to get all "homestead-ish" on you, but performing simple manual tasks with your hands (by this I mean dyeing a tank top or sewing—not plowing a field!) will nudge you into *real* time, where you notice the change of light and live within the actual pulse of a day.

four

Do It Gorgeously
in the Kitchen

Cooking from scratch is one of the most eco-friendly things you can do. It's better for your health, your pocketbook, and the planet because you'll be avoiding a plethora of unhealthy additives and unnecessary packaging. So many of the problems we face today are caused by modern food production. Take a box of sugary cereal: Despite the outlandish claims emblazoned on the box, some additives can actually contribute to health problems and obesity. The cardboard box itself is unnecessary, as you can buy a better cereal for less out of bulk bins. So it makes perfect sense to whip out your baking sheet, and, in a matter of minutes, make your own.

In this chapter, I'm going to show you how to make many of the basic foodstuffs that you would ordinarily buy. If you're as time-challenged as I am, a long and complicated recipe will just irritate you, so I've only included recipes that are extremely quick and easy to make.

There's something enormously satisfying about really *knowing* every ingredient that you are serving your family. It's also quite a relief not to have to cram your already overstuffed trash cans with any packaging that isn't recyclable. Try your hand at some of these recipes—recipes your grandmother and her grandmother used to cook—and you'll never look back.

Condiments and Pantry Staples

PREPARATION

I recommend stocking up on glass jars and containers to keep all your homemade goodies in. Glass is the most eco-friendly choice because it's odor- and stain-resistant and won't react with the contents. The problem with some plastic containers is that they can leach the hormone-disrupting chemical called bisphenol-A (BPA) into your food, especially if the food is acidic or warm. So start saving old jelly and condiment jars. I also recommend investing in a good set of glass containers of different sizes. I love Pyrex (www.pyrex.com); they carry a massive selection of tiny to large glass containers, which all come with BPA-free plastic or glass lids. As most of the following recipes yield one jar, you may want to triple or quadruple recipes and store the extra jars for later use or as gifts.

Mayonnaise

Homemade mayo is the best. Some people are a little scared of using raw eggs because of the fear of *Salmonella* poisoning. If you want to play it super safe, the recipe below is cooked, so all your fears can be put to rest.

4 organic egg yolks	1½ cups extra virgin olive oil,
2 tbsp. filtered water	cold-pressed
1 tbsp. white wine vinegar	Salt and pepper to taste

1. Combine the egg yolks, water, and vinegar in your food processor or blender and blend until they are combined.

2. As the processor is whirring, begin to add the olive oil in a *slow* and steady stream. If you add it too quickly, the mixture could separate or curdle.*

3. Transfer the mayo to a double boiler. If you don't have one, pour it into a metal bowl set over a large pan of boiling water. Heat until a thermometer reads 160°F.

4. Remove from the heat and, when cool, transfer to a jelly jar or a glass container and store in the fridge for up to 5 days.

* If your mayo does curdle, try adding 1 tsp. of boiling water, as it often does the trick. If it doesn't, you may need to chuck everything and start again.

MAYO VARIATIONS

For a **garlicky mayo,** otherwise known as aioli, add 1 tsp. of crushed garlic after step 3.

For a **low-calorie mayo,** add 2 tbsp. of plain low-fat yogurt (see p. 205) and 1 tsp. of lemon juice. Stir in well before storing.

For a **spicy mayo,** add ½ tsp. of smoked paprika and ½ tsp. of red chili powder when mayo is ready.

For **pesto mayo,** add 3 tsp. of fresh pesto (see p. 200) when mayo is ready.

Tartar Sauce

My husband cannot eat fish without tartar sauce. It's hard to find a good one that isn't filled with additives and extremely expensive. Mercifully, it's very easy to make. For a spicy variation, toss in ½ tsp. of fresh minced jalapeño pepper.

Yields: 1½ cups

Do It Gorgeously
in the Kitchen

183

½ cup homemade mayo (see p. 182)	2 large dill pickles, minced
	1 tbsp. lemon juice
½ cup low-fat yogurt (see p. 205)	½ tbsp. capers
3 scallions, minced	½ tbsp. Dijon mustard

1. Combine all the ingredients in a bowl.

2. Transfer to a jelly jar and store in the fridge for up to 5 days.

EASY CANNING

If you think canning is a labor-intensive project for the farm-to-table type, think again. It's relatively easy and enormously satisfying. I used to get freaked out by the whole "canning bath" thing, imagining that I'd have to purchase an enormous tin tub (the kind they washed themselves in on *Little House on the Prairie*). However, you can purchase an entire nine-piece canning kit (I like the one from Granite Ware, which you can find on www.amazon.com) for less than the price of a pair of jeans. I often use a very large stock pot for canning. As long as it's large enough to hold all your jars and deep enough to allow them to be completely submerged in water, you'll be fine.

You can also purchase canning jars with self-sealing lids. I like the flint glass mason jars with self-sealing "plastisol" lids (find them at SKS Bottle and Packaging, www.sks-bottle.com).

If you're interested in learning more about canning, I highly recommend the Web site of an organization called Pick Your Own (www.pickyourown.org). You can find out where your nearest pick-your-own farm is, buy canning supplies, and find detailed instructions on canning and freezing just about every food you can think of.

The whole deal with canning is that you have to heat the food in the jars hot enough to make sure that all the bacteria is killed so the food won't spoil. The other thing that's important is to sterilize the jars before use. Fortunately, the hot cycle of your dishwasher will do the trick.

The most important step in the process, to prevent spoilage, is to make sure your jars are properly sealed. As the jar seals, it should pull the center of the lid down. If it doesn't, it isn't sealed and you should start again. If you want to make sure, unscrew the jar ring and make sure that the lid doesn't budge. I like to hear the sound of the lid when it pops down, indicating that it's fully sealed.

You can "raw pack" your foods into the jars, which means you can skip the whole cooking and boiling step. However, the following is the recommended method for canning acid foods, such as tomatoes, fruits, and pickles.

1. Sterilize your jars by running them through the hot cycle in the dishwasher, and keep them in the dishwasher on the dry cycle to keep them warm (they need to be warm when you fill them). Alternatively, you can sterilize them in your canner or a large pot by boiling them in water for a couple of minutes. Leave them in the hot water until you are ready to fill them. When ready, remove them carefully with a pair of canning tongs.

2. Fill your canning pot with 4 inches of water (for quart-size jars). Heat the canner on your stove to get the water boiling. It's also a good idea to boil a full teakettle of water and keep it on hand.

3. Warm up the foods you are about to can by placing them in a large pot and covering them with juice or syrup. Bring to a boil and simmer tomato products for 5 minutes and fruit for 3 minutes.

4. Pack the food into the warm jars and stir in ½ tsp. of salt for a pint-size jar or 1 tsp. of salt for a quart-size jar.

5. Fill the jar with the hot juice or syrup up to the recommended level. Most recipes indicate the exact "head space" that you need in the jar. However, generally speaking, it will be ¼ inch from the top rim of the jar to the food. The reason you need to leave this space is because the fruit or veggies can swell, forcing the cap to open or leak. It's useful to have a ruler at hand to make sure your measurements are exact.

6. Wipe the rims of the jars and screw on the lids.

7. If the water is boiling in the canner, turn down the temperature until the water is exactly 180°F (just below boiling). Carefully place the jars in the canner. The water level should be 2 inches above the jars—if it's not, add some boiling water from your teakettle. Cover the canner with its lid.

8. The water should be boiling as you start counting your processing time, as specified in the recipe. When the time is up, remove the cover from the canner and leave the jars in the water for an additional 5 minutes.

9. Cool the jars for 24 hours before labeling and storing in a cool, dark cupboard.

Tomato Ketchup

Making old-fashioned tomato ketchup is not only hugely impressive when guests pop over for a cozy supper, but it's also divinely delicious. Make it in the summer when you can get pounds of overripe tomatoes cheap from your farmer's market. As this recipe makes 3 pints of ketchup, you may want to give a jar or two to your friends. Tie a gingham ribbon around the lid of the jar, design a pretty label, and take a jar as a hostess gift to a dinner party or a brunch.

Yields: 3 pints

3 10-oz. mason jars with 2-piece lids	1 tsp. mustard powder
4 lbs. ripe (can be overripe) tomatoes	1 tsp. ground mace
	1 tsp. ground cinnamon
2 cloves garlic, minced	¼ tsp. ground allspice
⅔ cup cider vinegar	½ tsp. ground black pepper
2 tsp. salt	¼ tsp. ground cloves
	¼ tsp. cayenne pepper

1. Combine all the ingredients in a large saucepan and bring to a boil.

2. Reduce heat and simmer for 1 hour. Keep stirring throughout this simmering process to prevent the mixture from sticking and burning.

3. After 1 hour, the mixture should have thickened considerably. If not, simmer for another half hour.

4. Either use a food mill to process the mixture or force it through a fine-mesh sieve.

5. The consistency of the mixture should be like a thick tomato sauce. If you think it's still too thin, you can return it to the pan and simmer another half hour.

6. Pour into the mason jars (put them through a hot cycle in your dishwasher prior to using) and cover loosely with 2-piece lids.

7. When the ketchup cools, the lids should slightly indent; screw them on firmly and refrigerate. Your ketchup will keep for up to 3 weeks, so write today's date on the label.

Organic Mustard

I've always been put off buying organic mustard at fancy grocery stores because it's so expensive. Now that I know how easy it is to make, I'll never have to spend so much again. You can make rather uninspiring mustard by simply adding water to mustard powder to make a paste. We are going down a more gourmet route. If your mustard works out, make dozens of little pots for holiday presents. This recipe calls for *ground* mustard seeds. I suggest using either a spice grinder or a coffee grinder. As you don't want your morning coffee to taste of spices, use a separate one for this purpose only. A pepper mill works well. You can also use a mortar and pestle, but it will take a lot longer and your mustard will be less smooth.

2 tbsp. ground yellow organic mustard seeds	2 tbsp. white wine vinegar
	1 tsp. raw honey
2 tbsp. ground brown organic mustard seeds	¼ tsp. ground turmeric
	¼ tsp. ground allspice
1½ tbsp. water	¼ tsp. salt

1. Place all the ingredients in a small bowl and mix into a paste.

2. Spoon your mustard into a 2-oz. glass jar.

3. Store for up to 3 months in the fridge.

Spicy Barbecue Sauce

This is better than any BBQ sauce you would typically find in a gourmet store. Perfect with burgers, veggie burgers, and grilled meat.

Yields: 12 ounces

1 cup organic tomato sauce	1 tbsp. Worcestershire sauce
1 6-oz. can tomato paste	2 tsp. smoked paprika
2 garlic cloves, minced	1 tsp. chili powder
⅔ cup packed dark brown sugar	1 tsp. mustard (see p. 187)
1 tbsp. molasses	1 tsp. salt
3 tbsp. cider vinegar	

1. Combine all the ingredients in a small saucepan and simmer over medium heat for 15 minutes, stirring every now and again.

2. Transfer into a jelly jar and allow sauce to cool before screwing on the lid. It will keep for up to 3 weeks in the fridge.

Fall Apple Chutney

This simple chutney can be made from bruised cooking apples or Granny Smith apples that you may be able to pick up cheap at your farmer's market. It's delicious when eaten with cold cuts, roast chicken, or roast pork. It's also wonderful with curry.

Yields: 2 ½-qt. mason jars

4 medium cooking apples, peeled, cored, and chopped	¼ cup brown sugar
	½ tbsp. orange zest
½ medium onion, minced	½ tbsp. grated fresh ginger
¼ cup red wine vinegar	½ tsp. ground allspice

1. Combine all the ingredients in a medium-size saucepan and bring to a boil.

2. Turn down the heat, cover, and simmer very gently for 30 minutes.

3. Uncover and continue to simmer until any excess liquid is eliminated.

4. Spoon into a glass jar and allow to cool before screwing on the lid. It will keep in the fridge for up to 2 weeks.

If you want to store your jars for longer or give them as gifts, you'll need to go through the following canning steps once you've completed step 3.

1. Sterilize your mason jars by running them through the hot cycle of the dishwasher or boiling them for a couple of minutes in a pot of boiling water. Thoroughly wash and dry the lids.

2. Spoon the warm apple mixture into the sterilized jars, leaving a ¼-inch headspace. Wipe the rims with a clean rag and screw on the lids tightly.

3. Place the jars in your canner or a large pot of boiling water. Have a teakettle of boiling water at hand.

4. Make sure the jars are fully submerged; the water needs to be 2 inches above the jars (you may need to top up with water from the kettle). Bring the water back to a boil and boil for exactly 10 minutes.

5. Carefully remove the jars from the water with a pair of canning tongs and set them on a dish towel to cool.

6. When completely cool, label and store the jars in a cool, dark spot. They will last for up to a year. Once opened, the chutney should be refrigerated and eaten within 3 weeks.

Mint Jelly

The bright green mint jelly that you may have seen at the store is made that emerald green color by adding food dye. As I don't like to use dye, I'm happy with the natural golden color that mint jelly is supposed to be. It is the perfect accompaniment for any lamb dish and makes a wonderful gift. Mint is also one of the easiest and most resilient herbs to grow.

Yields: 1 ½-qt. mason jar

4 lbs. Granny Smith apples, unpeeled, whole (including core and seeds), chopped	2 cups water
1½ cups fresh mint, chopped	2 cups white vinegar
	3½ cups organic sugar

1. Place apples, mint, and water in a saucepan over medium heat. Bring to a boil, reduce the heat, and simmer for 20 minutes.

2. Add the vinegar and cover the saucepan. Simmer for 5 minutes.

3. Smoosh up the apples with a potato masher.

4. Place a large piece of cheesecloth (doubled up) over a large measuring cup (tuck the edges of the cheesecloth under the cup). Carefully pour the apple mush mixture into the cheesecloth and leave it to strain, without squeezing, for 4 to 5 hours. Put a saucer in the fridge to chill.

5. Discard the cheesecloth (into your compost bin, if you have one) and combine the strained juice and the sugar in a saucepan over medium heat, stirring constantly.

6. Bring the mixture to a boil. Continue to boil for 15 minutes while you skim the scum off the top with a metal spoon.

7. Take your chilled saucer out of the fridge and drop ½ tsp. of the boiling mixture onto it. Put it back in the fridge for a minute. If the jelly wrinkles up when you touch it, that means it's done. If not, continue to boil for another 5 minutes and repeat the test.

8. Pour the jelly into sterilized jars (the hot cycle in the dishwasher will do it), leaving a ¼-inch space at the top of each jar. Screw lids on tightly. Keep the jelly in your fridge for up to 3 months.

Pickles

It's so satisfying making your own pickles. These are the kind that you'll want to eat with sandwiches and salads, and even add to chicken or tuna salads.

25 medium (approximately 5 inches long) pickling cucumbers, cut into ¼-inch slices	½ cup kosher salt
	4 cups crushed ice
	4 cups white vinegar
	4 cups sugar
6 large yellow onions, halved and thinly sliced	1 tbsp. mustard seeds
	1 tbsp. black peppercorns
1 medium red and 1 medium yellow pepper, seeded, cored, and chopped into cubes	1 tbsp. ground turmeric
	1 tsp. ground ginger

1. Set a large colander over a large bowl and fill the colander with the cucumbers, onions, and peppers.

2. Cover the veggies with the salt.

3. Cover the salt with a 2-inch layer of crushed ice and set in the fridge for at least 4 hours (if the ice melts, add more to make sure there's always a 2-inch layer).

4. In a large saucepan, combine the vinegar, sugar, mustard seeds, black peppercorns, turmeric, and ginger. Bring the mixture to a boil and continue to boil for 10 minutes.

5. Rinse the salt off the chilled veggies. Stir in the chilled cucumbers, onions, and peppers and bring back to a boil, then remove from the heat.

6. Ladle the vegetables and the liquid into sterilized jars (put them through a hot cycle in your dishwasher prior to using), leaving ¼-inch head room.

7. Run a spatula or spoon around the insides of the jars to release any air bubbles.

8. Wipe the rims of the jars dry and screw on the lids.

9. Carefully place the jars in a canner or a large pot of boiling water. When the water is boiling, boil for exactly 10 minutes.

10. Use canning tongs to remove the jars from the water and set them aside to cool.

11. Check that the seals around the lids are airtight. Set aside for 24 hours before you label and date the jars.

12. Store in a cool, dark cupboard to up to 1 year. Once opened, they must stay in the fridge.

Homemade Instead of Deli-made

Every grocery store now boasts an enormous refrigerated case containing platters that are groaning with salads, pasta dishes, meats, cheeses, dips, and salsas. The premade sandwiches, resembling colorful door stops, are packed with enough sliced meat to feed a family of five, and the muffins on the adjoining coffee counter are not only way too big to finish, but they're typically dry and have that made-from-a-mix taste. All in all, these deli counters can be a little off-putting, especially once you realize that you can make every single item at home—and make them far more delicious for half the price.

If you work in an office and run to the deli every day to grab your lunch, you won't believe how easy it is to make your own deli-style lunch. It'll be better quality, less expensive, and won't involve packaging that would otherwise end up in a landfill.

Old-Fashioned Egg Salad

I just adore homemade egg salad. It's a delicious way to make sure you get your protein quota for the day.

Yields: 2 servings

3 organic eggs	Sea salt and freshly cracked
1 tbsp. mayonnaise* (see p. 182)	pepper to taste
1 tsp. Dijon mustard	
1 tsp. fresh chives, chopped (optional)	

If you want a low-fat version, use ½ tbsp. mayo and ½ tbsp. low-fat yogurt (see p. 205).

1. Boil the eggs for 6 to 7 minutes, remove from the water with a spoon, and run cold water over them as you remove their shells.

2. Place them in a small bowl and mash well with a fork.

3. Add the other ingredients and allow the salad to cool before storing in a sealed container in the fridge. It'll keep for up to 3 days.

Tuna Salad

Mercury is a very serious concern in tuna, especially for children and women of childbearing age. If you do eat tuna, make sure it's *canned light*, as opposed to *albacore*. Albacore is a larger, fleshier fish and contains much more mercury. Better still, substitute canned salmon for tuna. It's a really healthy choice because salmon contains very little mercury and has the healthy omega-3s that we need for brain function. If you and your family are used to the taste of tuna, you can gradually make the switch by making your salad with half tuna and half salmon. After a while, no one will notice.

Yields: 2 servings

* 1 4-ounce can light tuna or pink salmon (or half a can of each)	½ stalk celery, minced
½ tbsp. mayonnaise	1 dill pickle, minced
½ tbsp. plain low-fat yogurt	Sea salt and freshly cracked
1 tsp. lemon juice	pepper to taste

* If you are vegan, tempeh (fermented soybeans) works really well as a substitute for the fish in this salad. Also substitute Vegenaise for the yogurt.

1. Mash up the tuna, salmon, or both in a small bowl. Mix in the rest of the ingredients.

2. Transfer to a storage container with a lid and store for up to 3 days in the fridge.

For variety, try adding one of these:

½ tbsp. dried cranberries

½ cup diced apple

½ cup red onion, diced

Greek Salad

Yield: 2 servings

2 tbsp. extra virgin olive oil	4 oz. feta cheese, cubed
1 tbsp. balsamic vinegar	2 medium ripe tomatoes, diced
Sea salt and freshly cracked pepper to taste	½ cucumber, seeded and cubed
	10 to 12 black Kalamata olives

1. Mix the oil, vinegar, and seasonings in a medium bowl.

2. Add the rest of the ingredients and toss gently.

3. Transfer to a container with a lid and allow to chill in the fridge for up to 3 days.

Tabbouleh

This is a traditional Lebanese recipe that couldn't be easier. The common mistake is that not enough parsley is used. Make sure you use flat-leaf parsley, also called Italian parsley.

Yields: 2 servings

	Dressing
1 cup bulgur wheat or couscous	1 garlic clove, crushed
2 large, ripe tomatoes, chopped	¼ tsp. cinnamon
4 scallions, trimmed and chopped	¼ tsp. turmeric
2 cups flat-leaf parsley, roughly chopped	Sea salt and freshly ground pepper to taste
½ cup mint, chopped	2 tbsp. lemon juice
	3 tbsp. extra virgin olive oil

1. Prepare the bulgur wheat or couscous according to the directions on the box.

2. Add the tomatoes, scallions, parsley, and mint, and combine well.

3. To make the dressing, add the garlic, cinnamon, turmeric, salt, and pepper to the lemon juice and stir. Then slowly add the olive oil.

4. Combine the dressing with the salad and enjoy with some beautiful black olives.

Waldorf Salad

Every time I make this salad, I wonder why I don't eat it more often. It's crunchy, refreshing, and really satisfying. It's a salad to make in the winter, when you can't face out-of-season hothouse tomatoes and cucumbers.

Yields: 4 servings

½ cup plain Greek yogurt (p. 205) or sour cream	1 unpeeled apple, cored and cut into cubes
½ cup homemade mayonnaise (p. 182) or Follow Your Heart's Vegenaise	1 cup celery, thinly sliced*
2 tbsp. lemon juice	½ cup raisins
1 tsp. agave syrup	½ cup toasted walnuts
	2 large handfuls baby spinach

In winter months, substitute 1 cup celery root, grated.

1. Whisk together the yogurt, mayo, lemon juice, and agave syrup in a small bowl.

2. Place the fruits, nuts, and veggies in a large bowl and toss in the dressing—simple and delicious!

White Bean and Edamame Hummus

This is an incredible dip for crackers, toasted pita bread, and crunchy veggies. It makes a great alternative to the regular chickpea hummus.

Yields: 4 servings as a dip or small appetizer

¾ cup white beans, cooked or canned, drained, and rinsed	2 tbsp. lemon juice
	1 tbsp. tahini
¾ cup edamame beans, shelled and cooked as per directions on packet	½ cup extra virgin organic olive oil
	Sea salt and freshly ground black pepper to taste
2 large cloves garlic, finely chopped	Pinch paprika

1. Place beans, garlic, lemon juice, and tahini in the bowl of a food processor and process until smooth.

2. With the machine running, slowly add the olive oil until emulsified.

3. Season with sea salt and pepper to taste and sprinkle with paprika.

Classic Three-Bean Salad

A three-bean salad is very easy to prepare and is packed full of protein. I love to eat mine with a warm whole-wheat tortilla.

Yields: 4 servings

1 15-oz. can cannellini beans	½ cup fresh cilantro, chopped (optional)
1 15-oz. can kidney beans	
1 15-oz. can garbanzo beans (chickpeas)	**Dressing**
½ large red onion, minced	¼ cup extra virgin olive oil
2 celery stalks, minced	⅓ cup apple cider vinegar
1 cup flat-leaf parsley, chopped	⅓ cup agave syrup (or sugar)
	Sea salt and black pepper to taste

1. Combine all the salad ingredients in a large bowl or container with a lid.

2. In a small bowl or measuring cup, whisk up the dressing ingredients.

3. Pour the dressing onto the bean salad and gently toss. Chill. You can keep up to 4 days in the fridge.

Tricolore Pasta Salad

I love this salad so much that I eat it at least once a week. It makes a hearty and delicious lunch.

Yields: 2 servings

3 tbsp. extra virgin olive oil
1 tbsp. balsamic vinegar
1 garlic clove, minced
½ tsp. sugar
Sea salt and black pepper to taste
4 to 5 oz. dried penne pasta,
   cooked according to directions
1 cup cherry tomatoes, halved
   (in the winter, substitute 1 cup
   sundried tomatoes, chopped)

½ cup black olives, pitted and
   halved
1 cup fresh basil leaves, torn into
   small pieces
½ cup mozzarella or feta cheese,
   cut into small cubes
½ cup pine nuts

1. Combine the oil, vinegar, garlic, sugar, and seasonings in a large bowl and whisk.

2. Add the rest of the ingredients to the bowl and gently toss with the dressing.

3. Transfer to a large container with a lid and store up to 3 days in the fridge.

Homemade Pita Bread

I don't know anyone who doesn't love pita bread. It's so versatile and just delicious when warmed and drizzled with a little fruity olive oil. It's easier than you think to make and far more delicious than the store-bought kind.

Yields: approximately 16 pita breads

1 tbsp. dry active yeast	1 cup whole-wheat flour
1 cup warm water	½ tbsp. salt
4 cups unbleached all-purpose flour	

1. Dissolve the yeast in the water. Add 1 tbsp. all-purpose flour and let the mixture stand until it gets bubbly.

2. Mix the flours and salt in a large bowl. Add the yeast mixture and enough water to make a stiff dough.

3. Mix with your hands and knead until the dough is smooth.

4. Cover with a clean dish towel and let it rise in a warm spot until it's doubled in size (about 3 hours).

5. Punch the dough down and divide it into small 3-inch balls.

6. Preheat oven to 500°F. Roll out the balls on a floured surface.

7. Bake pita breads one batch at a time on a greased baking sheet until the bread puffs up (about 4 minutes). Flatten with a spatula. Remove from the oven and cover with a clean dish towel until you're ready to serve them.

8. They will keep 4 to 5 days in a sealed bag in your breadbox, or you can freeze them for up to 1 month.

Classic Italian Pesto

This is a basic basil pesto that can be used for many different dishes. You can drizzle it on soups, pizzas, or baked potatoes, or the classic way—on pasta. In the summer I make buckets of it with fresh basil from my garden.

Yields: 4 to 6 servings for pasta

2 cups fresh basil leaves	½ cup extra virgin olive oil
¾ cup pine nuts	Salt
1 cup parmesan cheese, grated	

1. Place all the ingredients except the salt in the blender and whiz it up until it forms a thick paste. You should still be able to see tiny pieces of the pine nuts. If it's too thick, add a little more olive oil.

2. Add a little salt just before serving. You want to avoid adding salt before, as it can darken the bright green color of the basil.

3. You can add a few arugula leaves or 5 or 6 sundried tomatoes for variety.

4. The pesto should keep for up to a week in an airtight container in your fridge.

Toasted Almond Pesto

This is a great variation on the regular basil pesto that we know and love. I like to add a dollop of it to almost any soup. It's also delicious when mixed with a little mayo for your salad or sandwich.

Yields: 4 to 6 servings for pasta

2 cups flat-leaf parsley	1 cup extra virgin olive oil
¾ cup toasted almonds, slivered	1 tsp. lemon juice
1 cup parmesan cheese	½ tsp. sea salt

1. Put all the ingredients in your food processor and blend until it forms a thick, crunchy paste.

2. Add a little more olive oil if it's too thick.

3. Store in an airtight container in your fridge for up to 1 week.

Fresh Garden Salsa

Who doesn't love a fresh, homemade salsa? The great thing about making your own is that you can customize the spiciness.

Yields: approximately 1½ cups

1 medium green pepper, chopped	½ cup water
2 celery stalks, chopped	½ cup tomato sauce
1 medium tomato, diced	3 garlic cloves, minced
1 small onion, chopped	1 jalapeño pepper, diced (optional)
1 medium carrot, chopped	1 tablespoon lemon juice
½ cup cilantro or parsley, minced	2 tsp. lime juice
1 14.5-oz. can diced tomatoes, drained	¼ tsp. freshly ground black pepper

1. In a bowl, combine green pepper, celery, tomato, onion, carrot, cilantro or parsley, and diced tomatoes.

2. In a separate bowl, combine water, tomato sauce, garlic, jalapeño, lemon juice, lime juice, and black pepper. Stir into vegetable mixture.

3. Serve immediately or cover and refrigerate for up to 1 week.

Garlic and Parmesan Potato Chips

Buying organic, gourmet potato chips can be quite expensive. You may not realize that it's really easy to make your own at home. If you bake them, instead of deep-frying them, they won't be as greasy.

Yields: 2 servings

2 medium organic potatoes, scrubbed and unpeeled	1 tsp. garlic salt
2–3 tbsp. olive oil for baking	2 tbsp. Parmesan cheese, finely grated
	1 tsp. sea salt

1. Ideally, use a mandoline to slice your potatoes. You can use a really sharp knife, but either way, you want to try to create extremely thin (1/16 inch) slices.

2. Rinse the slices in a colander under cold water and pat dry with a kitchen towel.

3. Line a large baking sheet with parchment paper. Place the potatoes in a large bowl with the olive oil and garlic salt. Use your hands to coat each slice.

4. Lay the slices out evenly (in a single layer). Bake for 15 minutes or until crispy brown.

5. Sprinkle the warm chips with the cheese and sea salt, then carefully transfer them to a serving bowl.

Crispy Coconut and Chocolate Protein Bars

These are my favorite bars/snack because they contain every nutrient I need for optimal health and they are simply delicious. It's a good idea to spend some time gathering the ingredients that I recommend, as once you have them, you'll be able to make quite a few batches. The brown puffed rice is sold in bulk by Nature's Path Organic (www.naturespath.com) so it's very budget-friendly. You can also find puffed rice in bulk bins in health food stores—just make sure it's unsweetened.

Yields: 10 to 12 bars

4 tbsp. virgin coconut oil*	2 tbsp. unsweetened cocoa powder
4 tbsp. brown rice syrup**	1 tbsp. shredded coconut
1 tbsp. unsulphured molasses	2 scoops whey or hemp protein
2 cups puffed brown rice	powder***
2 tbsp. ground flaxseed	2 tsp. ground cinnamon

Find virgin coconut oil at Spectrum (www.spectrumorganics.com) or Tropical Traditions (www.tropicaltraditions.com).

**Find brown rice syrup at Lundberg Family Farms (www.lundberg.com).*

***Find hemp protein powder at Living Harvest (www.livingharvest.com).*

1. Preheat the oven to 325°F.

2. Melt the coconut oil, brown rice syrup, and molasses in a small saucepan over low heat.

3. Mix all the other ingredients together in a large bowl. Add the syrup mixture and combine really well, making sure that each puff of rice is coated.

4. Press into a 9x9-inch baking pan and place in the center of the oven for 10 minutes. Cool on a wire rack. The bars will keep up to 10 days in a sealed container.

Make Your Own Dairy

Ricotta Cheese

I make a lot of Italian recipes that require ricotta cheese. It's expensive to buy and easy to make. Ricotta, drizzled with a little honey or agave syrup and a pinch of grated lemon zest or a handful of summer berries, makes a satisfying dessert.

Yields: approximately 1 pint

| Unbleached cheesecloth* | 2 cups buttermilk |
| ½ gallon whole milk | |

Available at most health food stores.

1. Rinse the cheesecloth in cold water, squeeze out excess moisture, and set it in a double layer over a large colander in your sink.

2. Place the milk and buttermilk in a large pot on your stove on a low heat. Stir continuously to prevent the milk from burning on the bottom of the pot. When the temperature has reached 100°F (you have to use a thermometer for this), stop stirring and allow the milk to continue cooking for 10 to 15 minutes more, or until curds start forming on the top of the milk. When the milk reaches 175°F, turn off the heat and let it sit for 5 minutes.

3. Use a slotted spoon to scoop up the curds and place them in the cheese-cloth-covered colander. Let the curds drain for 10 minutes.

4. Gather the cheesecloth around the curds and tie up the bundle with a rubber band. Hang the bundle from either your faucet or the arm of a ladle set across a cooking pot. Leave the ricotta to drain 45 minutes.

5. Empty the ricotta into a container with a lid. It will keep in your fridge for up to 4 days.

Yogurt

The taste and texture of my homemade yogurt is so good that I cannot eat the store-bought kind anymore. Homemade plain yogurt is terrifically tart, so it pairs well with sweet, crunchy granola and fruit. I also mix it into mayonnaise to make a lower-fat mayo, and add it to soups and chili instead of sour cream.

You will need a yogurt maker. I love the Yogourmet, which comes with all the accessories you'll need, from Lucy's Kitchen Shop (www.lucyskitchenshop .com). It'll cost you less than a pair of jeans and will make you and your family exquisite yogurt for years. It comes with a plastic container, but I prefer to use glass.* I recommend purchasing an extra *glass* container when you buy your kit. It also comes with a box of Yogourmet freeze-dried starter powder.

You can follow the directions that come with the yogurt maker. However, having made gallons of the stuff with a little trial and error, here's what I've found works best.

As the container is being heated, glass is safer; it won't leach BPA (Bisphenol A), a hormone disrupter.

Yields: 1 quart

1 quart whole milk	½ package yogurt starter powder

1. Pour milk into a large saucepan and heat until a thermometer reads exactly 180°F. Be careful not to let it boil over.

2. Remove from the heat and set the pan in a sink filled with cold water to speed up the cooling process. Make sure the water level comes only halfway up the pan.

3. Test the temperature after 10 minutes. When it reads 110 to 112°F, ladle about ½ cup of milk into a measuring cup. Empty 1 5-gram package of the powder starter into the cup and whisk to make sure it's dissolved and well combined. Pour into the large glass container.

4. Pour in the rest of the cooled milk.

5. Add lukewarm water up to the bottom marker line in your yogurt machine and set the glass jar inside.

6. Plug it in and leave it for approximately 8 hours to transform into yogurt.

7. Transfer the container to your fridge and chill for at least 8 hours before eating. It will keep for up to 3 weeks in the fridge.

Butter

Homemade butter melting over steaming buckwheat pancakes is a taste that you will never ever forget. You may remember shaking up cream in little jars to make butter at school—this is a similar method, minus the elbow grease. You'll need a standing mixer (if you don't own one, borrow one), unbleached cheesecloth, and a quart mason jar.

Yields: 3 cups of butter

3 pints whole organic cream

1. Pour the cream into the mixing bowl and begin mixing on high. You will begin to witness a few transformations: You will see whipped cream, then this will turn into lumpy curds in a watery liquid, and finally, the curds will clump on the beaters, leaving the buttermilk in the bowl.

2. Transfer the butter from the beaters into a large piece of cheesecloth and squeeze out the remaining buttermilk. Squeeze hard, because you want to get out as much buttermilk as you can.

3. Discard the buttermilk from the mixing bowl and replace it with the butter. Add 1 cup of cold water and begin mixing again.

4. Repeat the rinsing process by pouring the watery butter mixture into the cheesecloth and squeezing out the excess water. Repeat once more or until the water runs clear.

5. Spoon lumps of the butter into a large mason jar. Your butter will keep better in an oxygen-free environment, so squeeze each lump of butter firmly down into the jar. Fill the gap at the top of the jar with cold water and close. During the cooler months, you should be able to keep your butter this way out of the fridge. When it gets warmer, especially here in Southern California, I put the jar in the fridge.

Easy and Healthy Breakfasts

Nutty Granola

This is a family favorite. When we're out of it, there's an outcry for the canisters to be refilled. It's sweet, crunchy, and nutty, but unlike the store-bought versions, it is not filled with sugar. It also works as a great little afternoon treat.

Yields: approximately 8–9 cups

½ cup raw honey	½ cup pumpkin seeds
½ cup virgin coconut oil	½ cup shredded, unsweetened
4 cups rolled oats	coconut
½ cup raw almonds (almonds that	1 tsp. vanilla extract
haven't been roasted or salted)	1 cup raisins
½ cup walnut pieces	½ cup dried cranberries or
½ cup sunflower seeds	apricots, cut into small pieces

1. Preheat the oven to 375°F.

2. Place honey and coconut oil in a small saucepan over a low heat and warm until liquefied.

3. Put oats, nuts, seeds, and coconut in a bowl and mix in the honey mixture and the vanilla. Mix well and spread over a baking sheet.

4. Bake for 10 minutes, or until crispy and lightly browned. Add the dried fruit.

5. Let it cool and then store your granola in a large glass or stainless steel container.

Homemade Almond Milk

When you try the homemade version, you'll never want to buy it from a store again. It pairs beautifully with the Nutty Granola.

Yields: about 4 cups

1 cup raw almonds	Filtered water

1. Put the almonds in a glass bowl or pitcher with 4 cups of water and place in the fridge overnight.

2. Rinse with water, then put in the blender with filtered water.

3. Strain the mixture through cheesecloth into a pitcher.

4. If you want to make it sweeter, you can put it back in the blender and add 3 or 4 dates (they must be soaked in water for a couple of hours), or make a delicious, gorgeously green shake by adding half a banana, 1 tsp. of any leafy greens, and 1 tsp. of agave syrup.

Coconut Banana Protein Pancakes

Everyone is crazy about my coconut pancakes. They are not only scrumptious, but they'll keep you going until lunch because of the coconut oil and protein.

Yields: 2 to 3 servings

1½ cups all-purpose flour	3 eggs
2 tsp. baking powder	1 cup cottage cheese
½ tsp. baking soda	2 tbsp. honey or agave nectar
½ tsp. salt	1 ripe banana, mashed
1 tbsp. shredded unsweetened coconut	2 tbsp. virgin coconut oil

1. In a large bowl, mix the dry ingredients together.

2. In a small bowl, whisk up the eggs and mix in the cottage cheese, honey or agave, and banana.

3. Pour the egg mixture into the large bowl with the dry ingredients and blend well.

4. Heat the coconut oil in a large skillet and drop in a tablespoon of batter for each pancake. When the tops of the pancakes start to bubble, flip them over and continue to fry until both sides are gently browned.

5. Serve with a little maple syrup or Brown Rice Syrup (see resources, p. 379), and sliced bananas and/or organic berries.

Easy Flaxseed Loaf

You can bake a loaf of bread in 10 easy steps. Alternatively, you can sling all the ingredients in a bread maker and go watch television or meditate. The process of hand making the bread is very therapeutic for me, so on a bad day I whip out my loaf pan and indulge in this soothing activity.

Yields: 1 loaf

¾ cup warm water	1 tbsp. butter, softened
1¼ oz. package active dry yeast	½ cup whole milk
1 tsp. salt	3 cups bread flour
1½ tsp. sugar	½ cup ground flax meal

1. Put the warm water in a large bowl. Slowly stir in the dry yeast until it's dissolved.

2. Add the salt, sugar, butter, and milk and stir.

3. Mix in 2 cups of the flour.

4. As you stir, add a little more flour and the flax meal (1 tbsp. at a time), until the dough forms a ball.

5. Turn the dough onto a floured board and knead for 3 to 5 minutes (dig your fists in to flatten the dough, fold it over, turn, and repeat). Add more flour as needed to prevent the dough from becoming sticky.

6. Place the dough in a greased bowl. Cover the bowl and leave it in a warm spot for 45 minutes.

7. Preheat the oven to 375°F.

8. Form the dough into a loaf shape and place it into a greased loaf pan.

9. Let it sit for 30 minutes.

10. Bake in the center of the oven for 45 minutes.

Homemade Almond Butter

Almond butter is the most nutritious of all nut butters, and it's ridiculously easy to make. You don't have to add any sugar or preservatives. And given the fact that it's very expensive to buy, this one is a real winner.

Yields: approximately 2 cups

4 cups raw almonds

1. Preheat the oven to 375°F.

2. Spread the almonds on a large baking sheet and bake for 10 to 15 minutes.

3. When they have cooled down, put them into your food processor and begin to blend. You need to process them until they reach the requisite creamy butter texture. Every 30 seconds, stop your processor so that you can scrape the sides down with a spatula.

4. Store in a glass container with a lid. It'll keep for up to 3 months in your fridge.

Low-Sugar Strawberry Jelly

In the summer months, take advantage of the abundance of berries and make up a few jars of jelly to remind you of summer when it's freezing outside. It's easier to make than you think. Since jelly typically uses a great deal of sugar, I love to make this version for a guilt-free indulgence. To make low-sugar jelly, you will need to use Pomona's Universal Pectin (www.pomonapectin.com), which is available at many large grocery and health food stores.

Yields: about 6 cups (4 to 5 half-pint jelly jars)

4 cups strawberries, crushed	¾ cup sugar
2 tsp. calcium water*	2 tsp. Pomona's pectin powder

You will get a small packet of calcium powder along with your Pomona's pectin. To make the water, add ½ tsp. of calcium powder to ½ cup of water and store in a clear glass jar with a tight-fitting lid in the fridge.

1. Place the crushed strawberries in a large stainless steel saucepan and add the calcium water.

2. Place the sugar in a small bowl and add the pectin.

3. Bring the fruit to a boil and add the sugar mixture.

4. Stir vigorously for 1 or 2 minutes to dissolve the pectin.

5. Bring back to a boil and then remove from the heat.

6. Fill your sterilized and warm jars, leaving ¼-inch headspace. Screw on the lids.

7. Place your jars in your canner or a large pot of boiling water. Have a teakettle of boiling water on hand.

8. Making sure the jars are fully submerged (the water level needs to be 2 inches above the jars), bring the water back to a boil and boil for 10 minutes.

9. Carefully remove the jars from the water with canning tongs and place on a dish towel. Test the seals.

10. When cool, label and store the jars. The jelly will last for 3 weeks after opening. Store in a cool dark spot for up to 1 year.

Foodie Gifts

Here are a few wonderful homemade recipes that your foodie friends will love to receive as gifts.

Herb-Infused Oils

Herb-infused oils can be used for dressings, marinades, or just drizzled over grilled veggies. They're also wonderfully decorative on a kitchen counter. Your first job is to find a good bottle. You may have some luck finding what you need in your local discount store. Keep an eye out for pretty-shaped bottles with corks or well-sealing lids. If you have trouble finding what you need, check out the great glass bottle selection at Specialty Bottle (www.specialtybottle.com). You can make infused oils with dried herbs. However, I think fresh herbs deliver a much deeper flavor.

Yields: 12- to 17-ounce bottle of oil

2 sprigs fresh rosemary	2 bay leaves
½ cup fresh thyme (leave the tiny leaves on the stems)	1 tsp. whole black peppercorns
3 lemon slices	12- to 17-oz. glass bottle, with swing or cork top
½ cup white vinegar	1 large bottle the best quality extra
½ cup water	virgin olive oil you can find

1. Wash the rosemary, thyme, and lemon slices in cold water and place them in a glass measuring cup overnight, steeping in the vinegar and water.

2. Rinse off your herbs and lemon and leave them to air dry for at least 8 hours on a paper towel.

3. Insert the herbs, bay leaves, peppercorns, and lemon into the bottle* and pour in the olive oil, leaving a 1-inch space (or more if the bottle has a cork) at the top of the bottle.

4. Make a pretty label that you can tie with raffia or string around the neck of the bottle. Be sure to put the "best used before" date on the back of the label. The oil should be good for up to 6 months when stored in a cool, dark spot.

Make sure you sterilize the bottle before using by running it through a hot dishwasher cycle.

Gourmet Herb Salt

This makes a perfect holiday/hostess gift. Use mason jars and spend some time creating pretty labels. You can use a mixture of any herbs you have on hand. Some of my favorites are basil, oregano, thyme, marjoram, and parsley.

Yields: 16 ounces

1 cup mixed fresh herbs	1 pint-size mason jar
2 cups sea salt (coarse-grain, rock, or flakes work best)	

1. Place the herbs in your blender or food processor and pulse for only a few seconds. You just want to break the herbs into little pieces, so be careful you don't overprocess them into a mush.

2. Place the salt in a large bowl and mix in the herbs with your hands.

3. Leave the bowl uncovered in a warm spot overnight.

4. Fill your mason jar with your herb salt.

Creamy Walnut Fudge

This fudge is heavenly. A generous bag could patch up even the sourest of friendships!

Yields: about 3 cups of fudge squares

4 cups soft brown sugar	1 stick butter, cut into small chunks
1 14-oz. can evaporated or condensed milk (for a richer fudge, I recommend condensed milk)	1 cup semisweet chocolate chips
	1 cup chopped walnuts
	2 tsp. vanilla extract

1. In a heavy saucepan, combine the sugar and milk. Bring to a boil over medium heat, stirring constantly to avoid scorching. It's very important to stir this mixture constantly. Boil for 10 minutes, stirring constantly. Remove from heat and stir in butter.

2. Place the chocolate chips and nuts in a large bowl. Pour the sugar mixture over the chocolate chips and nuts. Stir until well blended, then stir in vanilla.

3. Pour into a well-greased 9x9-inch baking pan.

4. When the fudge has set, cut it into little squares.

5. Pack your fudge into cellophane bags and decorate with pretty labels and ribbons. It will keep for up to 1 month; no need to refrigerate.

Kitchen and Beyond

Sassy Little Apron

A cute and sexy little apron is a must for the gorgeously green girl. An apron is just about the easiest thing you can ever hope to sew, so don't even think about buying one. This apron is eco-friendly because you are making it out of an old men's shirt. You could also use a child's shirt for a little girl's apron.

YOU WILL NEED
- ☐ 1 old men's shirt
- ☐ Bias binding in a cute, bright color
- ☐ Ribbon
- ☐ Basic sewing supplies

HOW TO

1. Lay the shirt out face down on a flat surface. Cut the side seams, around the armholes, and below the collar.

2. Spread out one of the front halves of the shirt and cut out a half circle for the apron pocket. Decide whether you want to have buttons or buttonholes at the top of the pocket.

3. Carefully pin your bias binding all around the edges of the apron and the pocket. I suggest picking out a bright, contrasting color. I had a muted blue and green shirt, so I used a bubblegum pink bias binding.

4. If you have a sewing machine, you may want to pick a zigzag or a fancy stitch to sew on the binding. If you are hand stitching, use a simple backstitch all the away around. Make sure the last length of binding you sew on is the piece around the armholes, and extend the binding 18 inches beyond the edge of the apron to create a tie.

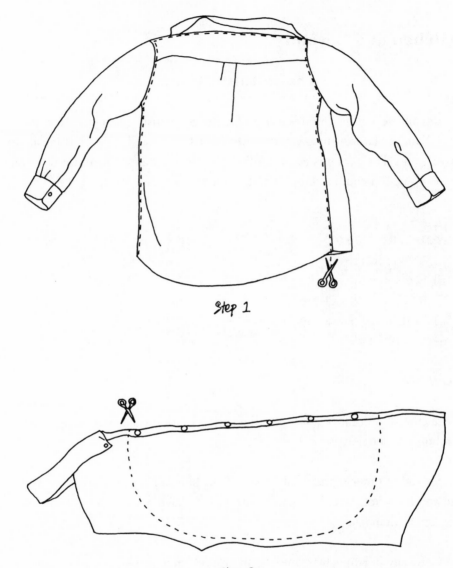

Step 1

Step 2

5. Find a pretty length of ribbon for the neck loop. When buying the ribbon, measure it around your neck to see how much you need. I measure to just below my collarbone, as I like my apron to come up high to avoid grease splattering my clothes. Turn the ends of the ribbon under to prevent fraying and sew each end onto the apron as shown.

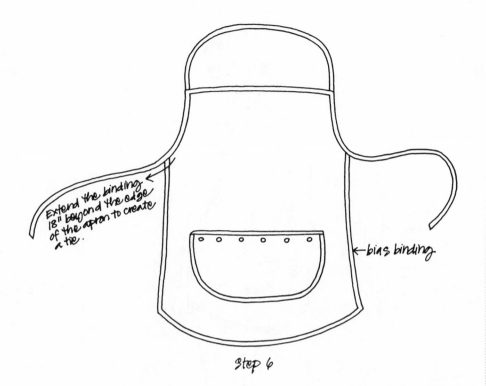

Extend the binding 18" beyond the edge of the apron to create a tie.

←bias binding

step 6

6. Sew binding around the pocket as you sew the pocket to the apron.

7. If you really want to get fancy, you may want to decorate your apron pocket with a couple of unusual buttons (odd buttons look cute).

Gift tip: For a lovely gift, you could wrap your apron around a pair of bamboo salad servers or wrap it up with a jar of homemade jelly (see p. 190). If it's a child's gift, wrap it around a bag of homemade fudge (see p. 216).

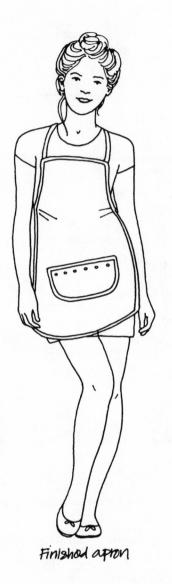

Finished apron

Grocery Bag Keeper

If you hang on to grocery bags that find their way into your kitchen, you'll need an efficient way to store them. I love this fabric tube, as it's so pretty. It's a great sewing project for a beginner and also makes a wonderful gift. You'll probably find the perfect fabric for it in the remnant bin at your local sewing shop.

HOW TO

1. Lay out your fabric on a flat surface and cut a rectangle measuring 11x16 inches.

2. To make the casings (the turned-over bits at the top and bottom through which the elastic will go), press under the top and the bottom edge ¼ inch and then another ½ inch. Pin to keep in place and then either hand or machine stitch the casings in place.

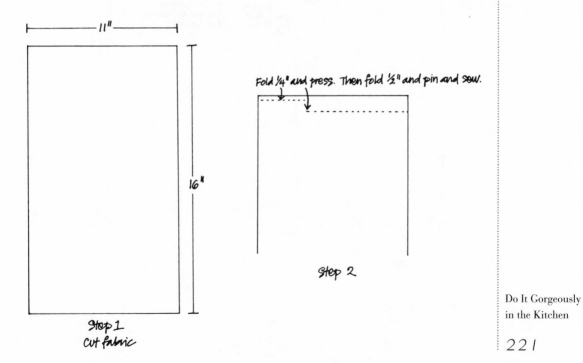

Step 1
Cut fabric

Fold ¼" and press. Then fold ½" and pin and sew.

Step 2

3. Cut your piece of elastic in half. Attach a safety pin to the end of one piece and thread it through the top casing, leaving 1 inch of elastic sticking out of each side. Pin in place. Repeat for the bottom casing.

4. Make a loop with your ribbon and pin it at an angle to the right side of the fabric, about 1 inch from the top of the tube.

5. Fold the panel in half lengthwise (right sides together), pin, and stitch the long sides together.* You'll be sewing over the elastic and the ribbon to sew them in place.

You need to back tack at the beginning and end of your stitching. This means that you sew to the end and then go back half an inch over the stitches you've just done.

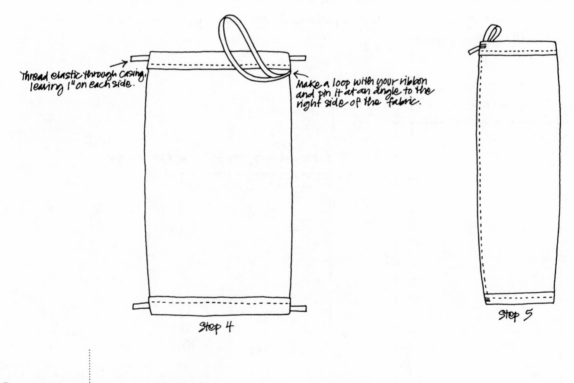

Thread elastic through casing, leaving 1" on each side.

Make a loop with your ribbon and pin it at an angle to the right side of the fabric.

Step 4

Step 5

Recycled "I *am* a plastic bag" Grocery Tote

This is a must-do craft for the gorgeously green girl. It's really therapeutic to make, and because of the whole recycled plastic thing, toting it around is a serious badge of honor. It's up to you how detailed and creative you get with it. The look depends on what color plastic bags you end up with. As I use reusable totes, I ask my friends to give me their old plastic bags for this project.

You need basic knitting skills for this project, so if you can't knit ask a friend to show you how. I taught my 8-year-old daughter to do it with ease.

YOU WILL NEED

- ☐ 30 to 40 old plastic bags (flimsy grocery store ones are perfect)
- ☐ 2 bamboo handles (find them at a craft or sewing store)
- ☐ Knitting needles (10½ inch)
- ☐ Polypropylene thread

HOW TO

1. Lay out a plastic bag on a flat surface.

2. Fold it in half lengthwise and then in half again.

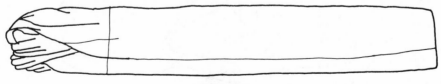

Fold the bags in half lengthwise and then in half again.

Step 2

3. Cut off the top handle.

4. Cut the bag into 1-inch strips, discarding the strip at the end (bottom) of the bag.

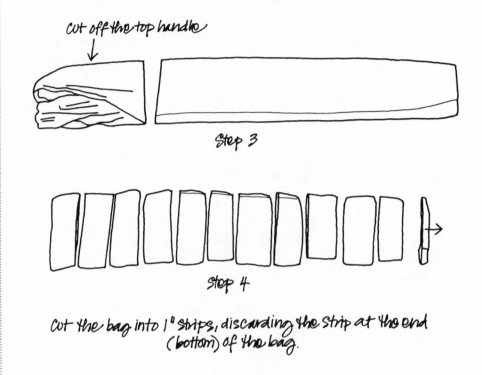

Cut off the top handle

Step 3

Step 4

Cut the bag into 1" strips, discarding the strip at the end (bottom) of the bag.

5. Take 2 strips and lay them out as shown in the illustration. Loop one over the other, pulling the bottom through, and pull gently to form a knot.

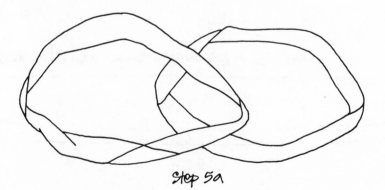

Step 5a

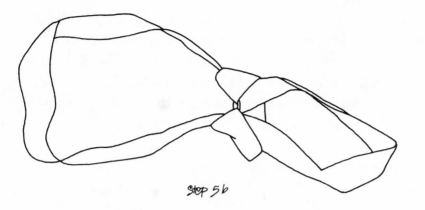

step 5b

6. Continue knotting all the strips together in long strings. Cut up more bags until you have a couple of balls of yarn, or "plarn."

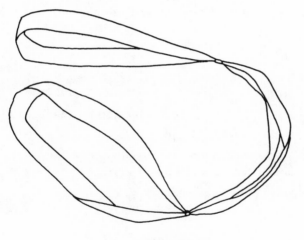

step 6

Continue knotting all the strips together
until you have a couple of balls of "plarn."

7. Using your 10½-inch needles, cast on 44 stitches for the back of the bag. Knit in garter stitch (every row is a basic knit stitch) until it measures 15 inches. End with a wrong-side row and cast off.

8. Repeat step 7 for the front.

9. For the gusset (bottom panel), cast on 20 stitches and knit in garter stitch until it measures 42 inches. End with a wrong-side row and cast off.

10. Now you're ready to sew the pieces together. Start at one end of the gusset and pin it to the back all around the 3 edges. Repeat on the front panel. Using your polypropylene thread, sew the 3 pieces together.

11. Sew on your bamboo handles.

Wine Cork Kitchen Board

My husband loves our kitchen corkboard because he can look at the corks of many of his favorite bottles of wine. I'm not a drinker, but I love the rustic look of it anyway.

YOU WILL NEED
- ☐ 1 square of plywood (your local home improvement store should be able to cut it for you)
- ☐ 60 to 100 wine corks, depending on the size of your wood board (ask your local wine store for extras)
- ☐ Wood glue or a glue gun

HOW TO

1. Decide on the size board you want and take the measurements to your home improvement store. Alternatively, you may have an old piece of wood that you want to use.

2. You may want to play around a bit, deciding on the look you want in terms of how you arrange your corks. You can lay them on their long side, vertically, horizontally, or in a brick-laying pattern.

3. Apply glue to the back of each cork, making sure the writing is on the front, and stick firmly to the board.

Beautiful Beeswax Candles

Candles can be horribly toxic. Regular paraffin wax candles are made from the sludge waste product of the petroleum industry, which is then bleached and textured with acrolyn, a known carcinogen. When a paraffin wax candle is burned, it releases benzene and toluene (both carcinogens).

You've probably heard a lot of good press about soy candles. Soy is a much healthier alternative and it burns at a much lower temperature, so it doesn't produce soot or burn marks. Most of the soy used in candles is genetically modified (GM), if that bothers you. I like to avoid GM crops on principle.

My absolute favorite wax is natural beeswax. It looks stunning, gives off a honey-like scent, and can also help relieve symptoms of allergies such as hay fever and asthma.

Rolled beeswax candles are very quick and easy to make. You won't need to fiddle around with melting and pouring, and you'll have beautiful candles in minutes—for a fraction of what you'd pay in a high-end store.

I love to use candles even on an informal dinner table. They can make an everyday supper seem cozy and special, and are essential in creating a lovely, warm ambiance at a dinner party. The following project will create candles that you would use in place of regular taper candles.

YOU WILL NEED

☐ 8x16-inch beeswax sheets* (each sheet makes 2 candles)
☐ 1 roll candlewick spool*
☐ Good plastic cutting board
☐ Sharp knife or box cutter
☐ Hair dryer

*Find beeswax sheets and candlewick at a crafts store, or try Candle Wic (www.candlewic.com).

HOW TO

1. Place one sheet of the beeswax on the cutting board.

2. Cut the sheet in half, so that the length of each candle will be 4 inches. Put aside half the sheet.

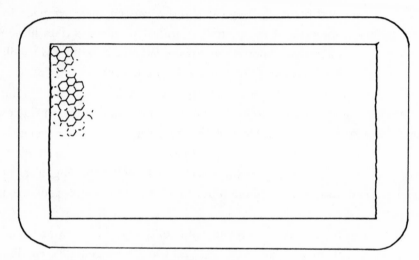

Step 1

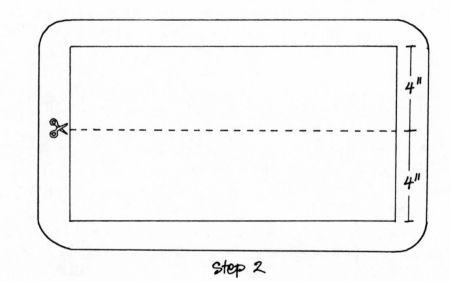

Step 2

3. Cut a length of the candlewick to be 2 inches longer than your candle—that is, 6 inches.

4. Place the wick along the length of the sheet, about 2 inches away from the edge.

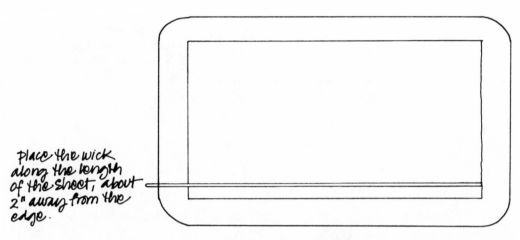

place the wick along the length of the sheet, about 2" away from the edge.

step 4

5. Warm the entire sheet with your hair dryer, until you can feel it softening.

6. Beginning with the edge closest to you, roll the wax very tightly over the wick. Continue to roll. It's similar to rolling up a yoga mat or making sushi—you have to constantly make sure that the bottom of the candle is straight. If you make a mistake, you can always warm the wax a little more and redo a few inches.

7. Once you have rolled about half the sheet, check for size by putting the candle in a candlestick. When it fits, cut off the remaining wax in a straight line.

Tip: To keep your candle pliable and workable throughout the process, you can keep heating it with your hair dryer.

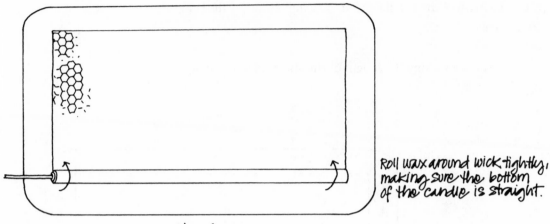

Roll wax around wick tightly, making sure the bottom of the candle is straight.

step 6

TABLECLOTHS AND NAPKINS

How often have you wished you had the perfect tablecloth to go with the seasonal table setting you had in mind? Purchasing fine-looking tablecloths with matching napkins can be extremely pricey—but not if you do it gorgeously! Moreover, making your own will guarantee you the specific dimensions of your table.

I committed a few years back to ditching the paper and plastic when it comes to tablecloths, and especially napkins. I've made a bunch of cute cloth napkins for everyday use. Every couple of days I toss them in the laundry pile, and we don't waste any paper. It also feels a little more elegant than dabbing at your mouth with a paper towel.

Everyday Napkins

You should be able to find some really fun fabric at your local big box chain or fabric store. Since you need only a little fabric, you can afford to splash out a bit. Ask your fabric store if they carry any organic cotton. A good size for everyday napkins is a 14x14-inch square.

HOW TO

1. Lay out your fabric on a large table and, with your ruler and tailor's chalk, mark out 9 16x16-inch squares (I have allowed an extra inch on all sides for the seams). With 1½ yards of fabric, you should get 9 squares with a little left over.

2. Using sharp fabric scissors, cut out the squares.

3. With a steam iron at the ready (best to do this on the ironing board), fold over ¼ inch and then another ½ inch on one side of the square and press. Repeat on the remaining 3 sides. If your fabric is cotton, you'll be fine with only ironing. If your fabric contains any polyester or silk, you'll have to pin it, too.

4. Carefully sew the seams. You can hand sew with a running stitch (see p. 136), but it will take a while, so I recommend whizzing through them with a sewing machine.

DINNER PARTY TABLECLOTH AND NAPKINS

For a special occasion, you may want to go out and hunt for some fabric that's either seasonal or that fits your theme. If you can get to a fabric store, plan to spend some time browsing, and always look in the remnant bin. If you can't get to a fabric store, check out Near Sea Naturals (www.nearseanaturals.com) for a great selection of organic fabrics. For a massive selection of conventional fabrics, you can visit Fabric.com (www.fabric.com). Always check out the clearance/sale pages on both these sites, as great bargains can be found.

Here are some shopping tips.

- It seems obvious, but make sure to take your measurements with you. Allow an extra inch on all sides for seams. Keep in mind that your tablecloth should have a 12-inch hang down all sides of your table.

- For fancy dinner party napkins, you may want to go for a slightly bigger size. I recommend 16x16 inches for the finished napkin.

- Get creative and add some rickrack or ribbon as edging on your tablecloth. I love the Ribbon Jar (www.theribbonjar.com). Consider using a bright, contrasting color thread for sewing on your embellishments.

Designer Terrarium

A beautifully made terrarium can become the centerpiece of a dining room or kitchen table, or an accent on a hall or side table. They are really fun and easy to make.

YOU WILL NEED
- ☐ Glass container with a lid*
- ☐ River rocks or stones (hardware or pet supply store)
- ☐ Activated charcoal (nursery or pet supply store)
- ☐ Peat moss
- ☐ Sterile, soilless potting mix
- ☐ Plants**

I found a great selection at a local discount store. Make sure the container is as wide as possible, as you want to fit in at least 2 or 3 plants without their leaves touching the glass. (See resource section for where to find glass containers.)

**Perfect plants for your terrarium are button fern, creeping fig, miniature holly, miniature sinningia, bird's nest fern, English ivy, weeping fig, and miniature violet. I also love to put herbs in my terrarium, as they add a lovely scent.*

HOW TO

1. Place 2 inches of stones in the bottom of the container.

2. Add a ½-inch layer of activated charcoal, which will help with drainage and odor control.

3. Add a 2-inch layer of peat moss.

4. Add a 3- or 4-inch layer of potting mix. At this point you may need to measure to see if your plants will fit in the container.

5. Remove plants from their pots and gently tease out their roots.

6. Use a spoon to dig a small hole in the terrarium substrate. Plant your plant and pat soil around it. Repeat with your remaining plants.

7. With a water sprayer, mist your plants until the leaves, stems, and soil are damp, not dripping.

Maintenance: Check your plants every week or so to see if they need a little more water. If you see condensation on the sides of the container, it means that it's become a little too damp, so remove the lid and leave off for a day or two to dry out.

five

DIY Diva

Whether or not DIY in the home and garden department is your thing, it makes sense to get a few simple projects down—ones that will save you enough cash to buy that eco-purse you've got your eye on. I've taught myself to successfully complete easy tasks that will make my home a bit more eco-friendly. I'm not talking about scaling my roof to single-handedly install solar tubes or refining restaurant grease into gas for my car—these tasks are more suited to a contractor or a hemp-sandaled nerd. I'm talking about simple tasks that will take you under an hour to complete and will save you a few hundred bucks a pop in labor.

Saving Energy

You've heard it before and you'll hear it again: Conserving energy is just about the most important ecological step we can take. It's amazing the difference that just a few simple steps can make.

HOME ENERGY AUDIT

I know—a home energy audit sounds awfully tedious. I'd rather be painting my toenails. But when I realized that I could save up to $800 a year by getting on the case, I figured it out.

Use the following checklist to walk through your home. In the blank boxes, check off where you are fine and make a note of what needs further investigation. To check air leaks efficiently, I recommend that you make sure all windows and doors are closed and then light an incense stick and hold it by all the windows, doors, and outlets that you feel could have a problem. If you see a steady line of smoke going up toward the ceiling, that door or window is working properly. If the smoke blows all over the place, or horizontally, you've probably got some weather stripping to take care of.

I also love the Thermal Leak Detector by Black & Decker. It's a really cool handheld device that you point toward the cracks in your windows, door, light fixtures, etc., and different colored lights will detect cold or hot spots (www .blackanddecker.com).

AIR LEAKS

Electrical outlets: Are they well sealed?	
Switch plates: Have they been insulated?	
Window frames: Do they rattle? Can you see any light coming through the cracks? Have they been recently weather-stripped?	
Baseboards: Are there gaps between the walls and the baseboards?	
Weather stripping around doors: Does the door fit tightly when closed? Does light come though the cracks?	
Attic hatches: Are they well sealed?	
Window- or wall-mounted air conditioners: Are they well sealed?	

Pipes, wires, electrical outlets: Are there any holes, gaps, or crumbling plaster around them?	
Foundation seals: Is there a gap where the baseboard meets the floor?	
All exterior corners of your home: Do you see any cracks?	
Roof, where chimney meets siding: Are there any cracks or holes?	
Whole house foundation, where the brick meets the foundation: Are there cracks or holes?	

GENERAL ENERGY USE CHECK

Furnace filters: Do they look dirty?	
Heating and cooling vents: Are they dusty or dirty? Have you shut off the ones in the rooms you don't use often?	
Coils behind the fridge: Are they clean and is the fridge door well sealed? Is the fridge temperature set at 37°F and the freezer at 3°F?*	
Do you have low-flow aerators in all your faucets and showers?	
Are you using power strips that you switch off when not using?	
Have you checked how many watts your major appliances use?	
Have you replaced all your incandescent light bulbs with compact fluorescent bulbs?	

*I recommend putting a thermometer in your fridge, rather than relying on the thermostat.

ENERGY AUDIT PROBLEM SOLVERS

Electrical outlets, switch plates, and any nooks and crannies that are letting in air: If, during your audit, your incense smoke detected drafts and you realized that you have no idea what a switch plate insulator is, there are a couple of really easy actions you can take.

- Get yourself a tube of OSI GreenSeries Acryclic Urethane Indoor/ Outdoor Sealant and get busy sealing any cracks, holes, or leaks you detected. You can buy it from Energy Federation (www.energy federation.org).

- Purchase some AM Foam Switch Gaskets to insulate your switch plates (also available at Energy Federation).

Weather stripping and insulation for windows and door: I live in an old, rattling home that was built circa 1920. I can't bear to replace the lovely old windows, so the price I have to pay is a lot of weather stripping annually. A couple of the windows are really drafty, so I have covered them with an Ace Indoor Window Insulation Kit (www.acehardware.com). This little kit is a lot of fun and it's quite a bit easier to install if you can get a friend to help you. Basically, it's double-sided tape and a sheet of plastic. Imagine sealing your window with Saran Wrap—not that different! You stick the tape all around the window and then mount the plastic (this is where it's useful to have a helping hand). The fun part is using a hair dryer to shrink and seal the plastic. You need to get the nozzle of the dryer very close to the plastic or it'll take you hours, so don't be afraid to get your turbo dryer up close and personal with the plastic. You don't want to put this kind of insulation on a window that's the main focal point of your living room (you can kind of tell that it *is* plastic), so use it on windows that are less visible and in rooms that you use infrequently.

Weather-stripping doors and windows can be a breeze if you follow these simple suggestions.

- Measure, and measure again, before you go shopping. There's nothing worse than coming home and realizing you're a few inches short.

- Nail-on weather stripping, such as Ace Spring Bronze Weatherstrip (www.acehardware.com), is the best bet if you have wooden window

HOW TO INSTALL SPRING BRONZE WEATHER STRIPPING

1. Measure the sides and the top of the window and door frames.

2. Transfer the measurements to the bronze strip with a marker and cut with metal snips or shears.

3. Nail the metal strips along the line where the window or door meets the frame when closed.

4. Bend the outside half of the strip in to form a seal.

frames. Nail-on will last longer. When you're in the hardware store, remember to ask a salesperson to help you make sure you have the correct nails and enough of them.

- If you have steel or vinyl windows, you will need to use felt, foam, rubber, or vinyl weather stripping. The good news is that it's easier to install. The bad news is that you may have to replace it every season. In my experience, the longest lasting of these products uses EPDM, a type of synthetic rubber. I like the V-flex EPDM Weatherstripping Tape available at some hardware stores and from Greater Goods (www.greatergoods.com). As with all of these products, you simply peel the adhesive off the back and push it into place. For a better stick, make sure you have removed as much dirt and dust as possible from your window frames before installing the weather stripping.

Dirty filters: It's so important that every single filter in your home be clean. This will help your heating/cooling system work more efficiently, and dramatically improve your air quality.

Furnace filter: Take a look at your furnace filter and if it looks dirty, you need to change it immediately. I didn't even know that a furnace *had* a filter, never mind what kind it was. Here's how to figure it out.

1. Locate your furnace filter. This is not as obvious as it sounds. Many people really don't know where to find it. Most furnaces will have a built-in furnace filter rack with a service cover in the unit. If yours doesn't, I recommend that you call the manufacturer. Some furnace filters can be hidden in unlikely places. Mine is miles away from my actual furnace.

2. Remove the service panel, which is normally at the front of the furnace. You should be able to lift or slide off the panel. Worst-case scenario, you may need a screwdriver.

3. Find the furnace's power switch and turn it off. If you know the right breaker (the switch in your electrical panel that turns off the electricity), you can go ahead and turn it off to be safe.

4. Remove the filter, either by sliding it or popping it out.

5. You will know that it's disposable if it has a cardboard frame. Take measurements and call your local hardware store to see if they carry filters of these dimensions. When you've found the correct filters, purchase a few of them, so you'll have them in stock. If the filter has a metal frame, it's probably permanent. If this is the case, take it outside, hose it down, and wait for it to dry completely before putting it back.

6. You should clean or replace the filter every 90 days.

Heating and cooling vents: It's a great idea to vacuum out your heating/cooling vents every once in a while. If you want to further improve your home's air quality, I recommend sticking little dust filters to 80% of your filter grates. You can buy a DustChek Vent Filtration Kit (available from NationalAllergy, www .natlallergy.com). It's a porous mesh that you cut to size and stick on with the tape provided. The mesh removes any dust coming out of the duct work. It's recommended that you use it on the vents in the rooms where you spend the most time, such as bedrooms and the living room.

Fridge coils: You've heard it before and you'll hear it again: Squeaky clean fridge coils will reduce the heavy energy demands of the SUV of your kitchen. Make it a habit to vacuum the coils out once a month. While you're at it, vacuum behind your clothes dryer, as it always gets dusty back there and stray pieces of lint could cause a fire.

Low-flow aerators: These little guys cost less than a latte. They are about $1 to $2 at most stores and can save you a considerable amount in water rates. They mix air into the water, helping to reduce the actual volume of water pouring down the drain. The cost of water is only going to go up, so you may as well make this easy change. They can cut your water usage by up to 50%, and they're also really simple to install.

1. You may need a pair of pliers or a crescent wrench to loosen the existing aerator on your faucet. Once loosened, you should be able to twist it off with your fingers.

2. Pop out the old aerator and washer and replace with the new low-flow one. Don't forget to replace the washer.

3. Screw the aerator back onto the end of the faucet. Turn on the water and if you notice a leak, tighten the aerator with your pliers.

Low-flow showerhead: To test whether or not you need a low-flow showerhead, place a 5-gallon bucket under your shower. Turn on the shower for exactly one minute. If the bucket is half full, you are fine and don't need to change your showerhead. If the water has reached the top or is overflowing, you should head to the store to pick up a low-flow model. There is a huge variation in price and you do get what you pay for, so I recommend choosing a midpriced model.

Appliances and gadgets: I highly recommend purchasing a Kill-A-Watt EZ power usage-monitor (Amazon has them, www.amazon.com) to test how much energy each and every gadget and appliance in your house uses. I was astonished at how much energy my beloved hair dryer uses—ugh, that's the one electrical device I can't live without! You just plug your appliance into the front of this handy little monitor and the results show up in the LCD screen. You may need a flashlight to read the results.

This monitor might persuade you to switch out some of your heavy guzzlers for more energy-efficient models. I'm still looking for an energy-efficient

DRAFT STOPPER

Old-fashioned insulation at its best comes in the form of good, solid draft stoppers. I love to make my own because I can customize them to suit the decor of whatever room they'll be in.

YOU WILL NEED

The amount of fabric will obviously depend on the width of your door. However, you won't need more than half a yard (18 inches) of whatever fabric you choose. You can use practically any thick fabric. I suggest browsing the remnant bin at your local fabric or drapery store. You can also use an old piece of clothing. An old pair of children's pants or jeans makes a perfect draft stopper.

You can easily hand sew your draft stopper, but if you have a sewing machine, you can whip it up in a jiffy.

It's a good idea to stuff your draft stopper with rice or beans (dried, of course). You should be able to buy some inexpensive bulk bags at your local discount store—and in the event of a terrible food shortage, you'll know where your dried foods are stashed!

HOW TO

1. Simply measure the width of the bottom of your door. Most standard doors are about 30 inches wide.

2. Lay out your fabric on a table and mark the length of the rectangle you need, using a piece of tailor's chalk or a pen. If your door is 30 inches

30"

18"

step 2

wide, the long side of your rectangle will be 30 inches and the width 18 inches.

3. Fold the rectangle in half, right side on the inside, so that the width now measures 9 inches.

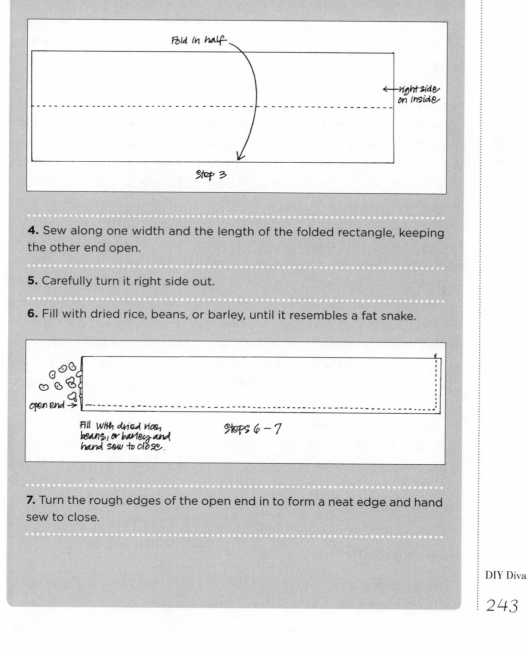

Fold in half

←—right side on inside

Step 3

4. Sew along one width and the length of the folded rectangle, keeping the other end open.

5. Carefully turn it right side out.

6. Fill with dried rice, beans, or barley, until it resembles a fat snake.

open end →

Fill with dried rice, beans, or barley and hand sew to close.

Steps 6 – 7

7. Turn the rough edges of the open end in to form a neat edge and hand sew to close.

hair dryer with the same turbocharge (sounds like an airplane taking off) that my current "salon style" model produces. I guess that's like wanting a power shower with a low-flow aerator—but I'll pick the power hair dryer over the power shower every day of the week!

Compact fluorescent lightbulbs: By now almost all of us have replaced at least a few incandescent lightbulbs (the old rounded ones) with new, energy-efficient compact fluorescent (CFL) bulbs. You have probably heard that CFL bulbs contain mercury. Given that many countries are currently planning to stop production of incandescent lightbulbs, should we be concerned about the mercury in the new bulbs?

Compact fluorescent bulbs contain a tiny amount of mercury—less than would fit on the tip of the point of a pencil. The biggest source of mercury pollution globally is coal-fired power plants. This means that over its lifetime, an old-school energy-guzzling bulb will potentially emit more mercury into the atmosphere than its curly cousin. So if you're concerned about poisoning the soil and water with mercury, you're better off reducing the amount of energy you use by switching every bulb in your house to a CFL. If your bulb breaks, just open the windows in the room, carefully sweep it up, and place it in two or three plastic bags, which you should seal and take to your nearest hazardous waste disposal. To find where your nearest one is, visit Earth 911 (www.earth911.com). Type in "hazardous" and your zip code. It will show you the nearest drop-offs to your home. Many stores now collect used CFL lightbulbs, or you can go to Earth 911 to find out where to recycle them. Keep in mind that certain brands of bulbs contain less mercury than others, so read the packaging. I also recommend buying a name brand, as the cheaper bulbs burn out quickly and often contain more mercury.

I suggest going around your home and making sure that every CFL bulb is the lowest wattage possible. If you can get away with a 14-watt CFL bulb (equivalent to 60-watt incandescent bulb) instead of a 24-watt CFL (100-watt incandescent), make the switch.

Bathroom Bliss

To my great pleasure, I've discovered that I don't need to hire an expensive plumber or handyman for the following boring but important tasks.

DISCOVERING AND FIXING A LEAKING TOILET

One of the most alarming ways in which hundred of gallons of water can be wasted is through a leaking toilet. The really annoying thing is that these leaks are often "silent" and so hard to detect. On the other hand, your toilet might keep running after it's been flushed—very annoying!

To find out if there's a sneaky leak, take the following steps.

1. Remove the lid from your toilet tank.

2. Drop a few drops of food dye or some instant coffee into the tank—anything that will give the water a deep color.

3. Wait 30 minutes and make sure nobody uses the toilet.

4. If you find any of the colored water in the toilet bowl, your toilet is leaking.

How to fix the leak: If you see water leaking from your toilet onto your bathroom floor, take immediate action and call a plumber. If, however, the problem is water leaking into the bowl, you can definitely take care of this yourself. The usual symptom of this problem is that you can hear water running periodically as your toilet tank refills long after the last flush, or the water is running constantly. If this is what you hear, you'll need to adjust the water level in your toilet tank. I can think of many things I'd rather do than fiddle around with a ball cock or refill valve—yes, I know, even the mere mention has me running to Mr. Rooter—but learning these simple fixing tips below has saved me hundreds of dollars over the years.

Adjusting the water level: First, take the lid off your toilet tank and look for the overflow tube. Worry not, this is easy to detect and is, as it sounds, a large white hollow tube in the center of the tank. If the water level gets too high in the tank, it flows over the top of this overflow tube and drains into your toilet bowl.

It's all about the float: The float either looks like a big plastic softball attached to the end of a metal rod, or it'll be a plastic cylinder that slides up and down a plastic shaft.

If lifting the float shuts off the water, you'll need to adjust the float so it shuts off the water at a lower water level.

To adjust the plastic-ball type, you can either turn the adjusting screw at the end of the rod opposite the float, or you can actually bend the rod slightly downward. Bending it will often work, but obviously be careful not to snap it in half.

To adjust the cylindrical-float type, look for the thin metal rod connecting the float to a valve-arm. The metal rod has an adjusting clip you can pinch, allowing you to move the float farther down in the water.

After making this adjustment to the float, flush your toilet and observe the tank as it refills. The valve should shut off when the water is about ¼ inch below the top of the overflow tube. Readjust the float if needed.

If, however, when you lift the float, you see water overflowing into the overflow tube, the float is not working to shut off the water when the tank is full, so the refill assembly needs to be replaced.*

Fill valves are inexpensive and relatively easy to install. When you buy a replacement fill valve, it will include detailed installation instructions. The only thing you need to know when you go shopping for your replacement fill valve is whether your toilet has the ball or cylinder float (see above).

The flapper: If the problem is not water flowing over the overflow tube, it may be leaking through the stopper at the bottom of the tank. The stopper at the bottom is called a flapper. It looks like a large white bath plug that goes up and down.

When the flapper is leaking, the water level in the tank will go down very slowly until the float drops enough to start refilling the tank.

If this is happening, the flapper may not be sealing well because of (1) an improperly adjusted pull-chain, (2) an obstruction or built-up mineral deposits from the water, or (3) a deteriorated flapper.

To correct this, turn off the water supply to your toilet (using the valve handle on the wall or floor behind the toilet), and flush to empty the tank.

First, flush your toilet and have a look at the chain that pulls up on the flapper. When you release the handle allowing the flapper to fall back to its closed position, you should see a little slack in the chain and it shouldn't be getting hung up on anything to prevent the flapper from sealing completely. If this is the problem, adjust the chain.

Also, lift up on the flapper and observe the surfaces that form the seal, looking for any mineral deposits. Clean these surfaces gently with water and a scrubbing sponge.

The flapper could also be old and the rubber deteriorating. If the rubber is cracked, brittle, or warped, remove the flapper and buy a replacement from your hardware store.

If the flapper looks in good condition, but it's still leaking after you clean it and adjust the chain, replace it anyway.

Is your toilet low-flow? Unless you have a post-1992 toilet, it's likely to be low-flow. To check whether it is or not, put down the seat and check for a flush volume stamp between the seat and tank. If the stamp reads *"1.6 gpf/6.0 lpf,"* your toilet is a low-flow model. This stamp is sometimes found on the inner back wall of the toilet tank.

If by any chance you have an old high-flow toilet, you can make it low flow by taking a few easy steps, as follows:

1. Find an old 1-liter plastic water bottle.

2. Fill it with small rocks, stones, and/or sand. A funnel may come in handy for this.

3. Place it in at the bottom of your water tank, taking great care to make sure it's not obstructing any of the flushing equipment.

REGROUTING/RECAULKING YOUR TUB AND SHOWER

There's nothing more unsightly than stained or grimy grout. Regrouting your tub can give it a total face-lift. No need for a handyman here—I have regrouted mine and a few of my girlfriends' a number of times. Everyone's thrilled with the results.

You may also need to re-caulk around your tub, where the tub meets the tile. The caulk is important in providing a protective seal. Chipped or peeling caulk can be a breeding ground for mold.

Before you start, establish whether you intend to regrout the whole tiled area around your shower and tub, or just the caulking around your tub. If the tile grouting looks like it's seen better days, I recommend doing the whole thing.

Tip: Bathtubs expand when they are filled with water, so you need to start off with a tub full of water before you put in the new caulk. Wait half an hour after applying the caulk, then empty the tub. Leave the caulk for another hour and fill the tub again. Because of the expanding and contracting that's taken place, the caulk will be securely set and less likely to loosen or chip.

Regrouting

YOU WILL NEED

- ☐ Chisel
- ☐ Nontoxic grout (I recommend QuartzLock grout from StarQuartz, available at Green Building Supply, www .greenbuildingsupply.com)
- ☐ Grout float (a blade-like tool for smoothing grout surface)
- ☐ Nontoxic grout sealer (I recommend AFM Safecoat grout sealer, also available at Green Building Supply)

HOW TO

1. Choose your grout color. This is important, as you don't want to get neon white if your tiles are cream.

2. Scrub the existing grout and the tiles with a homemade grout cleaner (see p. 302).

3. Use a chisel to remove the dirty, chipped grout that needs to come out. You may need to remove all the caulk from the strip around the tub.

4. Vacuum out all the tiny chips and grout dust.

5. Clean the tiles and surrounding area with a bunch of old rags. Dry off the tile.

6. Spread the new grout all over the tiles using the grout float—this part is great fun! Use the float to push the grout into the empty spaces between the tiles.

7. Run the float across the top of the tiles, smoothing away the excess grout.

8. Wait 10 minutes and then wipe a wet sponge all over the surface of the tiles.

9. Leave the grout to set for 3 days without using your shower.

10. To seal the grout with the grout sealer, apply it to the grout liberally, using a sponge, a dry lint-free rag, a small brush, or any other tool that can be used comfortably. One coat is generally sufficient.

Important: Wipe off any sealer that has not penetrated into the grout within 10 to 15 minutes; do not allow sealer that has not soaked in to dry on the surface of the tile (simply wipe off with a slightly damp cloth or sponge).

Recaulking

YOU WILL NEED
- ☐ A single-edged razor in a razor blade holder*
- ☐ A sprayer filled with white vinegar
- ☐ A vacuum cleaner
- ☐ Old rags
- ☐ A sponge
- ☐ Non-toxic caulking compound—I like Safecout Caulking Compound, available at www.greenbuildingsupply.com

* If you are removing hard water-based (as opposed to rubbery silicone) caulk, you may need to use a heat gun to soften it before removing with your razor blade.

1. To remove the caulk, keep the razor angled low, so you don't scratch the bathtub. Ease the old caulk carefully out of the crack.

2. Use your vacuum cleaner with the narrow nozzle attachment to suck out any remaining caulk particles and dust.

3. Spray the crack with vinegar to kill any mildew and mold.

4. Wipe around the area with a damp rag, spritzed with vinegar.

5. LEAVE TO DRY OUT OVERNIGHT.

6. Cut a ***small*** opening at the end of the caulk nozzle (too big a hole will make your job messy).

7. Carefully squeeze out caulk into the crack, using your fingers to push in and smooth. Have a wet sponge at the ready to wipe your fingers on. This step requires an artistic touch—don't rush it.

8. Wipe away any mess with a rag dipped in a little of the vinegar.

9. Leave OVERNIGHT to dry.

Doing It Outside, Too

Refinishing Your Outdoor Furniture

This project is actually incredibly therapeutic. This is best done in the spring, when the days are a little warmer. It's important to use eco-friendly stains and sealers, as more than anything, you don't want to be breathing in toxic fumes while you're working. Be careful not to apply the stain finish on a windy day, as you'll get a full coat of dust sticking to your lovely new finish.

YOU WILL NEED
- ☐ Rubber gloves
- ☐ Sandpaper block or holder
- ☐ 5 sheets 120-grit sandpaper
- ☐ 5 sheets 220-grit sandpaper
- ☐ Wood filler*
- ☐ Stain finish**

*I recommend Elmer's Carpenter's Wood Filler, or PL FI:X Solvent Wood Filler, available from KenCraft Company, www.kencraftcompany.com.

**I recommend BioShield Aqua Resin Stain Finish, available from Green Building Supply, www.greenbuildingsupply.com, or Building for Health, www.buildingforhealth.com.

HOW TO

1. Pull on your gloves—this is a project that's hazardous to newly manicured nails!

2. Grab a bunch of old rags and give your furniture a good clean.

3. Get sanding. Use the 120-grit sandpaper first. Once you've gotten rid of any old varnish/stain, finish off with the 220-grit sandpaper. Keep in mind that this is the most time-consuming part of the task, so you may need to turn on your iPod and get going.

4. If you see any holes or crevices, use your wood filler to fill them in. Leave to dry for the time specified on the container.

5. Sand the wood filler until smooth.

6. Slightly dampen a rag and clean off the dust residue and all around the furniture.

7. Apply your stain finish and leave to dry.

GENERAL WOOD REFINISHING

Refinishing the wood surfaces in your home can give your kitchen, office, or child's room a total face-lift. Using the techniques outlined for refinishing your outdoor furniture in the previous section, you can refinish countertops, desks, kid's furniture, and more. I recommend paying the extra for nontoxic stains and sealers, especially for indoor use. Conventional sealers can off-gas toxic fumes for years. I love the BioShield Aqua Resin Stain Finish (available at Green Building Supply, www.greenbuildingsupply.com).

I wouldn't recommend refinishing:

- Antiques, unless you know they're not valuable!

- Any wood that is particleboard—this is particles or chips of wood that are bonded together with formaldehyde, a tough and toxic resin. This wood can off-gas formaldehyde for years.

Clean, Green, and Gleaming Windows

After having someone come to clean my windows a few years ago, at great expense, I realized that there's really nothing to it. I kept a beady eye out to see his technique and cleaning materials. Get the right tools and you're good to go.

YOU WILL NEED

- [ ] 2 or 3 squeegees*: You might need a small, medium, and large squeegee, depending on the size of your windows. I have 3, as my windows run from a large-paned picture window to very small-paned French doors.
- [ ] 2 or 3 microfiber cloths or old terry facecloths
- [ ] Sponge
- [ ] Bucket
- [ ] Water
- [ ] Throw towel (for interior cleaning)
- [ ] Unger concentrated glass-cleaning tablet** (you'll find this at many hardware stores or at Amazon, www.amazon.com) or liquid castile soap

* *It's vitally important that the rubber blade of your squeegee is in good shape, or you will get streaks. If you know it's old or if it looks warped, you'll need to buy either a packet of new squeegee blades or a new squeegee.*

** *This little blue tablet is eco-friendly and biodegradable and is used by many professionals.*

HOW TO

1. Prepare your cleaning solution: If you are using the Unger tablet, dissolve it in 2 gallons of water in your bucket. If you are using the castile soap, add 2 tsp. to 2 gallons of water.

2. If you are using a ladder to clean second-floor windows, *always* have an adult hold your ladder. When planning which windows to start with, the second-floor windows should be tackled first. Never clean your windows in direct sunlight, as they'll streak.

3. If you are cleaning interior windows, be sure to put down a throw towel to soak up excess water and drips.

4. Apply your cleaner with a sponge, making sure you slosh it all over the windows. If you are cleaning interior windows, you might be better off putting your cleaner in a spray bottle, so you can avoid too much excess water.

5. Drag your squeegee from side to side, starting at one edge and getting as close to the other as possible. Dry off the blade after each stroke with your microfiber cloth.

6. Create a point by wrapping the microfiber cloth over your index finger to mop up drips along the bottom edge and corners of the windows. *Never* use your microfiber cloth on the actual windowpane, as you'll immediately get streaks.

AIR-DRYING FOR EVERYONE

Air-drying laundry can be for everyone. I grew up in rainy England and we air-dried our laundry year-round. I have many memories of Mom and me legging it to the backyard to grab sheets and towels off the clothesline as storm clouds broke overhead, but we managed just fine and the short summer months were a breeze.

Retractable lines are the way to go: If you have a small backyard and you're resistant because you don't want to look at a clothesline, I suggest finding a good retractable line. Only a very small area of my yard actually gets sun, so I found a four-line retractable model, which is perfect (it's the Extendaline Quatro 4, available at Breeze Dryer, www.breezedryer.com).

Rotary rocks: If you have a lot of space, I recommend going with a rotary line, which is like a huge umbrella strung with clothesline. Your laundry will dry really quickly because it whirls around as it catches the wind. You can also buy a rotary line that can be folded up or even removed from the ground socket. Breeze Dryer has a good selection.

Homemade: A homemade clothesline will cost you very little and will do a great job. The only disadvantage is that you can't whip it in and out when the guests come over. If you have an out-of-sight space for your line, you'll need to use plastic-coated nylon (rope will sag and rot). You can drill a hole and screw a large hook into a wall or a tree to attach the rope.

Drying inside: If you live in an apartment, or a really rainy city like Seattle, you may want to invest in an indoor drying rack. I don't recommend getting a cheap rack, as they have a tendency to break really easily. Find one that's large enough for you to hang out a full load of laundry. If your space is limited, I highly recommend one of the following three models, all available from Urban Clothes Lines (www.urbanclotheslines.com): the D-Rack, the Frazier 3-Tier Mobile Airer, or the Kitchen Maid Ceiling Mounted drying rack. If you are heating your home during the winter, it makes sense to use this heat to dry your clothes, too.

Tips for line drying:

- Use wooden clothespins, as they last longer than plastic.

- Don't leave your clothespins out on the line, as rain and sun will rot them.

- Before hanging out clothes, wipe the line clean with a damp rag.

- Hang jeans and pants by folding the back waistband over the line and securing with clothespins.

- Hang shirts, T-shirts, and dresses from the hem to avoid clothespin indentations on the shoulders.

- Bring your laundry in before it gets bone dry. Smooth your garments out on a bed or a clean table and fold. You may be able to avoid ironing.

- If you have sheets or garments that you just cannot face ironing, bring them in while they're still damp and finish them off in your dryer.

DIY Car

Unless you have an old jalopy as your ride (and good for you if you do), it's likely you'll have a computerized system in your vehicle telling you when you need an engine tune-up, oil change, and just about anything else. Manufacturers also recommend that you don't fiddle around with the engine yourself, but take it to the dealer, a garage, or an oil-change place. That takes a lot of the DIY out of the equation. I remember the days in England when I had to change the oil (assuming I didn't forget), water, and windshield washer fluid myself. Back then you also had to know your way around an engine or you were considered to be a loser—and I most certainly *was*! I'm very grateful for the new technology, which doesn't even require me to put a key in the ignition of my new Prius. I'm also thrilled that there are still a few DIY things I can do that are extremely rewarding.

Changing a Headlight Bulb

I never realized how easy it was to change a burned-out headlight bulb in my car. First check to see if your headlights are covered under your warranty. If they're not, read on.

YOU WILL NEED

☐ New bulb (find it at your local auto shop or visit AutoAnything, www.autoanything.com)

HOW TO

1. Make sure the car is turned off.

2. Open the hood of your car and look for the plate at the back of the headlight. Different models have different mechanisms for opening the plate, but it should be pretty straightforward.

3. Unscrew the old bulb and place it carefully on the car seat to avoid breaking.

4. Screw in the new bulb.

5. Place the old bulb in the new bulb's box and dispose of it carefully.

6. Turn on your car to check that the new light is working.

DETAILING

Detailing is just a fancy word for cleaning your whole car, inside and out. You can save a lot of money by doing it yourself. All you need is a couple of inexpensive household ingredients. You'll also save time, as these recipes are super-efficient and you won't have to waste time driving to the car wash and waiting in line. Also keep in mind that the products that are typically used at most cash washes are extremely toxic.

For cloth upholstery: Pour 4 cups of hot water and 1 cup of washing soda crystals* into a clean bucket. Wet a clean rag in the water and gently dab away at any stains.

Washing soda crystals are an alkaline washing soda, commonly used in the UK. They are biodegradable and don't contain phosphates. They're a wonderful all-purpose cleaner and can be found under the brand name Arm and Hammer at Ace Hardware and Amazon (www.amazon.com).

To deodorize your cloth upholstery: Use carpet/upholstery powder (see p. 310). Apply liberally to the seats and carpet. Close the car and leave for half an hour. Then vacuum it off.

For interiors (vinyl dashboard, doors, etc.): Pour equal parts of distilled water and white vinegar into a sprayer. Use a clean, dry rag to wipe off after spraying.

For leather upholstery: Place 1 cup of cheap olive oil and 2 teaspoons of fresh lemon juice in a small plastic cup or bowl. Dip a clean, dry rag in the oil and rub gently into the leather. For an added lemony scent, add 10 drops of lemon or lemongrass essential oil to the mixture. Do not apply this oil mixture to the steering wheel, as it could cause your hands to slip while driving.

Deodorizing Car Spray

Never buy an interior car deodorizing spray or gadget from the gas station, as they are horribly toxic and smell pretty sickly anyway. Make your own beautifully therapeutic spray instead.

YOU WILL NEED
- ☐ 4-oz. dark glass bottle, with a sprayer (you can find these at Specialty Bottle, www.specialtybottle.com)
- ☐ 4 tbsp. vodka
- ☐ 2 tbsp. distilled water
- ☐ 20 drops each geranium and lavender, or grapefruit and sandalwood, essential oils

HOW TO

1. Mix the vodka, water, and essential oils in a glass measuring jug.

2. Use a small funnel to transfer the mixture into your bottle.

Rinseless car wash: This is the best car cleaner I have ever used—and I've tried them all! The beauty is that it uses very little water, and as far as conservation is concerned, I recommend that you never hose off your car or your driveway.

Simply shoot 2 squirts of liquid castile soap and 2 squirts of dishwasher rinse aid into 2 gallons of hot water. Wipe down your car with this solution using a soft sponge. There is no need to rinse. Before the water dries, polish with a microfiber cloth. You will need to use quite a bit of elbow grease to get a shine, but it's incredible exercise!

Tire care: Make a paste of 4 tablespoons baking soda and 2 tablespoons white vinegar in a plastic bowl. Use a large scrubbing brush to work the paste into your tires and rinse off with half a bucket of cold water.

Chrome: For all the chrome work, mix equal parts of distilled water and white vinegar in a sprayer. Apply with a clean, dry rag and polish with a microfiber cloth.

Six

Green Girls Grow!

The ultimate in DIY is gardening. It's right up there as my tippy-top most satisfying activity. I won't pretend it's the easiest, as gardening requires a certain amount of patience and perseverance, but it's ridiculously satisfying to sit down to a meal that includes produce from your own backyard. With food prices going through the roof, it also makes economic sense to pull your gardening gloves on as soon as possible.

You don't need an enormous backyard, either. The key to good gardening is to be creative with the space and tools you have. A tiny balcony or patio can yield more than you could ever dream of. Even if you live in an apartment, you can probably find a sunny windowsill for a planter in which you can grow herbs and cherry tomatoes. If you're in the middle of the city, I highly recommend joining a community garden. So no excuses—time to get dirty!

Keep It Simple

Many of us get put off or set ourselves up for failure by being a little too ambitious in the beginning. The key to success is to keep it really simple by:

- Choosing to plant only what you love to eat

- Making sure that your choice of seeds/seedlings is seasonally appropriate

- Making sure that the area in which your plants will grow has at least six hours of sunlight a day

- Creating raised beds

- Creating a stellar soil mix for your raised beds or planters

That's pretty much it. If you live in a region that gets cold and frosty in the winter and you have the room, you should also build a small cold frame (see p. 268). This will make it possible for you to enjoy greens from your garden year-round.

WHAT YOU LOVE

I happen to love arugula. I could eat it almost every day mixed with other salad greens and herbs, so I always make sure I have some at home. I also love home-grown tomatoes, so in the summer, I plant more tomato plants than I need. I quite like chard, but since I'm the only one in my family who does, I only plant a little—same with spinach.

Before you plant, look at your choices for the season you're in and plan according to your taste. Herbs are always a good idea, as they'll add a little something to even the most boring winter salad and you'll use them in many dishes. Herbs are also expensive to buy fresh in the store.

SEASONALLY APPROPRIATE

I have sometimes tried to plant lettuces when I know it's probably a bit too hot, or I'll shove some tomatoes in early, hoping I'll get lucky. Plants know their seasons and they won't budge, so if you want to succeed, only plant when the directions on the seed packet say you can. It's also a good idea to keep your eye out for seedlings in your local garden store or nursery. If they have the little plants in stock, it means they're in season.

Although every region differs considerably, here's what you may be able to plant in the three main planting seasons: early spring, early summer, and mid-summer.

In early spring, you can plant these seeds directly in the soil: arugula, bok choy, chamomile, chives, cilantro, dill, parsley, watercress, beets, broccoli, broccoli raab, carrots, chard, fennel, kale, leeks, lettuce, mache (lamb's lettuce), scallions, and spinach. Inside, you can start these seeds: basil, broccoli, eggplants, lavender, marjoram, oregano, peppers, rosemary, thyme, tomatillos, and tomatoes.

In early summer, you can plant these when you know the nights are staying above 50°F: arugula, basil, beans, beets, carrots, chard, cilantro, corn, cucumbers, melons, pumpkins, sage, soybeans, summer and winter squash, thyme, watermelons, and zucchini.

In midsummer, you plant outside the seedlings you have raised indoors. (If you live in an area with mild winters, you can plant outside midsummer through early fall.) These plants include: arugula, beets, bok choy, broccoli, cabbage, carrots, cauliflower, chard, chives, cilantro, dill, garlic chives, kale, leeks, lettuce, mache (lamb's lettuce), parsley, scallions, spinach, and watercress.

SIX HOURS OF SUNLIGHT

So many of my crops have failed because I thought I could get by on a little less sun. For example, I planted tomatoes in an area of my yard that gets about four hours of sun a day, and the plants barely yielded any fruit at all. You just can't cheat this part of the equation.

Raised Beds

Raised beds are the best for many reasons. Regardless of the quality of the soil in your yard, you can create perfect soil in a raised bed. They also keep everything really neat and orderly, and you can build a raised bed to suit any yard size.

The most wonderful thing about raised beds is that they are very easy to create. I have made four of them, all different sizes, for my own backyard. You can create a raised bed in any shape or size. I have rectangular and square beds in my yard. I love the square one best. The following directions are for a 4x4-foot square bed.

A home improvement store with a lumber department will cut this for you. If you are lucky enough to find reclaimed wood, use it instead of newly cut timber.

HOW TO

1. Drill 3 holes in the top at one end of each plank of wood.

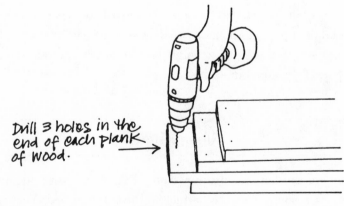

Drill 3 holes in the end of each plank of wood.

Step 1

2. Screw the wood screws through the drilled holes, attaching the boards end to end, until your square frame is completed.

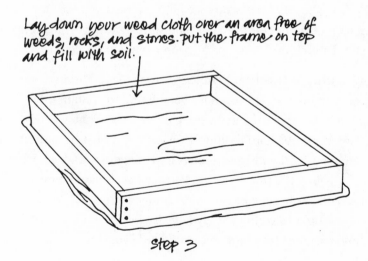

Screw the wood screws through the holes, attaching the boards end to end.

Step 2

3. On the area where you want the bed to be, remove existing weeds, rocks, and stones, and lay down your weed cloth.

Lay down your weed cloth over an area free of weeds, rocks, and stones. Put the frame on top and fill with soil.

step 3

4. Lay your assembled frame on top and you are ready to fill with soil.

STELLAR SOIL

The key to successful gardening is quality soil. It has to have the right texture and nutrient balance for the plants to be able to grow and thrive. It's much easier than you think to create perfect soil, especially with a raised bed.

To create your stellar soil mix, you'll need to fill your bed with ⅓ of each of the following:

1. **Compost:** If you make your own compost, you'll be all set. If, however, you need to buy it, see if you can buy your bags from different companies/manufacturers. If you need 3 bags of compost, see if your local nursery/hardware store carries 3 different kinds. The reason for this is because one company will make their compost from just *one* particular industry (wood, cotton, soybeans, etc.), so it's best to mix together a variety of by-products so you get as many different micronutrients and enzymes as possible.

2. **Coconut Coir:** Some people use peat moss instead of coconut coir; however, the more eco-friendly choice is the coir and it's less expensive. You can buy it in a brick, which will expand when water is added. The coir breaks up the soil, keeping it aerated. You can purchase coconut coir from pet food stores, nurseries, Planet Natural (www.planetnatural.com), or Amazon (www.amazon.com).

3. **Vermiculite or Perlite:** Vermiculite is a great addition to soil, as it retains moisture. However, it's been found to contain asbestos. Although most vermiculite in the United States is now considered to be safe, it may be hard to find. If you do use it, just be careful when pouring/mixing it with your soil, as it's really dusty and you want to avoid inhaling the tiny particles. Perlite doesn't retain moisture, but it helps with drainage, which is really important, too. If you can't get or don't want to use vermiculite, stick with just perlite. You will be able to find it at most large nurseries and hardware stores.

HOW TO DETERMINE HOW MUCH SOIL
YOU'LL NEED FOR YOUR RAISED BED

1. Measure the width of your raised bed planter box in inches, using a tape measure. Write that number down on a sheet of paper. Your tape measure will give you an exact measurement in inches, requiring you to do no math at all so far.

2. Measure the length of your planter box in inches. Write this number down.

3. Measure how deep you want your box to be. Measure from the bottom of the box to the level at which you wish your soil to end up. Measure this in inches as well and write that number down.

4. Multiply the three numbers you wrote down together on your pocket calculator. Let's assume the width of your box, like mine, is 48 inches and the length of your box is 48 inches and the depth of your soil is going to be 10 inches. On your calculator multiply 48 x 48 to get 2,304. Now simply multiply 2,304 by 10 for a final total of 23,040. Write that number down. That number is the number of cubic inches of soil you will need to fill your planter.

5. Now you need to divide 23,040 by 1,728. The reason for this is because soil is sold by the cubic foot and not by the cubic inch, so we need to change your cubic inches into cubic feet. The reason you divide by 1,728 is because 1,728 cubic inches (12 x 12 x 12 = 1,728) is 1 cubic foot. 23,040 divided by 1,728 equals 13.33 cubic feet. In other words, you'll need around 13 cubic feet of soil to fill a 4x4-foot planter 10 inches deep.

6. Finally, you'll need to divide your final number, 13, by 3, to determine how much compost, coir,* and vermiculite you need (remember you need equal parts of all 3). So 13 divided by 3 is 4.3 cubic feet. That means you'll need about 4 cubic feet of each of these ingredients.

Since a regular-size coconut coir brick will expand to 2.5 cubic feet, you could go with just 1 brick and add another 2 cubic feet of compost, or go with 2 bricks.

MIXING IT UP FOR YOUR RAISED BED

Once you have all your bags ready to fill your raised bed, you can either empty them straight into the bed and mix, or you can find a large tarp on which to mix everything up before sliding it into the bed. This is a job for the girl or guy who doesn't mind getting dirty. I'm not afraid of a bit of soil—remember, there's a huge difference between dirt and soil—however, soil can totally ruin your nails. I *always* wear gardening gloves for this task. Either way, you will first need to soak the coir in a large bucket of water and agitate it with your hands (rubber gloves for this step!) until it expands. When you add it to the mix, make sure you tease it out with your hands. Ultimately, all three ingredients must be really well blended.

Cold Frame

If you want to extend your growing season—think eating beautiful baby salad leaves from your garden through the winter—you'll need to put together a cold frame. It's like a mini-greenhouse. The best way is to use old windows. If you don't have any, send an e-mail blast out to all your friends or visit a salvage yard.

YOU WILL NEED
- [ ] 1 old window or doorframe with glass panels
- [ ] Breeze/cement blocks* (the number will depend on the size of your window or door)

If you don't like the idea of using breeze blocks (not the prettiest things in the world), you could always put together a wooden frame that will fit the size of your window in the same way that you created your raised beds (see p. 263).

HOW TO

1. Choose an area that is facing south. As this isn't the most elegant-looking cold frame, you might want to pick a spot that's out of sight.

2. Measure your window or door and calculate how many blocks you'll need for the width and length of your frame. Set out the blocks in a rectangle. Pile up the blocks 3 or 4 deep.

3. Fill with a stellar soil mix (see p. 266), plant your seedlings, and cover with your window.

4. If it gets super-sunny, you'll need to pull the window over an inch or so to one side to let in a little cool air.

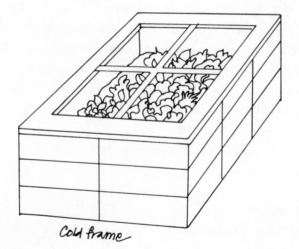

Cold frame

Compost Bin

You can easily make an outdoor compost bin with chicken wire or cement blocks, but these designs are open and I'm not crazy about them, as they tend to attract rodents. They are best used exclusively for garden waste such as leaves and clippings. However, if you are only interested in collecting garden waste for mulching, you don't really need to build any kind of structure. When I was growing up, my mom had a compost "pile"—all the garden or yard waste got dumped in this sweet-smelling mini-mountain behind a hedge. Layers upon layers of grass clippings, leaves, dead roses, and even veggie scraps weathered all manner of harsh British weather conditions to bring us tons of odorless compost yearly.

I don't have that kind of space in my urban backyard, and really, I'm more interested in finding a way to compost my kitchen waste. So a closed bin is a must for me if I don't want to encourage a small, furry nightly gathering. There are many great compost bins on the market. The simplest are the best—but they are expensive, so here's a way to do it yourself.

When picking out your old plastic bin or container, make sure you find the size that's right for you. If you live in an apartment and want to compost, you can find a smallish plastic storage box that you can keep on your patio or balcony. If you have a yard, you'll probably want to look for the largest one you can find. Your bin should produce compost in 4 or 5 months. You can use the compost as an amazing soil enhancer in your yard or on your houseplants. If you live in an apartment, ask the nearest community garden if they want it (they will!).

YOU WILL NEED

- [ ] Plastic storage container with a tight-fitting lid (since I want to discourage you from going out to buy plastic, I suggest asking around to see if any of your friends have any old storage containers, or check out Freecyle, www.freecycle.org)
- [ ] Drill
- [ ] Old newspaper
- [ ] Soil
- [ ] Sawdust

HOW TO

1. Drill at least 10 small holes in both long sides of the container and at least 5 small holes on the shorter ends. Drill 8 or 9 small holes into the lid.

2. Cover the bottom of the container with torn-up newspaper. Fill the container ¼ full with garden dirt. If you live in an apartment, you can buy a small bag of potting soil.

8 or 9 small holes in the lid

Drill small holes along sides and lid of container.

at least 10 holes in the long sides

at least 5 holes in the short sides

Step 1

Fill the container ¼ full with garden dirt.

Cover bottom of container with torn-up newspaper.

Step 2

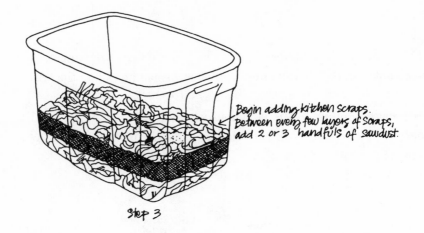

Begin adding kitchen scraps. Between every few layers of scraps, add 2 or 3 handfuls of sawdust.

Step 3

3. Begin adding your kitchen scraps. Between every few layers of scraps, add 2 or 3 handfuls of sawdust, which you can buy from most pet stores and hardware stores with nurseries.

COMPOST TIPS

- Turn your compost with a garden fork or stick every 2 weeks, to ensure the whole pile is oxygenated.

- If the compost becomes too dry (it should look slightly damp), add 2 or 3 cups of water, depending on size of your bin.

- If your compost starts to smell, you may need to add more sawdust. You can also add a cup of baking soda to every layer.

- Remember that making compost is like making a lasagna—*you have to layer* with brown matter (sawdust, soil/dirt, leaves, garden clippings, torn-up newspaper), and green matter (veggie scraps). You can also add bread and pasta (no oil or butter), coffee grounds, tea bags, paper towels, and anything that is biodegradable.

- Remember that you cannot add meat, fish, bones, dairy, pet waste, or anything that is covered with grease to your compost bin.

Worm Bin

A fantastic way to take composting to the next level is to create a worm bin. The worms will speed up the process by digesting the scraps and eliminating sweet-smelling compost. You can easily create an indoor worm bin. Worm-composting bins can be expensive to buy, so have a go at making your own.

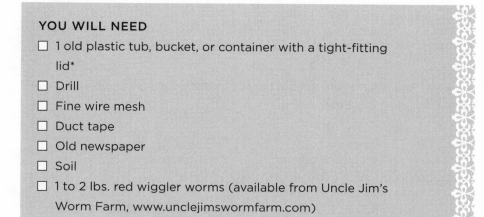

YOU WILL NEED

☐ 1 old plastic tub, bucket, or container with a tight-fitting lid*

☐ Drill

☐ Fine wire mesh

☐ Duct tape

☐ Old newspaper

☐ Soil

☐ 1 to 2 lbs. red wiggler worms (available from Uncle Jim's Worm Farm, www.unclejimswormfarm.com)

A storage container from a hardware or big box store will work perfectly. Get one as big as you have room for. It needs to be at least 24 inches high. (You can use wood or galvanized steel. However, the steel is expensive and the worms eventually eat through the wood, so plastic, although not my favorite, is more convenient and cost effective.) If you're buying a new container, make sure it's recyclable plastic with the numbers 1 or 2 in the chasing arrows on the bottom. A bin that measures 2x3x1 ft. is large enough to compost the kitchen scraps from a family of 4.

HOW TO

1. Take the lid off your container and drill 12 ½-inch holes evenly all over the lid.

2. Cut a 1-inch square of wire mesh for each hole you've drilled. With the underside of the lid facing up, cover each hole with the mesh and tape down all 4 sides with duct tape.

3. Drill 4 or 5 holes in the bottom of the container and repeat the hole/screening process.

4. Fill the bottom of the container with a couple of inches of torn-up newspaper. Add 3 inches of soil and then add your worms.

5. Place the whole container on a tray with a lip, so you can collect the "worm tea," which will drip out of the container and can be used for fertilizing houseplants.

6. Once you've added your worms, give them about 4 days to settle in before you add food.

7. It will take 3 or 4 months for the vermicomposting (that means compost made by worms) process to take place.

HARVESTING YOUR WORM COMPOST

The first thing you can harvest is the worm tea, which will gather in the tray that your bin sits on. When it becomes full, you can either remove the tray and carefully take it outside and empty it into a bucket, or you can use a turkey baster to suck up the liquid and transfer it to a jug. This "tea" is the most potent fertilizer imaginable. Keep it in an old plastic bottle and give to a green-thumbed friend, or use in your own garden.

HOW TO

1. When you think you've got enough compost to harvest (it just looks like potting soil), start to feed your worms only on one side of your bin for a week.

2. Get a large trowel and carefully scoop out the compost from the side of the bin opposite where your veggie scraps were last buried. Scoop the compost into a bucket or a large black trash bag.

3. Alternatively, you can dump out all the contents of the bin onto a large plastic sheet. Direct a bright light to the top of the pile. The worms are photosensi-

HOW TO FEED THE WORMS

• Red wiggler worms will transform the following scraps into compost: vegetables, fruits, eggshells, tea bags, coffee filters, and shredded paper towels.

• Don't feed them any citrus fruits, as they're too acidic.

• You should never add meat, fish, or oily foods.

• A layer of food scraps *must* be covered with a layer of bedding (shredded newspaper or paper towels) to eliminate odor.

• Do not add more food scraps until you see that the previous ones have been eaten.

• It's best to cut up food scraps into very small pieces.

• When adding your food scraps, mentally divide your bin into six squares. Bury the first load of scraps in the first square, then move on to the second square for your next load, and so on. This method will ensure that one area gets composted by the time you get back to square one.

• Be patient with your worms. Sometimes they take a while to get settled in and happy. The optimal temperature for their comfort (and don't forget, they're guests in your home!) is between 50 and 84°F. That means an outside patio or balcony in midwinter is a no.

tive and will crawl away from the light to the bottom of the pile so that you can scrape off the top layers of compost.

4. When you're done harvesting (and don't worry if a few worms end up in the compost bag/bucket), put a fresh layer of bedding down and either even out the existing worms/compost or start over and add the worms from your plastic sheet back into your bin.

SEEDS OR SEEDLINGS

Having successfully prepared the soil in your raised beds, it's time to choose what you want to grow and get planting. Spring is obviously the best time to plant in most regions. However, you'll be surprised by how much you can plant at other times of the year, especially if you've prepared a cold frame for your raised beds.

The big question for me is always whether to plant the seeds directly into the soil in the raised bed or whether to grow or purchase a seedling first. Successfully germinating a seed requires some TLC. There are only a few seeds that you can toss in the soil outside and expect to grow. By taking care in the early stages, you'll have strong, healthy plants and a great harvest.

WHAT'S A SEEDLING?

A seedling is a tiny plant (2 to 12 inches high). The advantage of planting seedlings over planting seeds outside is that seedlings have already had a successful start in life, so they're more likely to survive. You can buy seedlings from your local nursery, farmer's market, or hardware store, but it's also really easy to grow them yourself. You can decide whether to start a seedling or plant a seed directly outdoors by reading the directions on the seed packet. I have a long growing season here in Southern California, so I've always got something happening in my garden. If you live in a cooler region, you might want to check out Ed Hume Seeds (www.humeseeds.com), which specializes in cool climate seeds.

Starting Your Seedlings

You can start your seeds in virtually any container. Use containers and cartons that you might ordinarily throw away. Cardboard egg cartons, waxed milk cartons (tops cut off), and old yogurt containers are perfect. If you are using a plastic container, punch holes in the bottom for drainage.

HOW TO

1. Prepare your containers. It's a good idea to set them in a tray or a large baking pan that can hold ½ inch of water.

2. Fill each container with some soilless potting mix. You get what you pay for with these mixes, so go with one from a reputable company. I like QuickRoot from Peaceful Valley Farm and Garden Supply (www.groworganic.com).

3. Sow the seeds at the proper depth (as indicated on the seed packet). This is really important, as sowing them too deep will result in a no-grow!

4. Set the containers in a bright spot, but not in direct sunlight. They need 14 to 16 hours of light a day. If you set your seedlings on a windowsill, be sure to turn them every day. You can also use a fluorescent light, which creates a more even light. The temperature should be about 65 to 72°F day and night, so for many of you this will be indoors.

5. Water your seeds with warm water from a sprayer for the first few days. Once the seeds have germinated (you'll see little green shoots and the first tiny leaves*), water with room-temperature water. As the plants grow to be an inch or so high, you can water from a watering can or a hose with a fine mist nozzle.

6. You need to fertilize your seedlings every 2 weeks. However, be careful because too much fertilizer can burn the tiny plants. I love PlanTea fertilizer from Ed Hume Seeds (www.humeseeds.com). It's inexpensive and very gentle.

7. Once your seedlings have reached a minimum of 2 to 3 inches, you're ready to transplant them into a bigger container or a planter. Be very careful how you dig them up. Try not to disturb the roots at all. A metal nail file is a good tool for scooping up the whole plant and transporting it. Have your larger container ready with lightly watered potting soil and an appropriate size hole. Gently drop your plant into the hole and pat the soil around it. Water and set it in a sunny spot.

* When your seeds first start to germinate, you'll see a set of two tiny leaves poking out of the soil. These are not the "true" leaves. Wait a few more days for the second set of slightly larger, more oval "true" leaves to appear. Now your plant is well on its way.

8. If you are going to plant them outside, they need to be "hardened off" first. This means that they need to acclimate to outside conditions. Simply place them outside in a shady spot for a few hours each day and then bring them in. After a week, they'll be ready to face the elements.

MULCHING

I recommend that you use mulch (a layer of organic matter) around your plants to discourage weeds and to insulate and keep your soil from drying out. Think of it as a protective blanket. You can use bark chips, pine needles, straw, sawdust, or small rocks. Cover the entire bed, especially around the plants, with a 2-inch layer of mulch.

IRRIGATION

We all need to conserve as much water as possible, so you'll need to find the best way to water your plants. Raised beds hold water better than large garden beds, as they're more contained. I just use a hose. I've tried all kinds of new-fangled drip-irrigation systems, but the very act of getting that hose out every day helps me pay attention to my plants and notice if anything is amiss. Make sure you have a shutoff valve at the end of the hose, so you can control the amount of water that comes out. A nozzle with different settings is also a good idea.

Water close to the roots and try not to get the plant wet at all. Always water in the early morning or early evening, when the sun is not direct. Sunlight will evaporate your precious water. Your soil should feel damp. If you pick up a handful and squeeze it, it should be wet enough to stay in a loose clump, but not so wet as to be dripping. Make sure it maintains this texture every day.

WEEDING

With raised beds and good soil, you'll barely need to weed. Once a month, you may have to kneel down and pull out a few little weeds. Because the soil is loosely packed, they'll come out easily. It's a great little chore for a child. Even Lola manages to un-lazy herself for this satisfying little task, especially when a tasty treat is involved.

Organic Pesticides

It has always astonished me how many pests seem to want to aggravate the organic gardener. This is the huge part of organic gardening, and it can be frustrating. You have to be vigilant or all your hard work could be devastated overnight. Having grown my own vegetables, I now have the utmost respect for the organic farmer. When you really understand the work and ingenuity that goes into protecting crops naturally, you'll never balk at paying a few extra dollars for pesticide-free food.

Why shouldn't we use regular pesticides? It's tempting, especially when you're dealing with a seriously pesky outbreak. However, pesticides attack the nervous systems of the insects and then kill them. If they can do that to an insect, they can obviously adversely affect our health, too. I have heard firsthand horrendous stories of friends who have suffered pesticide poisoning from their own backyards. This kind of poisoning isn't like food poisoning, where you get sick for a few days—you can be sick for months or even years from just one poisoning. Children and pets are especially vulnerable.

The key to keeping pests at bay is to grow really healthy plants. Plants are like humans, in that when we are healthy and eat well, our immune systems are strong enough to fight off invading germs and parasites. If plants are grown in nutrient-rich soil and are thus well nourished, they'll be better able to put up a good fight.

There are literally hundreds of pests that could attack your plants. The most common are aphids, cabbage loopers, earwigs, tomato hornworms, and slugs. Make up one of the following sprays to fend off these hungry little critters. If you live in an area where there are deer or rabbits, I suggest you rig up a strong barrier made of chicken wire.

Smelly Pest Spray

Many pests will be disgusted by the smell of this wonderfully effective spray.

YOU WILL NEED
- ☐ 1 onion
- ☐ 1 whole garlic bulb
- ☐ 1 2-inch piece fresh ginger root
- ☐ 1 tbsp. cayenne pepper
- ☐ 2 cups water
- ☐ 2 tbsp. liquid castile soap

HOW TO

1. Place the onion, garlic, ginger, and cayenne pepper in a large mason jar and cover with boiling water. Leave overnight and then strain.

2. Add the onion liquid to the water and liquid soap.

3. Pour into a large sprayer and spray generously over the tops and bottoms of the plants' leaves and the stalks.

Smothering Spray

This spray is particularly effective for aphids. Be aware that it suffocates every insect as well as the aphids.

YOU WILL NEED
- ☐ 1 cup vegetable oil
- ☐ 2 tbsp. liquid castile soap
- ☐ 1 gallon water

HOW TO

1. Pour all the ingredients into a couple of large sprayers.

2. Give your plants (tops and bottoms of the leaves and the stalks) a good spray once a week.

COMPANION PLANTING

When you plan out your garden or raised beds, it's a great idea to figure out which plants make good companions for the ones you want to grow. These "companion" plants can help repel pests and enrich the soil with appropriate nutrients. Companion planting is the primary method used today for successful organic farming.

Visit any organic farm and instead of seeing massive fields and rows of monocrops (one crop only), you will see a variety of crops growing together. Not only do they serve each other as good companions in the pest department, but the taller plants also give necessary shade to cool-season crops. It's a science that every organic farmer will have taken years to perfect, but for the amateur gardener, it serves well to have a basic understanding of which are the best plants to plant near the ones you want. It's interesting to note from the list that follows that the plants that work well together are often the ones we like to eat together. For example, it's always a good idea to plant basil and oregano with tomatoes—that's why the Italians created marinara sauce!

Basil: tomatoes, peppers, oregano, asparagus

Beets: lettuce, onions, kohlrabi, garlic

Bell peppers: onions, potatoes, marjoram

Cabbage: celery, dill, onions, potatoes

Carrots: lettuce, onions, tomatoes

Chard: beans, cabbage, onions

Corn: beans, cucumbers, melons, morning glory, parsley, peas, potatoes, pumpkins, soybeans, squash, sunflowers

Cucumbers: corn, beans

Eggplants: beans, peas, spinach, tarragon, thyme, marigolds

Hot peppers: prevents root rot; great companions are cucumbers, eggplants, tomatoes, okra, chard, squash

Kohlrabi: cucumbers, onions, chives

Leeks: carrots, celery, onions

Lettuce: beets, bush beans, cabbage, carrots, cucumbers, onions, radishes, strawberries

Melon: corn, pumpkins, radishes, squash

Onions: carrots, leeks, beets, kohlrabi, strawberries

Parsley: asparagus, carrots, chives, onions, tomatoes

Peas: parsley, potatoes, radishes, spinach, strawberries, sweet peppers, turnips

Peppermint: repels aphids and cabbage moths

Potatoes: bush beans, cabbage, carrots, celery, corn

Pumpkins: corn, melons, squash; marigolds will deter beetles

Radishes: repel many pests; plant them around squash, corn, broccoli, spinach

Rosemary: cabbage, beans, carrots, sage

Sage: broccoli, cauliflower, rosemary, cabbage, carrots

Spinach: peas, beans, cabbage, cauliflower, celery, eggplants, onions, peas, strawberries

Squash: corn, cucumbers, radishes, melons, pumpkins

Strawberries: beans, lettuce, onions, spinach, thyme

Tarragon: great general insect repellent

Thyme: deters cabbage worms

Tomatoes: asparagus, basil, beans, borage, carrots, celery, chives, cucumbers, garlic, lettuce, marigolds, mint, onions, parsley

Planning Your Garden

Now that you know which companions your favorite fruits, veggies, and herbs favor, plant your garden accordingly. I recommend making a plan on paper. I like to allow 1 square foot for each crop, unless I want to grow a lot of one particular kind, in which case I'll plan for about 4 square feet for that crop.

You can also divide up your bed into 1-square-foot squares, which makes for a very orderly bed. You can use long bamboo sticks, or have some lengths of lath cut at the lumberyard to fit your garden bed. Just lay them across the bed, delineating the squares. Mel Bartholomew has written a wonderfully useful book on this method called *All New Square Foot Gardening* (Cool Springs Press). He has taught me that although 1 square foot seems like too small a space for a vegetable, you'll be surprised how much you'll harvest from that one square.

Other gardeners prefer orderly rows. I teach a Garden-to-Table class at a local charter school. The sixth graders, who have taken proud ownership of the vegetable beds, prefer rows. Each group has their own row that they planted from seeds, watered, weeded, and eventually harvested.

Think about what you and your family will eat the most. It's a waste of precious space to put in cabbage or radishes when you know that nobody will really eat them.

EARTHBOXES

If you are challenged spacewise and/or have a hard time finding enough sun (remember, all edibles need at least six hours of sun a day), you might want to consider purchasing an EarthBox from Two Dog Organic Nursery (www .twodognursery.com). These genius boxes come with everything you need to grow a box full of your veggie of choice. You can attach casters to the bottom so you can push the box around to follow the sun, which is so useful in the winter months when the angle of the sun is lower.

The really cool thing about the EarthBox is its irrigation system. It has a patented tank with a watering tube underneath the soil. You simply fill the tank through the tube every couple of days and that's it. It's also a great design for anyone with back or hip problems. My aunt loves gardening but cannot bend down because of back issues, so she has her EarthBoxes on tables (obviously with the casters removed).

Taking a Cutting

I remember thinking my mom was a bit strange when I was little, as she would ask for "cuttings" whenever we visited someone with a stunning yard. I couldn't understand what the excitement was about, much less the obsession with bringing these bits of cut-off plants back home wrapped carefully in a damp cloth. Now I understand. It's how to get the plant you want without having to pay for it! Just ask for a "cutting."

It turns out to be a little more complicated than just whipping out a pair of scissors and hacking off a stem—there is a little science to it. My mother doesn't believe in fiddling around with razor blades and rubbing alcohol (as in the Scientific Method described on p. 286), but others swear you have to take these steps. I'll give you my mom's method and the more scientific one—you pick!

WHAT IS A NODE?

A node is a tiny bump where a leaf is or was attached. It's the joint on the stem. You want to find a node on a nice green stem (not a woody one). It's important that you cut through the middle of the node when you take a cutting, as the new roots will emerge from it.

Mom's Method

YOU WILL NEED
- ☐ Sharp pair of scissors
- ☐ Plant pot or large yogurt container with holes for drainage
- ☐ Potting soil
- ☐ Pencil
- ☐ Rooting hormone powder (find it at any nursery)
- ☐ Plastic bag (an old grocery store or large resealable one will be perfect)

HOW TO

1. Pick out your "mother" plant—the one from which you want to create many plants—and, using a sharp pair of scissors, cut through the center of the node.

2. Fill your pot or container with potting soil and jab a pencil into the soil, creating 2-inch-deep holes. Try to fit 3 or 4 cuttings in one pot (spacing them 2 inches apart).

3. Dip the stem of the cutting in the rooting powder and then drop it into the hole, firming the soil around the stem.

4. Water gently, then place the pot in a plastic bag and either seal the bag or tie the top of it with a rubber band.

5. Cuttings will take root in warm, humid conditions. You could set the pot on top of your fridge or in a warm laundry room. Every now and then, open the bag and test the soil to see if it's still damp. If not, add water. A cutting can take anywhere from 10 days to 3 months to take root, so be patient. My mom tests by gently pulling on one of the plants.

Scientific Method

This is more fiddly, for sure, but might be more your thing.

YOU WILL NEED
- ☐ Sharp pair of scissors
- ☐ Rubbing alcohol
- ☐ Razor blade
- ☐ Rooting hormone stimulator
- ☐ Pot
- ☐ Potting soil
- ☐ Pencil
- ☐ Plastic bag

HOW TO

1. Pick your "mother" plant. This should be a plant with plenty of greenery.

2. Look for the node.

3. Sterilize your scissors in the rubbing alcohol and snip the stem just below the node.

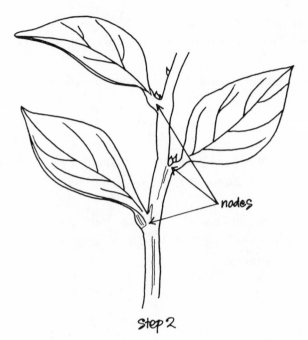

nodes

step 2

Snip just below the node
with sterilized scissors.

step 3

4. If you are taking your cutting from a friend's yard, pop it into a small, clean plastic bag with a wet paper towel in it and seal it until you get home.

5. Sterilize the razor blade and cut a clean cut through the center of the node.

6. Remove all but a couple of the leaves on the stem.

7. Have a small plant pot ready and filled with potting soil. Push a pencil down a couple of inches into the soil to make a hole for the stem.

8. Pour a little water into one glass and the rooting stimulator into another. Dip the cut node into the water first, then into the rooting solution. Tap off any excess liquid (less is more).

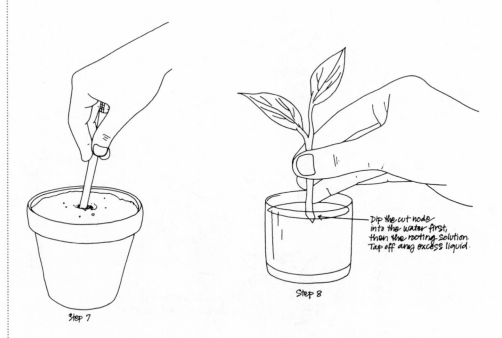

Step 7

Dip the cut node into the water first, then the rooting solution. Tap off any excess liquid.

Step 8

9. Carefully drop the stem into the hole you've created and gently pack the soil around the stem. Water well.

10. Place a plastic bag over the pot and tuck the edges under. You don't want to seal it completely.

←Place a plastic bag over the pot and tuck edges under.

Step 10

11. Place the cutting in your home, out of direct sunlight. Make sure the soil stays damp until the cutting has established roots (you can tell by gently tugging on it—if there's resistance, you have roots). Once roots are established, you can plant your cutting either in your yard or in a planter.

Medicinal Garden

You can grow your own medicine chest right in your backyard. I find this incredibly exciting, because herbal remedies can be very expensive to buy and by growing your own, you're ensuring yourself a supply of remedies to help with many common ailments. Many of these herbs, flowers, and roots can be grown in the United States, but you'll have to research the temperature and soil conditions needed for each individual plant before choosing it for your specific region.

You will need to start most of these plants from seeds, as seedlings will be hard to find. You will then harvest and dry the flowers, leaves, roots, or seeds to prepare medicinal tinctures, powders, teas, or pastes.

MY MEDICINE CHEST

These are some of the herbs that I love to grow in small raised beds in my yard.

- Violets: These beautiful purple flowers have a plethora of medicinal benefits. I make an infusion from the leaves to maintain good breast health and to help with congestion from a cold.

- Calendula: I use the dried calendula flowers to make an infusion for many of my homemade skincare preparations, as it's great for irritated or dry skin.

- German chamomile: I use the dried flowers to make infusions for my skincare preparations, and also as a tea to aid digestion and sleep.

- Lemon balm: An infusion or tincture from the leaves makes a great mosquito repellant and works well on inflamed skin conditions, such as herpes, sores, and insect bites.

- Milk thistle: I prepare a tincture to help with liver dextoxification, or just munch on the flowers.

- Echinacea: I prepare a tincture from the roots to help strengthen my immune system.

- Feverfew: The flowers (dried or fresh) can be steeped in hot water to make a tea for headaches, migraines, and arthritis.

- Evening primrose: I eat the leaves as salad greens, which is great for PMS, menstrual problems, and even for treating multiple sclerosis.

- Peppermint: An infusion from the leaves can relieve gas, bloating, and all kinds of digestive disorders.

- Valerian: A great herb to grow for those with insomnia. I chop up the roots and steep in boiling water as a sleep aid.

- Hyssop: I use the fresh or dried leaves to prepare a hot infusion for nasal congestion and bronchial irritation.

- Slippery elm (the bark): This is my go-to herb for sore throats or an irritated digestive tract. When growing my own, I use the dried inner bark to prepare a fine powder, which can be added to teas, soups, and oatmeal.

You should be able to buy all your medicinal herbs from Garden Medicinal and Culinaries (www.gardenmedicinals.com).

PLANNING YOUR MEDICINAL GARDEN

It's a good idea to spend a little time researching the herbs you might want to include in your backyard pharmacy. If you have kids, you may favor herbs that will deal with coughs and colds, such as sage and thyme, whereas if you are menopausal you may want to include black cohash and red raspberry leaf. To further research the medicinal benefits of a huge variety of herbs, visit Plants for a Future (www.pfaf.org).

The illustration on page 292 shows how I planned my medicinal garden. Obviously, try to plant the taller, bushier plants at the back of the bed and the smaller ones at the front. I always plant mint separately in planters, as it takes over the entire bed. I also plant calendula separately, as it attracts aphids.

HOW TO HARVEST AND USE MEDICINAL PLANTS

Harvesting: As far as harvesting is concerned, it depends upon which part of the plant you will be using—flowers, leaves, seeds, or roots.

Flowers: If you need the dried flowers for your medicines (chamomile and lavender), pick them as soon as the flowers blossom.

Leaves: If you are using the leaves (red raspberry, sage, thyme), gather them throughout the growing season.

Roots: If you are using the roots (echinacea and black cohosh), harvest in the fall.

Seeds: If seeds are what you need (milk thistle and rosehips), harvest when the fruit is ripe.

20'

3'

◉ Chamomile – 12"
◊ Thyme – 8"
☒ St. John's wort – 10"
◬ Milk Thistle – 8"–10"
⊠ Lemon Balm – 8"

⑥ Feverfew – 12"
☆ Sage – 12"
§ Rosemary – 18"
⊗ Hyssop – 12"
⊡ Evening primrose – 24"

Medicinal garden

Drying and storing: Unless you are going to use your herbs right away, I suggest drying them. Here's how to do it in the oven.

1. Put your oven on its lowest setting.

2. Line a baking sheet with parchment paper and evenly spread out your herbs.

3. Place the sheet in the oven for 3 to 5 hours, leaving the oven door ajar.

4. Allow the herbs to cool, then crumble them up and store in an airtight, dark glass container for up to 1 year.

To air dry them, try this method.

1. Gather your herbs in bunches and tie with either twine or a rubber band.

2. Hang them upside down in a warm room for 2 to 3 weeks, or until they feel dry and crispy.

3. Strip the leaves and flowers off the stems and store them in an airtight, dark glass container for up to 1 year.

Infusion or tea: An infusion is a fancy name for a tea. Here's how to make an herbal infusion.

1. Place the washed and chopped or dried plants in a glass measuring cup and cover with boiling water (2 tablespoons of herbs needs approximately 2 cups of water).

2. Leave to steep for half an hour.

3. Strain through a cheesecloth-lined sieve. Drink right away.

Tincture: Tinctures use alcohol to extract the healing properties from a plant. This method works well when using roots.

1. Fill a mason jar with the root or herb and cover with 80-proof vodka.

2. Run a spatula around the inside edge of the jar to disperse any air bubbles. Seal and leave the jar in a cool, dark spot for 3 to 4 weeks.

3. Strain through a cheesecloth-lined sieve and pour into small, dark glass bottles. Will keep for up to 5 years.

Infused (macerated) oil: This is a similar method to the tincture, only oil is used instead of alcohol. Prepare the oil this way.

1. Pick out a base oil in which to infuse your herbs (it can be any base oil, but I like to use olive, sweet almond, or jojoba).

2. Place 2 cups of oil in a heavy saucepan. Add 3 tablespoons of the herbs and heat over a very low heat for about 20 minutes.

3. Strain through a cheesecloth-lined sieve and pour into dark glass bottles. Will keep for 6 months.

Balm: You won't believe how easy it is to make herbal lip balms or ointments.

1. Prepare an infused oil, as detailed on the previous page, but use just 1 cup of oil and 2 tablespoons of herbs.

2. Before you take the oil off the heat, add 2 tablespoons of beeswax and allow it to melt. (If you are making a lip balm, halve the amount of wax and add 1 teaspoon of raw honey along with the beeswax.)

3. Pour into a dark glass jar or a tin. Will last for 1 year.

COLD SORE BALM

This is a healing balm for anyone who suffers from cold sores. It's made with lemon balm, which is easy to grow.

Yields: approximately 11 oz. of balm

Application: use liberally on and around cold sores

Storage: 1-oz. dark glass bottle or tin in a cool, dark cupboard

Shelf life: 1 year

1½ cups fresh lemon balm leaves
½ cup olive oil
3 tbsp. wheat germ oil
1½ tbsp. raw honey

1 tbsp. beeswax
5 drops tea tree essential oil
5 drops peppermint essential oil

1. Strip the leaves off the stems and place in a small saucepan with the olive and wheat germ oils. Warm over low heat for 10 minutes.

2. Remove from the heat and strain through a cheesecloth-lined sieve.

3. Pour the oil back into the saucepan and add the honey and beeswax. Stir until the beeswax has melted. Remove from the heat.

4. Add the essential oils and pour into your jar.

Medicinal Salad

One of the most delicious ways of eating some medicinal herbs is to make a salad from their leaves and flowers. Here is my favorite salad, which is not only wonderful for your skin, digestion, and immune system, but also incredibly pretty.

Yields: 2 servings

2 cups dandelion greens (leaves)	2 tbsp. extra virgin olive oil
1 cup violet leaves	1 tbsp. fresh lemon juice
½ cup violet flowers	½ tsp. agave nectar
1 cup mixed salad greens	Salt and pepper to taste
½ cup crumbled feta cheese	
¼ cup almonds, toasted and slivered	

1. Mix all the greens, cheese, and almonds in a large bowl.

2. Add the olive oil, lemon juice, agave, and seasoning.

3. Toss well and enjoy with a slice of warm sourdough baguette.

1. Cover the bottom of a large glass baking dish (Pyrex is perfect) with a sheet of aluminum foil.

2. Lay out your pieces of tarnished silver on the foil, taking care that none of the pieces overlap.

3. Generously sprinkle baking soda all over the pieces.

4. Add boiling water, so that all the pieces are submerged.

5. Leave for 15 minutes.

6. Rinse your silver under cold water and polish dry with a clean rag.

If you have a piece of silver that's difficult to submerge in water (a photo frame, a box, or candlesticks), you may want to try one of the following tricks.

- Cut a potato in half, dip the cut side in baking soda, and use it to polish your silver.

- Use regular toothpaste and a rag. Work the toothpaste into the silver and buff off with a clean rag. Toothpaste is also great for polishing gold.

Computer Screen Cleaner

We buy a lot of little cleaners that are extremely expensive, because we don't think there's an alternative. One such item is a computer screen cleaner. I used to buy very pricey little foil packets containing moistened paper cloth. I thought I'd ruin my LCD (liquid-crystal display) by using anything else—at least, that's what they told me in the store! Now I know different. Here's how to do it.

YOU WILL NEED
- ☐ ¼ cup distilled water
- ☐ ¼ cup isopropyl alcohol (also known as rubbing alcohol, available at drugstores)
- ☐ 1 lint-free cloth
- ☐ 1 sunglasses/eyeglasses cloth

HOW TO

1. Turn off your monitor.

2. Gently remove excess dust with a dry microfiber cloth.

3. Mix the water and alcohol in a small glass bowl.

4. Dip in the lint-free cloth, squeeze out excess moisture, and gently wipe your screen.

5. Use your sunglasses cloth to gently polish the screen.

Five Great Uses for 15 Common Household Items That You Probably Already Have

BAKING SODA

1. Create a dry shampoo for your dog by shaking 1 cup of baking soda over your dog's fur. Leave for 5 minutes and then brush out.

2. Use as a fire extinguisher by keeping an opened box of baking soda near your stove. Toss handfuls on any unanticipated flare-ups.

3. Control compost bin/pile odor by pouring a cup of baking soda on top of the pile.

4. Neutralize kitchen garbage pail odors by sprinkling baking soda in the bottom of the can before you insert a liner.

5. Create a deodorant sachet for any stinky tennis shoes by placing ½ cup of baking soda into the toes of old, clean pantyhose. Tie a knot just above the baking soda and cut off. Insert into the toe of each shoe. To add a lovely scent, put 5 drops of lavender essential oil on each sachet.

ELECTRICAL TAPE

1. Wrap your hand with electrical tape, sticky side out, to remove lint or pet hair from your clothes and furniture.

2. Pick up little splinters of broken or shattered glass (after you have removed the larger pieces) by wrapping your fingers on one hand with electrical tape, sticky side out.

3. Create an ant barrier by surrounding the item you want to protect with a circle of electrical tape, sticky side up.

4. Repair the spine of a book by picking a matching color tape and pressing along the book's spine.

5. Clean a comb by pressing a length of electrical tape along the length of the comb and removing. Next, submerge the comb in a solution of equal parts water and hydrogen peroxide to disinfect.

RESEALABLE PLASTIC BAGS

1. Package fragile items for shipping by blowing up bags with a straw, sealing, and then using them as padding in place of Bubble Wrap or packing peanuts.

2. For chopping nuts, fill the bag with whole nuts, seal it, and use a wooden rolling pin to bash up the nuts.

3. For an icing bag for muffins and cupcakes, fill one corner of the bag with icing, cut off the tiny point of the corner with a pair of sharp scissors, and squeeze icing through the hole.

4. Keep silver jewelry from becoming tarnished by storing it in a sealed plastic bag.

5. Protect a leaking or exploding shampoo or lotion from ruining the contents of your toiletries bag (when on an airplane) by packing each bottle in a separate sealed plastic bag before packing it into your toiletries bag.

ALOE VERA JUICE

1. Create a mouthwash for great oral health by gargling and then swallowing 2 ounces of aloe vera juice daily.

2. Use as a toner for oily skin by dipping a cotton ball in aloe vera juice and wiping it over your face.

3. Dab aloe vera juice on an insect bite to take away the sting.

4. Drink 2 ounces of aloe vera juice mixed with 2 ounces of water and 1 teaspoon of fresh lemon juice for a liver-cleansing tonic.

5. For a soothing after-sun spray, add 1 cup of aloe vera juice to 2 cups of distilled water in a sprayer. Add 20 drops of peppermint essential oil.

HAIR CONDITIONER

1. You can use it to shave your legs! If you run out of shaving cream, hair conditioner is as good, if not better.

2. Conditioner is better than laundry detergent for washing silk. Make sure you use a nontoxic conditioner and rinse the silk items well with cold water.

3. If you have shrunk a sweater by putting it in the washing machine by mistake, unshrink it by soaking it in a bucket of water with 2 teaspoons of hair conditioner for half an hour. Rinse with cool water and stretch out to reshape.

4. Hair conditioner is one of the best leather shiners. Place a little on a clean, dry rag and work into your leather jacket, shoes, or furniture.

5. Shine up large-leafed houseplants with a drop of conditioner on a clean, dry rag.

EPSOM SALTS

1. Create the most relaxing bath on earth by adding 2 cups of Epsom salts to the hottest water you can bear.

2. Use as an extremely effective laxative. Add 1 tablespoon to an 8-ounce glass of water and swig. It tastes awful but totally does the trick.

3. Sprinkle a little on the soil of your houseplants every week before watering and watch your plants go bright green.

4. Soak a splinter in a bowl of warm water and 1 cup of Epsom salts, before easing it out by gently squeezing or having someone do it for you.

5. Treat toe fungus or athlete's foot by soaking your feet in a tub of warm water and 1 cup of Epsom salts for 15 minutes.

LEMONS

1. Clean a wooden cutting board by cutting a lemon in half and rubbing the cut side in circular motions over your board. Wipe off with a clean, damp rag.

2. Freshen up wilting lettuce leaves by soaking them in a sink of icy cold water and the juice of a lemon.

3. Keep avocados and apples from going brown by soaking cut edges with lemon juice and placing in an airtight container.

4. Stop rice from sticking to the bottom of the pot by adding a teaspoon of fresh lemon juice to the boiling water.

5. Freshen up your garbage disposal by running half a lemon (cut into very small pieces) and a cup of ice through it.

MILK CARTONS

1. If you don't have a compost crock, just slice off the top of a milk carton and leave it on your counter to collect scraps. Transport to your compost bin when it's full.

2. To start seeds, cut off the top half of the carton and, using a metal skewer or a screwdriver, punch four holes in the bottom. Fill with potting soil and plant your seeds.

3. Cut off the top of a carton and half fill with water as a convenient holder for dirty paintbrushes while you are painting.

4. Use as a mini trash can under your sink in your kitchen or bathroom to collect the yucky, sticky stuff. When it's trash day, you can throw the whole thing out.

5. Cut off the top of the carton and use as a cooking oil holder, to prevent oil from dripping down bottles and creating oil rings in your cupboards.

PLASTIC MUFFIN/CUPCAKE TRAY (FROM STORE-BOUGHT MUFFINS)

1. Cut the top off. The indentations in the bottom are the perfect size for your daily vitamin bottles.

2. Cut the top off and set in your top office drawer to tidy up paper clips, thumbtacks, small sticky notes—whatever rattles around in your drawer.

3. Cut the top off but keep for a kid's paintbrush tray. Use the cups to hold six different colors of paint.

4. Make a snack'n'dip tray for the kids' snack time. Cut the top off. Fill half of the cups with chips, pretzels, or nuts, and the other half with dips (hummus, cream cheese, etc.).

5. For recipe prep, cut the top off, then cut out each bottom cup. Place the exact measurement you need of seasonings (salt, pepper, garlic, herbs, baking powder, and so on) in the individual cups.

PILLOWCASE

1. When you're traveling, use a pretty pillowcase as a lingerie bag to store your bras and panties.

2. Keep matching sheets and pillowcases together as a set in an old pillowcase.

3. Use as a cheap cover for a changing table pad.

4. Wash delicate bras and panties in a pillowcase.

5. Line a small wicker wastebasket with a lace-edged pillowcase to achieve a shabby chic/Pottery Barn look.

RUBBER BANDS

1. To stop paint drips, wrap a rubber band midway around an open paint can, making sure it runs across the center of the can. Use it to catch the drips from your brush before painting.

2. Use as a bookmark, so you're not tempted to fold down dog-ears.

3. Wind it around the center of your remote control horizontally, then double it up, to keep the remote from scratching your furniture.

4. Wrap around a honey jar to prevent drips.

5. Use instead of a chip clip by folding the bag down a few times and wrapping the rubber band around entire bag.

HYDROGEN PEROXIDE

1. Use as a nail whitening soak once a week.

2. Stave off colds and flu by dropping 3 drops in each ear once a day for 3 days. Let it fizz and then mop up whatever runs out with a cotton ball.

3. Use with equal parts of distilled water in a sprayer as a general home disinfecting spray.

4. Use as a mouthwash to prevent canker sores.

5. Add 1 cup to the rinse cycle of a white load of laundry to keep your whites brighter.

SALT

1. Prevent grease from spitting by adding a few pinches to the pan before frying.

2. Pick up a spilled egg or tomato seeds by sprinkling salt over them before wiping up.

3. Remove lipstick marks from glasses or mugs by rubbing a little salt over the mark before you put it in the dishwasher.

4. Mix with a little vinegar into a paste and use as a brass and copper polish.

5. Pour directly onto weeds and see them disappear. It's great to use between paving stones to keep weeds at bay.

WHITE VINEGAR

1. Get dingy dishcloths, socks, and rags bright and white by adding 1 cup of vinegar to a large pot of boiling water. Drop in items, remove from the heat, and leave overnight.

2. Clean out the pipes and hoses of your washing machine and dishwasher by running a cup of vinegar through for an empty cycle.

3. Keep your steam iron in good working order by once a month filling the chamber with vinegar and leaving for 15 minutes before pouring out.

4. Dip your eyeglasses in a glass of water with 1 teaspoon of vinegar. Dry with a lint-free cloth.

5. Before you apply nail polish, wipe your nails with a cotton ball soaked in vinegar.

CARDBOARD TUBES

1. Keep those old resealable bags from floating around your kitchen drawer by stuffing them into an old paper towel roll.

2. If you want to prevent creases on your pants, cut a paper towel tube lengthwise and hang the tube over the bar of a regular hanger.

3. Keep your child's homework assignments and artwork stashed tidily in a drawer by rolling them up inside a wrapping paper or paper towel tube; label the tubes.

4. Store loose bits and odd balls of string or yarn in an old toilet paper roll.

5. Use as a seedling starter. Cut into 3- to 4-inch tubes and sink them into a tray of potting soil. Sow a few seeds into each "pot." When the seedlings are 4 or 5 inches high, remove the tube and transplant the seedlings with a large spoon or a small trowel.

Eight

DIY Doggie (Kitty Too)

Bathing Your Dog

After buying an awfully expensive bottle of nontoxic doggie shampoo for my Maltese, Phoebe, from a fancy pet supply store, I knew that would be the first and last bottle of store-bought pet product I'd bring into the house! I experimented and found a way of making the perfect dog shampoo. It contains peppermint, which is fantastic for repelling fleas, and jojoba oil, which is great for dogs' skin and hair/fur.

YOU WILL NEED
- ☐ 1 cup liquid castile soap
- ☐ 1 cup distilled water
- ☐ 1 tsp. jojoba oil
- ☐ 5 drops peppermint essential oil

HOW TO

1. Combine all the ingredients in an old shampoo bottle and shake gently. (It should keep for up to 6 months in a cool, dark cupboard.)

2. Fill a tub or kitchen sink (depending on the size of your dog) with tepid (slightly warm water). Make sure your sink/tub has a shower attachment and a nonslip mat.

3. Place your doggie in the tub/sink, with the water coming up to his/her belly. Gently wet the rest of his/her fur with the shower attachment.

4. Squirt about 1 tsp. of shampoo on his/her back and work it into a lather all over his/her body. Avoid the dog's eyes and mouth area, as the peppermint oil could sting.

5. Thoroughly rinse off all the shampoo with the shower attachment.

6. Have a large towel laid out ready on the counter or the floor. Remove your pooch from the water and wrap him or her up in the towel. Most dogs love being dried, but after an initial rubdown you should let him or her run, shake, and go crazy before you attempt further drying. It's dogs' nature to want to roll and have a mad moment or two. If it's warm, I prefer to let Phoebe air-dry, but if it's cold I get the hair dryer going on its lowest/coolest setting. She hates it, so I'm pretty quick and don't get it anywhere near her face.

7. Most dogs don't need hair conditioner. However, if you have a long-haired pooch like Phoebe with dry hair, you can rub a few drops of jojoba oil in the palms of your hands and gently smooth over your dog's coat. You can also use a few squirts of the Fur Spritz (see following page).

8. The grand finale is the face washing. I take a damp (warm water) old facecloth and wipe around Phoebe's eyes and mouth.

Since I adopted Phoebe, pet supply shops have become like candy stores— my daughter and I have to stay away! The amount of stuff you can now buy, from bad-breath sprays to pedicure kits, is absurd. Having scouted out every major pet supply store in the area, I've realized that you can make virtually everything you need for your dog, and that much of what they sell can actually be harmful to your pet's health. Learning to do it yourself for your precious pet is the only way to go.

Fur Spritz

If your little pooch is anything like Phoebe, no matter how clean you keep them, it's normal for them to get a bit smelly now and then. This doesn't really pose a problem, unless they sleep very close to your face—which is the case with Phoebe. The fur spritz will make your pooch's fur smell sweet, as well as give it a conditoning shine.

YOU WILL NEED
- ☐ 2 oz. water
- ☐ 2 oz. aloe vera juice
- ☐ 1 tsp. vegetable glycerin
- ☐ 4-oz. dark plastic bottle with a sprayer
- ☐ 5 drops patchouli essential oil
- ☐ 5 drops lavender essential oil

HOW TO

1. Mix the water, aloe vera juice, and glycerin in a measuring cup and carefully pour into the bottle.

2. Add the essential oils and shake gently.

3. Store in a cool, dark spot when not using. It will last for up to 1 year.

DIY Doggie
(Kitty Too)

Fleece Doggie/Kitty Bed

You can make this out of an old fleece pullover. If you don't have one, you'll find a few tatty bargains at a garage sale or flea market. The size of the bed will depend on the size of the fleece you're working with. Use as big a fleece as possible for your dog. An XL fleece should work for a dog weighing up to 12 pounds. You can use a smaller fleece for a cat. If you have a large dog, look at the Large Dog Bed (see p. 331).

YOU WILL NEED
- ☐ 1 fleece pullover
- ☐ 1 large bag of filler (I like kapok). You can also use old grocery store plastic bags (you'll need about 80 of them).

HOW TO

1. Cut the sleeves off your fleece.

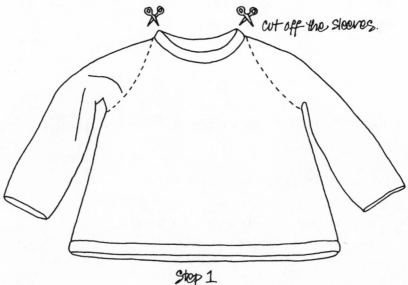

cut off the sleeves.

Step 1

2. Turn the body of the fleece inside out and lay on a flat surface, smoothing out the creases.

3. Mark a large half circle with a marker on the front panel of the fleece and carefully cut it out through both sides with a pair of fabric scissors.

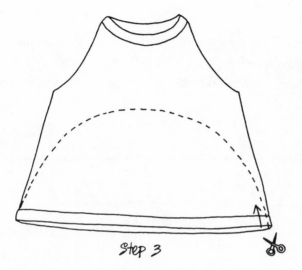

Step 3

4. Pin the edges together and sew a ¼-inch hem around the entire half circle, leaving a 6-inch opening for stuffing. Make sure you backstitch (see p. 137) both sides of the opening.

Sew a ¼" hem around the entire half circle, leaving a 6" opening for stuffing.

— 6" —

Step 4

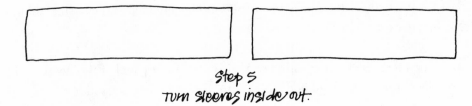

Step 5
Turn sleeves inside out.

5. Turn the sleeves inside out.

6. Pinch together the edges of the two cuffs (wrong sides facing each other) and carefully sew together, ½ inch away from the edge. When you have sewn around the circle, you should have a tube. Sew up one end of the tube.

Step 6

7. Turn the tube the right way out and stuff with your kapok or plastic bags. Tuck the edges of the open end in and hand sew to close.

8. Turn the half-circle the right way out and stuff with filling. Tuck the edges of the opening in and hand sew to close.

9. To assemble the tube and the base, set the tube around the round side of the base and use large stitches to hand sew either end of the tube onto the base. Then sew on the center of the tube. Go back to the first end of the tube and, using large stitches, go around the half circle, sewing the tube to the base.

step 9

LARGE DOG BED

You obviously need a bit more fabric for the big guy. You should be able to find inexpensive fleece fabric at just about every fabric store, or at fabric.com (www.fabric.com).

YOU WILL NEED

☐ 1 yard fleece fabric (if your dog is huge, you may need 1½ yards)

☐ Filling (kapok or about 200 grocery bags*)

In the parking lot of most grocery stores, you'll find a recycling bin for grocery store bags. This is where you might easily find your 200 bags!

HOW TO

1. Fold the fabric in half, right sides together, and lay out on a flat surface.

2. With a marker, mark the largest circle or oval possible on the fabric.

3. Cut out the shape and pin the edges together.

4. Sew around the edge, about ¼ inch away from raw edge. Leave a 6-inch opening. Backstitch both sides of the opening.

5. Turn it inside out and stuff with the plastic bags or the kapok filler.

6. Tuck in the edges of the opening ¼ inch and hand sew to close.

Doggie Placemat Day Coat

Have you noticed how overpriced dog's clothes are? My dog hates to be dressed, but my daughter thinks otherwise, and this little coat is a great alternative to some of the doll's clothes that she's tried to squeeze the poor dog into. It's easy to get on and off and lies lightly on the dog's back. This coat will fit a dog that weighs up to about 12 pounds.

YOU WILL NEED
- ☐ 1 placemat (the thicker the better—if you can find a quilted placemat, that would be ideal)
- ☐ Approximately 9-inch-thick fabric*
- ☐ 6-inch strip of Velcro
- ☐ 2 large buttons (odd buttons will look cute on this)

You want a contrasting color to your placemat, so if your mat is solid, go for a pattern, or vice versa. The remnant box in a drapery store would be a good place to look.

HOW TO

1. Turn your mat over, so the wrong side is facing up. With tailor's chalk, mark out an oval shape. Cut it out.

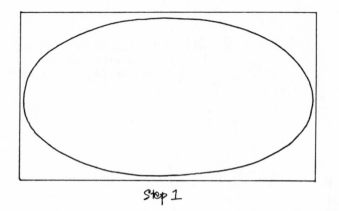

Step 1

2. Fold over the top third of the oval and cut out a circle 4 inches in diameter from the top edge.

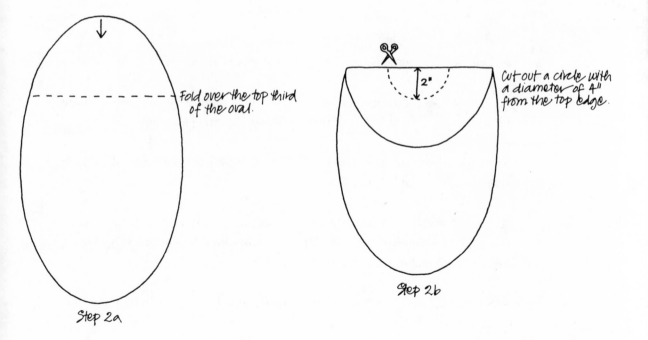

Fold over the top third of the oval.

Step 2a

Cut out a circle with a diameter of 4" from the top edge.

2"

Step 2b

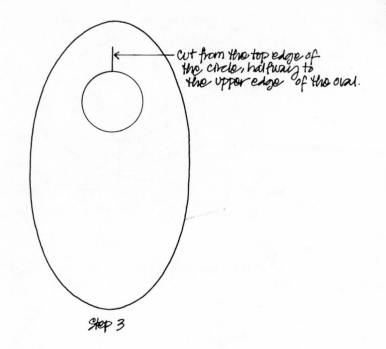

Cut from the top edge of the circle, halfway to the upper edge of the oval.

Step 3

3. Cut from the top edge of the circle, halfway to the upper edge of the oval.

4. Turn over ¼ inch and then another ¼ inch all around the oval. Pin and sew a hem. Repeat for the inside of the circle and the circle opening.

5. Measure your dog from the middle of his/her back to the middle of the belly to see how long the belt needs to be.

6. Fold your fabric in half, right sides together, and cut out a strip 5 inches wide and the length you measured (plus 2 inches for seams and a hem). For my dog, that's 20 inches total. Pin together.

7. Sew around both lengths and one end of the strips, then turn right side out, press, and sew up the open end.

8. Sew a square of Velcro to either end of the belt and to either side of the neck opening.

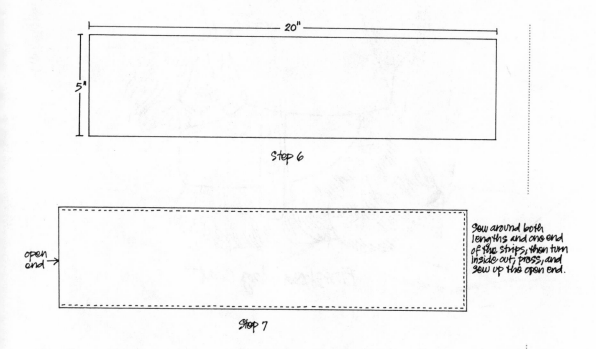

|← 20" →|

5"

Step 6

open
end →

Sew around both
lengths and one end
of the strips, then turn
inside out, press, and
sew up the open end.

Step 7

9. Stitch the belt onto the coat and sew a button on top of your stitches.

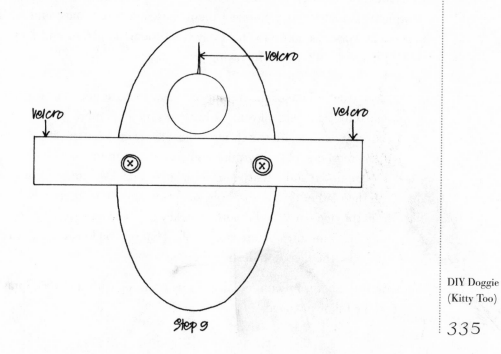

Velcro

Velcro

Velcro

Step 9

DIY Doggie
(Kitty Too)

335

Finished dog coat

Natural Flea Treatment Program for Dogs

Fleas are a nightmare, but even worse are most of the flea sprays, collars, and treatments available today. Some of them cause allergies at best and are carcinogenic at worst. I choose to stay away from them altogether and do my own thing. I have found that the following program works really well.

1. Weekly bath: One of the most effective ways of killing fleas is dish soap! Once a week, fill your bathtub or sink (depending on the size of your dog) with warm water. You need a spray attachment, if possible. Use 1 teaspoon of peppermint liquid castile soap for a small dog (up to 12 pounds) and 2 teaspoons for a larger dog. Wet your dog all over and then lather up the soap, obviously taking care to keep it away from the dog's eyes and mouth. The key is to let the soap stay on for a full 5 minutes before rinsing off. That will be long enough to suffocate the fleas and destroy their eggs.

2. After the bath: I recommend spraying your dog with the Flea Spray on the following page.

Flea Spray

YOU WILL NEED

- ☐ 4 oz. distilled water
- ☐ 10 drops peppermint essential oil
- ☐ 10 drops cedarwood essential oil
- ☐ 4-oz. dark glass bottle with sprayer top

HOW TO

1. Combine all the ingredients in a measuring cup and pour into the bottle.

2. Store in a cool, dark cupboard.

3. Flea comb: Always use a regular flea comb (available from most stores). If your dog has long hair, you may want to brush him/her first with your regular grooming brushes/combs and then, as the final step, comb through sections of his/her hair with the flea comb. As I have a little Maltese, I just use the flea comb.

4. Natural flea collar: Buy a cotton-covered or hemp collar. Place 5 drops of peppermint essential oil and 5 drops of cedarwood essential oil into the palm of your hand. Rub your hands together and then all over the collar. Reapply every 14 days.

Grub

Now that I know what is in most regular cans of dog food, I refuse to serve it to my dog. Without horrifying you with the details—think diseased animals unfit for human consumption, all ground up, and you're on the right track—

I make my own and Phoebe *loves* it. It also doesn't stink up my kitchen the way the cans do.

Yummy Dog Dinner

Yields: approximately 2½ lbs.

32 oz. ground beef, lamb, turkey, chicken, or a mix 2 cups cauliflower (cut into tiny florets and stalks, sliced), carrots, peas, or a mix (frozen is fine)	3 tbsp. old-fashioned uncooked oatmeal or cooked brown rice ½ tbsp. pet cod liver oil, available from Nordic Naturals (www.nordicnaturals.com)

1. Put the ground meat in a large cooking pot with 1 tbsp. water and cook over medium heat until the meat is brown all the way through.

2. Add the veggies to the pot. Cover and simmer for 20 minutes. Remove from the heat.

3. Stir in the rice or oatmeal and the oil.

4. If you have a big dog whom you know will consume this amount of food within 3 days, store in a covered container in the fridge. If you have a smaller dog, you may want to freeze dinner-size portions of the food in plastic snack bags. When you are ready to use, empty the bag into the dog's bowl (only glass or ceramic) and microwave for 50 to 60 seconds. Always wash and reuse the bags.

Dog Biscuits/Treats

When Phoebe is very well behaved, she gets one of her beloved treats. Be very careful with the doggie treats that you buy. My friend Sally bought her pooch some expensive snacks from a well-known health food store and her doggie got severe food poisoning. Upon investigation, she discovered that, despite being labled as "organic and natural," the treats had come from China, and it was therefore nearly impossible for her to trace the source. It's safer and less expensive to make your own.

Yields: approximately 2 dozen small treats

2½ cups whole wheat flour	1 tsp. dried parsley
½ cup powdered milk	1 tsp. beef bouillon granules
1 tbsp. wheat germ	½ cup bacon or meat grease*
1 tbsp. ground flax	1 egg
1 tsp. garlic powder	½ cup water

To avoid clogging up my drains, I keep a large jelly jar in my freezer for meat grease from frying bacon, chicken, or beef. I wait until it's full before disposing of it. This is a great way to use up some of that grease.

1. Preheat the oven to 350°F.

2. In a medium bowl, combine the first 7 ingredients.

3. Stir in the meat grease and egg.

4. Add the water, a little at a time, until the dough is sticky enough to bind together.

5. Flour a surface and roll out the dough to a ½-inch thickness.

6. Use a knife or cookie cutter to cut out shapes. Keep in mind that a regular cookie cutter will cut cookie shapes that are too big for dog treats. I use an

eggcup to press out small circles, or I cut out little squares and triangles with a paring knife.

7. Bake 25 to 30 minutes or until firm and lightly browned.

8. When cool, either store in an airtight container, where the biscuits will stay good for up to 10 days, or freeze half of them in a resealable bag.

Kitty Treats

These are moist and deluxe little treats for your cat.

Yields: approximately 24–36 small balls

½ lb. ground turkey	1 tsp. Pet cod liver oil (www
1 small carrot, finely grated	.nordicnaturals.com)
1 tbsp. grated cheese (any cheese	½ cup whole wheat flour
will do)	1 egg, beaten
1 tsp. dried catnip	1 tbsp. tomato paste

1. Preheat the oven to 350°F.

2. Combine all the ingredients in a large bowl.

3. Using your hands, roll the dough into tiny balls and place on a lightly greased baking sheet.

4. Bake 8 to 10 minutes or until the treats are hard and slightly browned.

5. Cool completely before storing in an airtight container in your fridge or freezing them.

Kitty Litter

This kitty litter will cost you pennies to make and will help you recycle your newspapers (ask your friends for their newspapers if you have a lot of cats!). Some cats just will not accept unfamiliar litter or litter with an unusual texture. To maximize the chances of kitty accepting it, change the litter gradually, mixing the old with the new. But if your cat stops using her litter box, you'll have to go back to the old litter.

YOU WILL NEED
- ☐ Pile of old newspapers
- ☐ Bucket
- ☐ Liquid castile soap
- ☐ Baking soda

HOW TO

1. Shred the paper (ideally, use a paper shredder).

2. Put the paper into a large bucket and cover with warm water and a squirt of dish soap (I like liquid castile soap).

3. Drain the paper in a large colander and repeat step 2, minus the soap.

4. Wearing a pair of rubber gloves, squeeze as much moisture as you can from the paper.

5. Lay it out over a screen or parchment-covered baking sheets and sprinkle liberally with baking soda. Leave in a warm place to dry. If it's hot outside, you can leave it in the sun, but cover with a dishcloth to keep it from blowing away.

6. Fill your kitty's litter box with 2 inches of your litter. Scoop the poop out every day and change the litter once a week.

Toys

Kitty Bonding Stock

This is a great toy for a kitten who is over 3 months of age.

YOU WILL NEED
- ☐ 1 old sock
- ☐ 2 tbsp. dried catnip

HOW TO

1. Wear your old sock around the house for an hour or so to get your smell into it.

2. Stuff the sock with the catnip and tie a knot just above the herbs.

3. Toss the sock on the floor and watch your kitty go crazy!

Crackle and Crunch Big Dog Toy

There's no need to buy expensive plastic dog toys when you can make toys your dog will love out of things you probably already have. This is best suited for a big dog. My little Maltese can't get her chops around it.

YOU WILL NEED
- ☐ 1 paper towel tube
- ☐ 1 sheet old cellophane
- ☐ Duct tape

HOW TO

1. Stuff the cardboard tube with the cellophane.

2. Cover the ends of the tube with duct tape, then wrap the duct tape around the tube, making sure it's secure and tight.

3. Show it to your dog and crackle it a few times—your dog will take over.

FOUR GREAT RECYCLED DOG TOYS

1. Don't clean out your old plastic peanut butter jar. Instead, let your dog have hours of fun licking it out.

2. Fill an old plastic water bottle with kibble and leave the top off. Then watch your doggie having hours of fun trying to get the kibble out.

3. Cut up an old garden hose into 12-inch lengths and let your doggie use it as a chew toy.

4. Save a bunch of catalogs, roll them up, and let your dog go crazy ripping them up—this is especially good for puppies.

Jumping Cat Toy

Instead of buying those expensive cat toys with teasing feathers or bells on them, this will cost you nothing to make and will drive your kitty nuts!

YOU WILL NEED
- ☐ 1 wire hanger
- ☐ Masking tape
- ☐ 10 to 15 pieces old yarn, cut into 10-inch lengths

DIY Doggie
(Kitty Too)

HOW TO

1. Unravel the hook of the hanger, straighten it out, and wrap the ends around the rest of the squeezed-together hanger.

2. Wrap masking tape around the entire length of your squeezed-together hanger. Double up the tape over the unraveled hook part, so that you cover and pull in the sharp ends of the wire. Work from one end to the other.

3. Leave the loop of wire at the end of your toy free of masking tape. Loop and knot the lengths of yarn around the loop (like tassels). Now you have the perfect cat toy.

4. For extra kitty interest, you can attach a bell to one of the pieces of yarn. The bell, however, can be a choking hazard, so make sure you put it somewhere the cat cannot reach when it's not in use.

Nine

DIY Mind/Body/Spirit

Taking care of *you* can be expensive and seriously time-consuming. How often have you implored a girlfriend who looks a bit frayed at the seams, "You need to take care of yourself"? How often have you promised yourself that *this* year you will really learn to take better care of yourself? We can have the greatest intentions in the world, but life happens. Our day gets packed to the max with kids, meetings, shopping, cooking, and e-mails—so much so that it often seems laughable to carve out time for meditation, much less exercise. The scary thing, however, is that the neglect will inevitably lead us to being less effective, healthy, and happy in the long run.

I'd love to be able to afford a personal trainer every day, someone who would ring my front doorbell and force me through a rigorous and sweaty routine before I had time to think twice about it. Most of us can't afford this luxury, though, and it's the "thinking twice" that kills us. I'll open my eyes first thing, thinking, "Right, as soon as I've packed my daughter off, the dumbbells are coming out." But then Phoebe, my little dog, needs some cuddling time and a girlfriend calls to chat. Before I know it, my precious 20 minutes that I'd earmarked for exercise or meditation has gone, and I'm legging it out to a meeting.

I've come to realize that every day I *don't* exercise is a day my muscles will lose strength and tone, making it increasingly harder to get away with a skimpy summer tank. Every day that I don't carve out time for quiet, meditation, or deep breathing, I put years onto my life with unnecessary stress. I want to look wonderful as I grow older. I want to look rested, with shiny eyes, glowing skin, and a toned behind. Thinking about it will accomplish nothing, so I've taught myself not to think twice, but to spring into action even with dogs and children participating. I've learned to surround myself with a bubble of "me" time that everyone has to respect.

Too Busy?

If you really don't think you have time to do a few exercises every day, you are wrong. The following arm, tummy, and butt exercises will take you all of 15 minutes total and then you're done. You'll feel fantastic when you've finished them.

These exercises are not intended to take the place of a full-on fitness program that you may have in place. They're not supposed to take the place of running, hiking, or walking—they are designed to supplement whatever else you have going. Bottom line, this routine is the *minimum* that I want you to do at least three times a week. If you want to be able to proudly don a skimpy bikini, a summer tank, and adorable skinny jeans at any age, there's no getting out of the little bit of effort required here!

DIY Fitness

You are going to become your own trainer, your own self-motivator. Because I've made this routine very easy, you should be able to learn it in two sessions and then you can plug into your iPod and have a blast doing it. You can save yourself a bunch of dollars by doing it yourself and becoming your own fitness trainer.

Awesome Abs

Aside from the six-pack that we all dream about possessing, getting your abdominal muscles strong and tight is paramount for keeping back problems at bay. If you suffer from lower back issues, it's likely that you need to seriously strengthen your stomach muscles. The following exercises are quick and simple.

AB TIP

When you're performing abdominal exercises, the key is to draw in your lower abs and keep them tight throughout. As you are sitting in your chair now, sit upright and draw your pubic bone in toward your spine, curving your tailbone up. Tighten your glutes (the muscles in your buttocks). This is the feeling you want to maintain throughout all of the following exercises.

LEG LIFTS

1. Start on your back with your knees bent and feet flat on the floor. Your arms should be by your sides, palms facing down. Straighten your legs to a 90-degree angle, making sure you feet are directly above your hips.

2. Lift your legs and buttocks off the floor. Keep your legs straight, up over your hips with your toes pointing upward.

3. Slowly return to starting position, while keeping your muscles contracted.

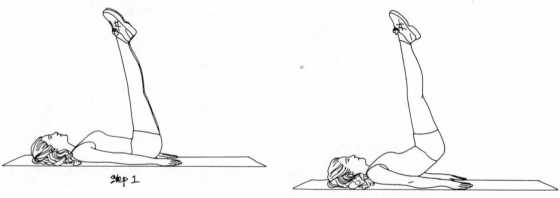

Step 1   Step 2

Tip: Keep your legs directly above your hips without letting them drop forward, toward you, or back.

Breathing: Exhale as you lift, inhale as you return.

Sets: 2 sets of 12 repetitions

CRUNCH IT UP

If performed diligently, the basic, traditional crunch will have you well on your way to a good six-pack.

1. Lie on your back with your knees bent and your feet hip width apart.

2. If you are a beginner, place your interlaced fingers behind your head. If you're intermediate or advanced, extend your arms overhead and place one palm over the other.

3. Draw your navel toward your spine and curl your torso up and toward your thighs until your shoulder blades are off the mat. Return *slowly* (keeping your abs tight) to the floor.

Step 1

Step 2

Tip: Look up toward the ceiling, so you limit tension in the neck.

Breathing: Exhale as you lift, inhale as you lower.

Sets: 2 sets of 12 repetitions

REACH BACKS

This is a great exercise for all the abdominal muscles.

1. Sit on your mat with your knees bent and your feet about 2 feet in front of your sit bones.

2. Extend your arms, palms down, fingers pointing forward and shoulder height.

3. Contract your abs, drawing your pubic bone toward your spine, forming a C curve. This helps to draw your tailbone up.

4. Lower your torso halfway to the floor and pause.

5. Making sure your C curve is still strong, reach your left arm out to the side and back, as if you are trying to reach something behind you.

6. Bring your left arm back to its starting position. Repeat with the right arm.

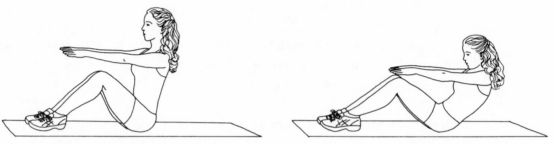

step 2   step 4

step 5

Tip: If you find yourself straining, gently hold the backs of your thighs with your hands.

Breathing: Exhale as you lower your torso and reach behind you. Inhale as you bring your arm back to center.

Sets: 3 sets of 15 repetitions

BICYCLE

This is one of the few ab exercises that I actually enjoy doing.

1. Lie on a mat with your knees bent toward your chest and your hands interlaced behind your head.

2. As you extend your right leg out in front of you, draw your right elbow up to touch your left knee.

3. Now extend your left leg as you pull your right knee up and touch your left elbow to it.

Tip: Your extended leg should be straight out and parallel to the floor. To increase the intensity of this exercise, hold your position for 4 breaths when your elbow meets your knee.

Breathing: Exhale as you extend your leg out in front of you. Inhale to come back up.

Sets: 3 sets of 10 alternating repetitions

Toned Tush

The glutes are massive muscles that need a lot of attention as we get older. No matter what your shape, you can dramatically improve the tone of your behind. Try to do these every day.

THE SQUEEZE

I actually enjoy this exercise, because you can feel it sculpting as you squeeze. You can keep going for quite a few rounds if you've got some great music on.

1. Lie on your back with your knees bent and your feet about 2 feet in front of your sit bones. Rest an 8- to 12-pound dumbbell on your lower stomach and hold it in place.

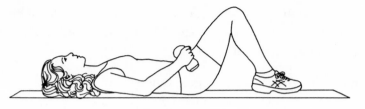

step 1

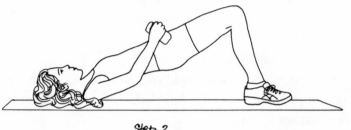

step 2

2. Lift your hips and contract your glutes as hard as you can as you press your heels into the floor.

3. Lower your pelvis to about an inch above the floor and repeat.

Tip: For extra sculpting, when you have lifted your hips up after your last set, pause and then do 20 small squeezes (almost as if you are pulsing in one place), then release.

Breathing: Exhale as you lift, inhale as you lower back down.

Sets: 3 sets of 15 repetitions

DEAD LIFT

Ever since a trainer with the most toned behind I've ever seen in my life taught me this, I've noticed a huge difference when I catch a glimpse of my behind in jeans.

1. Stand with your feet together, holding two 5- to 10-pound dumbbells in front of your thighs. Have your palms facing toward you. Draw your shoulders back and down.

2. Bend from your hips and, keeping your legs straight, lower your torso down as far as you can without bending your knees. It's vital that you keep your back straight, not arched. This will help to keep your shoulders back and down.

3. Push up through your heels, keeping the dumbbells close to the fronts of your legs, and return to starting position.

Tip: To challenge yourself, stand with one leg 2 feet behind the other, with your back toes touching the floor. Bend your front knee slightly. Keeping your shoulders down and back, lower the dumbbells toward your front shin and then return to the starting position.

Breathing: Inhale as you lower, exhale as you come up.

Sets: 3 sets of 12 repetitions

Step 1

Step 2

SQUAT

This exercise helps sculpt the inner and fronts of the thighs, as well as the glutes.

1. Stand with your feet a little wider than shoulder width apart and your feet turned out, so that when you bend your knees they will line up with your middle toes.

2. Hold an 8-pound dumbbell with both hands, cupping the top of the dumbbell, palms facing up.

3. Keeping your torso upright, shoulders back, and abs drawn in, lower down until your thighs are parallel to the floor.

4. Press into your heels to come up.

Tip: As you come up, squeeze your glutes as hard as you can.

Breathing: Inhale as you lower, exhale to come up.

Sets: 3 sets of 12 repetitions

Step 2   Step 3

LOVELY LUNGE

This is a vital part of your tush-toning regime. It also sculpts the entire hip and thigh area.

1. Stand with your feet together, holding an 8- to 10-pound dumbbell in each hand. Step your right foot about three feet behind you and rest on the ball of the foot.

2. Bend your right knee down to the floor at a 90-degree angle until the knee is a couple of inches away from the floor. Make sure your left knee doesn't overshoot your left foot (the knee should be directly above your left ankle). Return to your starting position and repeat with your left leg.

Step 1   Step 2

Tip: Make sure your front knee is aligned with the middle toes of your front foot.

Breathing: Inhale into the lunge, exhale to return to starting position.

Sets: 2 sets of 15 repetitions

Red Carpet Arms

Do you ever wonder how Hollywood actresses over a certain age manage to maintain their firm-looking arms? The answer is a lot of hardcore work. If you want to look great in an evening dress or a tank top, there's no gain without a little pain. These exercises are simple enough for you to master right away, and if done regularly, will have you wanting to show off those fabulous arms!

TERRIFIC TRICEPS

I suggest doing at least one exercise for your triceps every single day if you want to feel confident in a sleeveless dress. It's one of the first areas of your arms to show neglect, and is mercifully one of the quickest to get back into shape.

TRICEPS KICKBACK

1. Grab your weights (5- to 10-pound dumbbells, depending on your level).

2. Stand with your feet hip width apart with a dumbbell in your left hand.

3. Take a large step back with your left foot.

4. Bend your right knee and place your right hand on your right thigh.

5. Lean forward, keeping your hips square to the floor.

6. Keeping your abs tight, bend your left arm, holding the dumbbell just above your left hip with your elbow pointing back.

7. Extend your left arm behind you until your arm is straight.

8. Slowly lower the dumbbell to the starting position. Repeat on each side.

Tip: The only thing that should move is your forearm. Make sure your shoulders are relaxed and down.

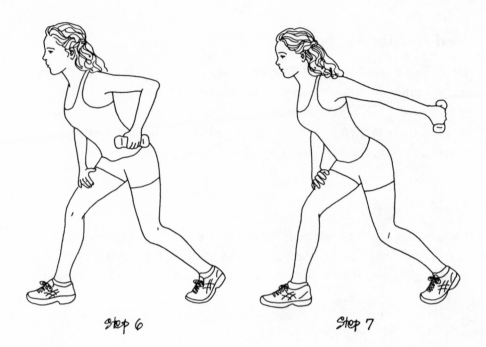

Step 6   Step 7

Breathing: Exhale as you straighten, inhale to come back to the starting position.

Sets: 3 sets of 12 repetitions

TRICEPS DIP

I love this exercise, as it's so easy to perform and will give the backs of your arms that "cut" look in just a few sessions.

1. Sit on a chair and place your hands, palms down, on the edge of the seat. Your fingers should be facing forward.

2. Draw in your abs and make sure your shoulders are back and down.

3. Scoot your sit bones forward and off the seat of the chair. You'll need to move your feet forward a couple of inches.

pull yourself up and lower down.

4. Bend your elbows as you lower your hips toward the floor, until your thighs are parallel with the floor.

5. Contract your triceps to bring you back to the starting position.

Tip: Keep your lower back as close to the chair as you can throughout. If this exercise becomes easy, try doing it with your legs straight out in front of you.

Breathing: Exhale as you lower and inhale back to the starting position.

Sets: 2 sets of 12 repetitions

BICEPS CURL

This is a very straightforward exercise that will deliver great results if done religiously.

1. Grab your dumbbells (5 to 12 pounds should be good, but this is one exercise where you should challenge yourself to go a little heavier than what seems comfortable).

2. Stand with your feet hip width apart and your knees slightly bent.

3. Draw in your abdominal muscles and release your shoulders down and away from your ears.

4. Hold the dumbbells at your sides with your palms facing inward.

5. Starting with your left arm, raise the dumbbell toward your shoulder. As it moves past your hip, rotate it so that your palm faces upward. Return to starting position and repeat with the other arm.

Tip: Tuck your elbow into your side to secure your upper arm (it shouldn't move). At the top of each movement, pause for a beat as you squeeze the dumbbell.

Breathing: Exhale as you curl upward and inhale to release down.

Sets: 2 sets of 12 repetitions

Step 4

Step 5

SHOULDER SCULPT ONE

The shoulders are viewed from all angles, and when toned can look extremely sexy in a tank or a top with spaghetti straps.

1. Grab your dumbbells (5 to 8 pounds are good).

2. Stand with your feet hip width apart and your knees slightly bent.

3. Hold the dumbbells in front of your thighs with your palms facing in.

4. Contract your abs and draw your shoulders down and back.

5. Lift both dumbbells until your arms are parallel to the floor.

6. Slowly return the dumbbells to the starting position.

step 3

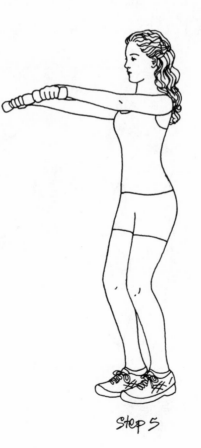

step 5

Tip: Kill two birds with one stone and combine this with a squat (see p. 353).

Breathing: Exhale as you lift and inhale back to the starting position.

Sets: 3 sets of 10 repetitions

SHOULDER SCULPT TWO

1. Stand with your feet together and your knees slightly bent.

2. Hold your 5- to 8-pound dumbbells by your sides, palms facing in.

3. Contract your abs and draw your shoulders back and down.

4. With your elbows slightly bent, raise your arms out to the sides until they are parallel to the floor.

5. Slowly lower them back to the starting position.

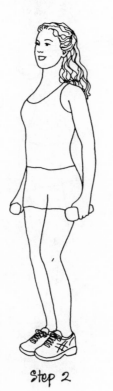

Step 2

Step 4

Tip: Make sure you keep your shoulders down and back, as you don't want to increase tension in your neck and shoulders.

Breathing: Exhale as you lift and exhale back to the starting position.

Sets: 2 sets of 12 repetitions

Yoga

There are three poses/stretches that you should do after the exercises I've just described. They should take no more than 10 minutes. Indulge in this time, as it should feel like a wonderful respite after your workout.

THREAD THE NEEDLE

1. Lie on your back on a soft surface with your knees bent. Cross your right foot over your left knee and flex your left foot.

2. Thread your left hand through the triangle in between your legs and grab the front of your right shin or the back of your right thigh with both hands.

3. Interlace your fingers and stay there, breathing deeply, for 3 minutes.

COBRA

1. Lie on your tummy on a soft surface. Turn your head to one side and place your palms on the floor in line with your bra strap—fingers facing forward and elbows pointing up.

2. Point your toes behind you.

3. As you gently press your tailbone into the floor, draw your shoulders down away from your ears and toward your spine.

4. As you inhale, raise your breastbone up toward the sky, gazing upward. Take 3 deep breaths.

5. As you exhale, release back down and turn your head to one side.

TRICEPS STRETCH

1. Kneel on a soft surface, sitting back on your heels. Extend your left arm out to the side, bend your elbow, and place your left hand up your back. Your fingers should point up toward your head and the back of your hand should be flat against your back.

2. Reach up with your right hand toward the sky, bend your right elbow, and crawl your right fingers down your back to try to catch your left fingers.

3. If you can't reach, grab a towel or a belt to hold on to between both hands.

Alternative Therapies

Alternative therapies can be very, very expensive, so it may come as some relief to know that you can perform many of these therapies safely on yourself and your partner at no expense.

You don't have to believe in any weird religion, cult, or outlandish philosophy for many of these simple techniques to work. Many alternative therapies concern themselves with our "energy" or "life force." This is hard for some people to wrap their heads around, because we can't actually see this energy. Many psychics and healers claim they can, but for the skeptical among us, we just have to trust that there's an invisible network of energy that can be manipulated or tweaked to assist in healing ourselves, mentally, physically, and spiritually.

I think this is best illustrated by the ancient art of acupuncture, which is now recognized even by insurance companies as an effective tool in healing all kinds of ailments. Acupuncture operates on the premise that this energy courses through invisible networks or channels called meridians. The meridians are like rivers that can get dammed up, so the acupuncturist will insert a needle to unblock these obstructions. Many other therapies, including yoga, chakra balancing, meditation, reflexology, and acupressure, also work toward the common goal of helping the body achieve perfect balance by removing obstacles to the energy or life force running freely through your physical and spiritual body.

I have had the fortune over the years to practice many of these therapies and

MEDITATION CUSHION

This is easy enough for a total beginner to make.

YOU WILL NEED

☐ 1 old XL fleece pullover*

☐ Large bag of filling (ideally kapok, but if you can't find it, you can use Poly-fil filler)

If you don't have one, go to your local thrift store or check out a few yard sales. If you can't find a fleece, you'll be able to purchase ½ yard of fleece fabric from your nearest fabric store.

HOW TO

1. Turn the fleece inside out and mark a large circle, 16 inches in diameter, with a marker. Cut it out.

2. Pin the edges of the circle, right sides together, and sew a seam 1 inch from the edge of the circle, leaving a 5-inch gap for adding the filling.

3. Turn right side out and stuff in as much filling as you can. It needs to be as thick and firm as possible.

4. To close the gap, turn the raw edges under ¼ inch and, pinching the seams together, hand sew the edges together (you may want to go back and forth a couple of times to ensure it won't come apart!).

to see some work and some not. I have found that the most valuable of all DIY therapies is simple meditation.

MEDITATION

I suggest that you carve out just 5 minutes a day to start with. Anyone can manage 5 minutes, and these 5 minutes might completely change your day.

It's up to you whether or not to use a timer. If you already meditate and know you can sit for more than 15 minutes, you may want to set an egg timer for a certain period of time. I try for 20 minutes. If you're a beginner, I would advise against using a timer, as you don't want to get shocked by the sound after only a few minutes of quieting down.

1. Make sure that you will be undisturbed. Turn off your computer and phone and tell your partner, kids, and pets that you are not to be disturbed. (Strangely enough, my dog doesn't really understand, but you'll find that pets love the meditation vibe and will likely lie lovingly at your feet.)

2. You need to get really comfy. The best position to meditate in is seated cross-legged on a firm cushion that's at least 6 to 8 inches high (when you are sitting on it). Sitting in this position encourages your spine to be erect and your head to sit where it's supposed to on your shoulders. Ideally, you should make a meditation cushion. If sitting cross-legged is out of the question, sit comfortably in a chair with your feet firmly planted on the ground and your back erect.

3. Close your eyes and relax your shoulders away from your ears. Draw the crown of your head up toward the ceiling and soften all your facial muscles.

4. Begin to deepen and lengthen each inhale and each exhale by breathing in for 5 slow beats and breathing out for 5 slow beats.

5. Each time your mind wanders, bring it back to focus on your breath.

6. You'll begin to notice a pause of a beat between each inhale and exhale. See if you can allow your mind/thoughts to become absolutely still in this beat.

7. If you haven't used a timer, you may just know when you're done. Open your eyes gently and take a few normal breaths before getting up.

MEDITATION BLANKET

During the cooler months, it's blissful to wrap yourself in a meditation blanket. When you meditate, your body temperature will drop, so you need to prepare. A blanket makes you feel very safe and cozy. A beloved friend of mine, Barbara, made one for me out of every imaginable shade of purple and blue. When I pulled it out of the bag, I burst into tears, as it was so gorgeous. Barbara is a passionate knitter, so she had a lot of leftover yarn to weave into her masterpiece.

Even if you are a complete beginner at knitting, you can make this easily—actually, it's a perfect beginner's project. Simply gather a bunch of yarn; different colors will look great. A chunky wool or cotton yarn will work best for this blanket. Ask anyone you know if they have any leftover yarn, or go looking in crafts stores or online. I always buy organic yarn. It's so worth the extra expense.

1. Use a 4.5 circular needle and cast on 150 stitches.

2. Simply knit each row (garter stitch) until your blanket measures 3½ feet.

3. Cast off.

CHAKRA BALANCING MEDITATION

I know that for many of you, the very notion of "chakra" anything conjures up images of weird crystal-swinging, long-ponytail-wearing men in Velcro-closed sandals. However, understanding the basics of how the chakra system works is worth a little investigation. As in acupuncture, the chakras are simply centers of energy. When they're out of balance, they mess up the free and even flow of energy throughout your body. The word "chakra" means "wheel"; and when in balance, they are thought to rotate in a clockwise direction.

As a beginner, all you need to understand is where your chakras are located, what each one facilitates, and how to restore their natural balance. Each chakra has a color, which makes them really easy to visualize. There are seven chakras; they start at the base of the spine with the root chakra.

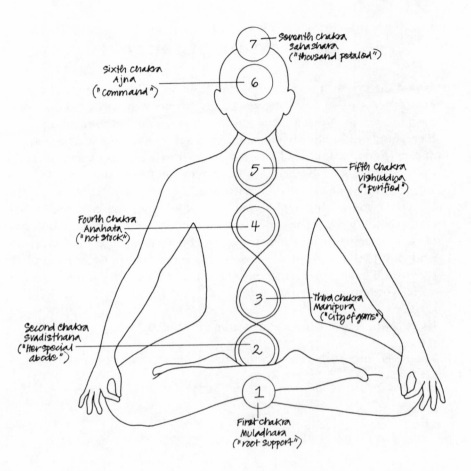

Seventh chakra
sahasrara
("thousand petaled")

Sixth chakra
Ajna
("command")

Fifth chakra
Vishuddha
("purified")

Fourth chakra
Anahata
("not stuck")

Third chakra
Manipura
("city of gems")

Second chakra
Svadisthana
("Her special
abode.")

First chakra
Muladhara
("root support")

- First chakra: The root chakra is stimulated by the color red and rotates at the slowest speed of all the chakras. It's located at the base of your spine and is concerned with survival and safety. When out of balance, you may feel fearful, anxious, and insecure.

- Second chakra: The sacral chakra is stimulated by the color orange and is located 2 inches below your navel. It's concerned with sexuality, creativity, intuition, and self-worth. When out of balance, you may feel emotionally blocked and explosive, and lack energy.

- Third chakra: The solar plexus chakra is stimulated by the color yellow and is located 2 inches below your breastbone. It is concerned with personal power, ego, passion, anger, and strength. When out of balance, you may lack confidence and feel depressed.

- Fourth chakra: The heart chakra is stimulated by the color green and is located behind the breastbone, in front of your spine and between your shoulder blades. It is concerned with love, compassion, and spirituality. When out of balance, you may feel self-pity, paranoia, and insecurity, and you may be afraid to let go.

- Fifth chakra: The throat chakra is stimulated by the color blue and is located at the V of your collarbone. It is concerned with communication, sound, and creativity. When out of balance, you may feel shut down, quiet, and unable to express yourself.

- Sixth chakra: The third eye, or brow, chakra is stimulated by the color indigo. It is located in the center of your forehead, above your eyes. It is concerned with higher intuition. When it's out of balance, you may lack assertiveness and be afraid of success.

- Seventh chakra: The crown chakra is stimulated by the color violet and is located just behind the top of your skull. It concerns itself with the inward flow of wisdom. When out of balance, you may feel frustrated and joyless.

Here is a simple meditation to heal all the chakras.

1. Imagine you are looking down through your body from above and there is a pole running through all of your chakras, head to toe. You want to visualize the chakras whirring *clockwise* around this pole.

2. Start with your root chakra and visualize it as a bright red ball spinning clockwise. Visualize inhaling and exhaling the color red for 2 minutes.

3. Move your way up through the chakras, visualizing them as the appropriate stimulating color ball. Continue to breathe in and out the corresponding color.

4. Finally, visualize a white light flowing down from above, through your crown chakra, and down through the other chakras as they spin in their vibrant colors, down into the earth. Visualize your entire body as a white, glowing being.

5. Take a few normal breaths and open your eyes.

MASSAGE

Who doesn't *love* a massage? It may be easier to perform a massage on your partner than you think. You just need to learn a few basics.

Good massage is all about the techniques you use. Here are some really effective ones that will make your partner very happy. The following chart shows the pressure points that you can focus on. Placing one thumb on top of the other and massaging in small circular motions is extremely therapeutic in dealing with areas that may be in need of a little healing.

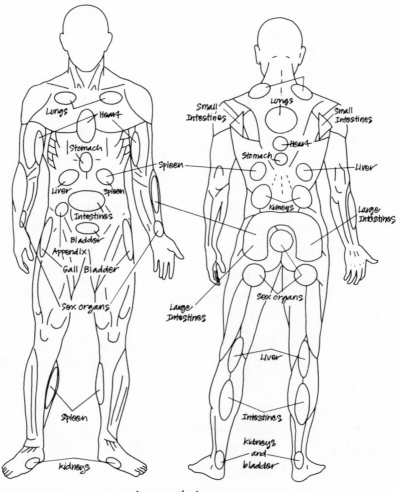

Massage chart

1. Effleurage (smooth, rhythmic stroking): Place a little oil in the palm of one hand and rub your hands together to warm the oil. Use the whole surface of both hands. Place them over the low back and stroke firmly up to the neck, then circle around back to the lower back. You can repeat this for a good 5 minutes.

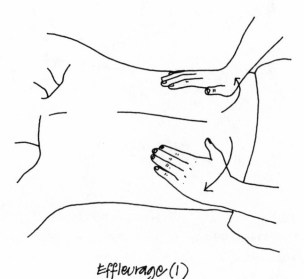

Effleurage (1)

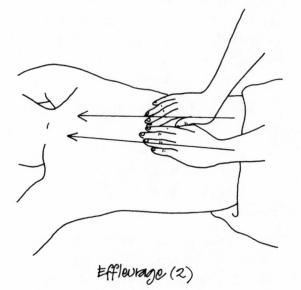

Effleurage (2)

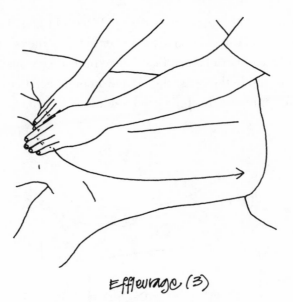

Effleurage (3)

2. Heel of the hand stroking: This is similar to effleurage, only you're using the heel of your hand, so you can exert a little more pressure. Work in circles with both hands at the same time. Move in a circle (out, up, and then back to the center).

3. Reinforced fingers: Stand on the opposite side of the side of the back that you're going to work on. Place one hand on top of the other and push down with the flats of your fingers, away from the spine (use a nice firm pressure), and then gently glide back to the spine. Start on the lower back and work your way up to the neck area.

4. Reinforced thumb technique: Start with one hand fanned out across the lower back and your thumb pressing into the muscle running alongside the spine. Press your other thumb on top of your massaging thumb for greater pressure and glide up the full length of the spine. Repeat on the other side of the spine with your other hand, and then repeat the whole process 3 times.

5. Forearm technique: Stand on the opposite side of the back that you're going to work on. Lean over, placing your forearms on the back (be careful that you're only pressing down on muscle, not on the

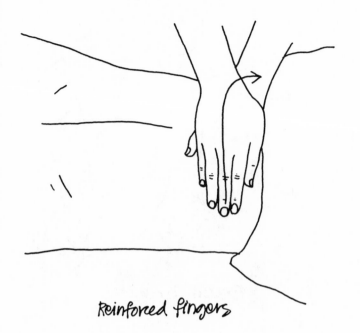

Reinforced fingers

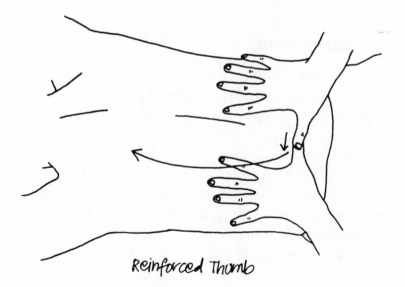

Reinforced Thumb

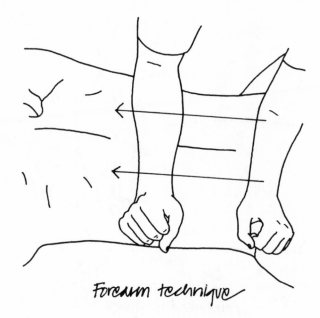

Forearm technique

spine). Move the arm that's closest to the head up to just below the shoulder blade, and then glide gently down. Repeat 3 times. Change sides.

MASSAGE PREPARATION

If you have a bad back, I don't recommend kneeling or crouching down to massage. Instead, lay some towels on your bed and have your partner lie across the bed with his/her chin hanging off the edge.

1. Choose the spot for your massage carefully. You need to have your partner on a surface that you can get to. A queen- or king-size bed is way too large and will make it difficult to move around your partner. I recommend taking the large pads off your couch and putting them on a carpeted floor. Cover them completely with a large sheet and then towels. Have some extra-large towels on hand to cover your partner with.

2. Prepare some lighting and music. Your partner will feel very nervous in bright light, so either dim the lights or use beeswax/soy candles.

Find some meditation or classical music that you know your partner likes.

3. Make sure the room is warm enough.

4. Make a horseshoe-shaped pad out of a rolled-up towel and set it (open end of the horseshoe facing your partner) at one end of the massage "table." Make sure the horseshoe pad is the same height as the massage pad.

5. Have your partner lie down on their stomach with their face in the horseshoe pad.

6. Pour some gently warmed massage oil (you can set the bottle in a cup of hot water) into the palm of your hand and rub your hands together. You're ready to begin.

REFLEXOLOGY

You can easily perform reflexology on yourself. I've always been a big fan. I think it can help to alleviate a host of symptoms. From sinus congestion to PMS, you should be able to provide some relief for yourself. Use the massage oil you can make yourself (see p. 375).

WHAT IS REFLEXOLOGY?

Each of the systems in your body corresponds to a specific zone on the sole of your foot (see the illustration). Applying pressure to a specific zone generates a signal through the peripheral nervous system. That signal then enters the central nervous system, where it is processed in the brain. Finally, it is relayed to the internal organs to make the necessary adjustments.

1. Using mainly your thumbs, work your way over the sole of your foot, from your heel to your toes.

2. Work your way over the top of the foot and the ankle.

3. As you go, notice tender spots, as these areas may signify tension or illness in a corresponding organ.

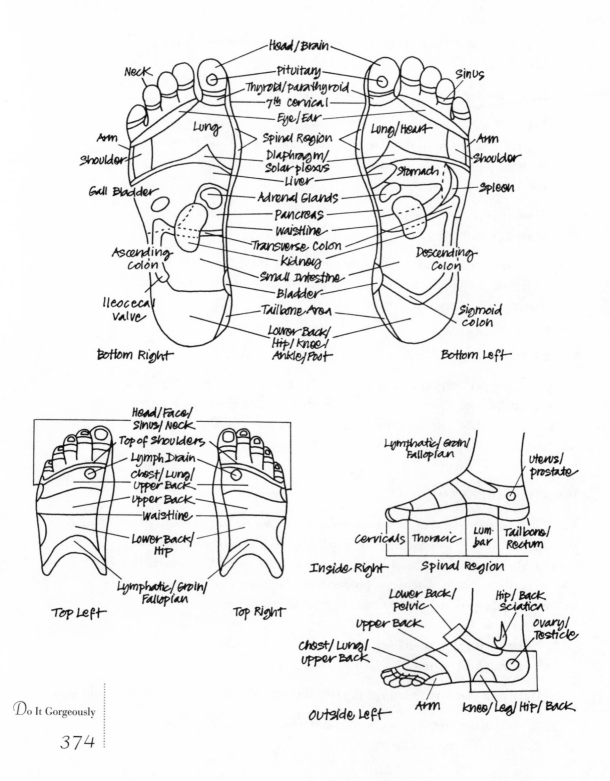

Head/Brain

Neck
Pituitary
Thyroid/parathyroid
7th cervical
Eye/Ear

Sinus

Lung
Spinal Region

Lung/Heart

Arm
Shoulder
Diaphragm/
Solar plexus
Liver

Arm
Shoulder

Stomach

Gall Bladder
Adrenal Glands
Pancreas
Waistline
Transverse Colon

Spleen

Ascending
Colon
Kidney
Small Intestine
Bladder

Descending
Colon

Ileocecal
Valve
Tailbone Area

Sigmoid
colon

Lower Back/
Hip/Knee/
Ankle/Foot

Bottom Right

Bottom Left

Head/Face/
Sinus/Neck
Top of Shoulders
Lymph Drain
Chest/Lung/
Upper Back
Upper Back
Waistline

Lower Back/
Hip

Lymphatic/Groin/
Fallopian

Lymphatic/Groin/
Fallopian

Uterus/
prostate

Cervicals Thoracic Lumbar Tailbone/Rectum

Inside Right   Spinal Region

Top Left

Top Right

Lower Back/
Pelvic
Upper Back
Chest/Lung/
upper Back

Hip/Back
Sciatica
Ovary/
Testicle

Arm Knee/Leg/Hip/Back

Outside Left

4. Using your thumbs, apply a steady pressure to the area of tenderness for about 30 seconds, or until the pain has been worked through. Make sure you take long, deep breaths as you work through this pain. See the chart to work out which organ you may be dealing with.

5. Repeat for the other foot.

REFLEXOLOGY MASSAGE OIL

½ cup sweet almond oil
3 tsp. wheat germ oil

10 drops tea tree essential oil
10 drops lavender essential oil

Blend the oils together in a small jug and use a funnel to pour into a 1-oz. dark glass bottle.

Epilogue

I have had a blast writing this book. My entire home has been turned into a massive workshop, where every recipe and project has been tested and then tested again. Everyone's been involved in this exciting and rewarding process—my husband, my daughter, and even my naughty little Maltese, Phoebe. They've had numerous skincare preparations rubbed into every available area of their body, they've smelled perfumes, tasted sauces, even tried on outfits and eaten all kinds of weird and wonderful plants from my garden.

The joy of doing it gorgeously is that you will inevitably come together as a family or a community. The many projects and recipes are to be discussed, shared, laughed about, savored, and then ultimately passed down to someone smaller than you.

I encourage you to experiment further with any project that you are drawn to. For many of you, this book will serve as a primer that will, hopefully, lead you deeper into DIY.

More than anything, I have realized through trial and error that beauty is in the imperfection of things. A homemade apple pie with part of its crust chipped off shows us that it has been home-made with love by a human being, not a machine. Everything I cherish—the things that I would gather together if I had three minutes to evacuate my home—are things that were *made* for me by people I love, and items that are outstanding in their imperfections: the tattered notebook containing poems that my husband wrote for Lola, the little baby cardigan with holes that my mom knitted for me when she was pregnant, and the Mother's Day pin that Lola created when she was only 4. I dare you to be imperfect and to have a go at creating something you've never made before—a chocolate cake tastes exquisite even if it's caved in, and a hand-knitted scarf that's studded with holes (from dropped stitches) will still keep your neck warm.

There's a tribe in West Africa whose definition of the word "prosperity" is to be supremely grateful for everything you have. This particular tribe has *very* little. The green revolution has nudged me a little closer to this way of thinking. As more and more of us realize that we can make do with what we already have or create the things we need out of sustainable materials, we can take steps toward *being* the change that we want to see in the world.

Resource Guide

Resources for Making Your Own Skincare Products

Plant-Based Oils, Essential Oils, Waxes, Butters, Emulsifiers, and Jojoba Flakes
Go to gorgeouslygreen.com and click on "Do It Gorgeously."

For All Dried Herbs and Flowers
Go to gorgeouslygreen.com and click on "Do It Gorgeously." These are companies that I implicitly trust in terms of their commitment to organic farming and producing the real thing:

Mountain Rose Herbs (www.mountainroseherbs.com)

Simplers (www.simplers.com)

Anti-aging Ingredients
For an updated list of anti-aging ingredients, go to gorgeouslygreen.com and click on "Do It Gorgeously."

Vitamin C crystals: www.cosmedix.com

L-ascorbic acid powder/crystals: These can be found at almost any health food or vitamin store. Keep in mind that it must be labeled L-ascorbic acid, as opposed to vitamin C.

Camu Camu: This potent vitamin C powder can be found at www.live superfoods.com.

Retinol: I recommend retinyl acetate from skinactives.com. I also love "Refine" by CosMedix (www.cosmedix.com).

Bottles, Jars, and Containers for Your Skincare Supplies
Go to gorgeouslygreen.com and click on "Do It Gorgeously." You should also be able to find everything you need from one of the following companies:

Mountain Rose Herbs (www.mountainroseherbs.com)

SKS Bottles (www.sks-bottle.com)

Specialty Bottles (www.specialtybottle.com)

For Your Chek It: Home Test Lab in a Box
Go to Snowdrift Farms (www.snowdriftfarms.com).

Water Filtration
I think it's vitally important to filter out chlorine and pollutants from your tap water. As mentioned in the beauty chapter, chlorine is horribly drying for skin and hair, so ideally a whole house filtration system is the answer. I highly recommend the LifeSource Water System (www.lifesourcewater.com), because it's an eco-friendly company that uses a granular activated carbon filter (only needs to be changed every fifteen years), and it's one of the few systems that filters out all the bad stuff but still keeps the valuable minerals in your water (important for drinking).

If you can't afford a whole house system, make sure you put filters on your showerheads. I recommend the Rainshow'r Shower Water Filter (www.amazon .com).

Pimple/Blackhead Removing Device
Go to www.venusworldwide.com.

Dry Skin Brush
I love the Tampico Skin Brush at Mother Nature (www.mothernature.com).

For My Favorite Nontoxic Nail Polishes

Sparitual (www.sparitual.com)

Zoya Polishes (www.zoya.com)

Deodorant
You can buy the zinc oxide to make your deodorant from www.naturalhealthsupply.com. It's sold as Deodorant Zinc Oxide.

Sunscreen
You will find powdered zinc oxide from www.soapgoods.com. My favorite sunscreens:

Solar Rx by www.keys-soap.com

Reflect by CosMedix (www.cosmedix.com)

Serious Protection by CosMedix

Zinc oxide (see above)

Remedies

Stevia as a Sweetener for Your Remedies
You can go to www.stevia.com. You can also find it in most large grocery stores/ health food stores.

Dried Herbs for Your Remedies

Starwest Botanicals (www.starwest-botanicals.com)

Mountain Rose Herbs (www.mountainroseherbs.com)

Labels

For making labels, I love the fountain pens from Lamy (www.lamy.com). You can find a great selection of decorative edging scissors from Fiskars (www.fiskars .com).

As a placeholder for decorative labels, or to help you stay organized as you prepare, use Post-it Greener Notes, available at most office supply stores.

Sewing

Sewing Machine
My favorite is the Brother CS-6000i (www.brother-usa.com).

Organic Fabrics

Near Sea Naturals (www.nearseanaturals.com)

Organic Cotton Plus (www.organiccottonplus.com)

Grommet Tape and Rings
FK Design (www.fkdesigninc.com)

Nursery Supplies

Nontoxic Mattress
Nirvana Safe Haven (www.nontoxic.com)
Naturepedic (www.naturepedic.com)

Neck Pillow
Serenity Pillows (www.serenitypillows.com)

Buckwheat Hulls for Your Pillow

Carolina Morning (www.zafu.net)

Buckwheat Hull (www.buckwheathull.com)

Mountain Rose Herbs (www.mountainroseherbs.com)

Baby Supplies

Zinc Oxide for Diaper Cream
Natural Health Supply (www.naturalhealthsupply.com)

Baby Cubes for Baby Food
Baby Cubes (www.babycubes.com)

Pigment for Shoe Polish
Earth Pigment (www.earthpigments.com)

Kitchen/Food Supplies

Yogurt Maker
Yogourmet (www.lucyskitchenshop.com)

Hemp Protein Powder
www.livingharvest.com

Brown Rice Syrup
www.lundberg.com

Virgin Coconut Oil
www.tropicaltraditions.com

Mustard Seeds
www.spicely.com

Pomona Pectin Powder
www.pomonapectin.com

Vegenaise
www.followyourheart.com

Terrarium

You can use glass fish bowls, large clear cookie/candy jars, or even a domed glass cake stand. For really beautiful terrariums I recommend using a large apothecary jar. They have a great selection at: www.save-on-crafts.com or www.englishcreekgardens.com.

DIY Around the Home Supplies

You will find most of the supplies that I mention from:

The Green Depot (www.greendepot.com)

Home Depot/Eco Options (www.homedepot.com)

Ace Hardware (www.acehardware.com)

Thermal Leak Detector
Black & Decker (www.blackanddecker.com)

Complete Sanding Kit
Black & Decker (www.blackanddecker.com)

Nontoxic Grout, Sealers, and Caulk

Green Building Supply (www.greenbuildingsupply.com)

Building for Health (www.buildingforhealth.com)

The Green Depot (www.greendepot.com)

Bio-shield Paint (www.bioshield.com)

Squeegees for Window Cleaning
Most hardware stores have great selections, or you can visit www.windows101.com.

Unger Window-Cleaning Tablets

www.windows101.com

Drying Racks

Urban Clothes Lines (www.urbanclotheslines.com)

All-Purpose Drill

I like the De Walt 12V VSR Drill and Driver Kit (www.greendepot.com).

Useful to Have at Hand

For screws and washers, get yourself the Midwest Fastener Handyman Kit (www.greendepot.com).

Sprayer Bottles

If you can't find what you need at the Dollar Store, try Specialty Bottle (www .specialtybottle.com).

Washing Soda Crystals and Baking Soda

Arm and Hammer (www.armandhammer.com)

Fels Naptha Soap

www.felsnaptha.com

Gardening Supplies

Coconut Coir for Making "Stellar Soil"

Planet Natural (www.planetnatural.com)

Amazon (www.amazon.com)

Worms for Your Worm Compost Bin

Uncle Jim's Worm Farm (www.unclejimswormfarm.com)

Seeds

Ed Hume Seeds (www.humeseeds.com)

Herbs

Horizon Herbs (www.horizonherbs.com)

Heirloom Seeds (www.heirloomseeds.com)

Index

abdominal exercises, 346–50
achy muscle soak, 66
acne gel, soothing, 62–63
acupressure face lift, 42–43
acupuncture, 362
aerators, low-flow, 241
air-drying laundry, 254–56
air fresheners, 298, 307–8
air leaks in the home, 236–37, 238
all-purpose cleaner, 299–300
almond:
   butter, homemade, 212
   milk, homemade, 209
   toasted, pesto, 201
almond oil, sweet, 14
aloe vera:
   and chamomile cleansing cream, 27–28
   and rose softening toner, 28–29
   toner, pure, 24
   uses for, 318
alpha hydroxy acids, 18
   skin-lightening mask, 39
alternative therapies, 362–75
   massage, 368–73
   meditation, 363–67
   reflexology, 373–75
antibacterial products, 118

antioxidants, 14, 17, 30
apple:
   chutney, fall, 188–90
   and walnut porridge, 131
appliances, energy usage of, 241–44
apricot and banana porridge, 130
apricot oil, 14
   and geranium moisturizer, 29–30
   and orange body cream for dry skin,
      47–49
apron, sassy little, 217–20
arms, exercises for, 355–61
auto maintenance, 256–59
avocado oil, 14

babies and children, 71–131
   boiled wool mittens, 106–8
   earache drops, 126–27
   easy gathered skirt, 105
   food for, 127–31
   haircutting, 113–16
   head lice treatment, 125–26
   jeans diaper bag, 95–98
   lavender cashmere comfort bear, 91–93
   making shoes last longer, 117–18
   no-sew perfect baby sling, 99
   patchwork comforter cover, 109–12